UNCANNY AVENGERS™

The Red Shadow

WRITER: RICK REMENDER
ART: JOHN CASSADAY (ISSUE #1-4)
AND
PENCILS: OLIVIER COIPEL (ISSUE #5)
INKS: MARK MORALES (ISSUE #5)

LETTERS: VIRTUAL CALLIGRAPHY'S CHRIS ELIOPOULOS
COLOURIST: LAURA MARTIN AND LARRY MOLINAR

ASSISTANT EDITOR: DANIEL KETCHUM
EDITOR: TOM BREVOORT
EDITOR IN CHIEF: AXEL ALONSO
CHIEF CREATIVE OFFICER: JOE QUESADA
PUBLISHER: ALAN FINE
EXECUTIVE PRODUCER: DAN BUCKLEY

COVER: JOHN CASSADAY

 Published by Panini Publishing, a division of Panini UK Limited. Mike Riddell, Managing Director. Alan O'Keefe, Managing Editor. Mark Irvine, Production Manager. Marco M. Lupoi, Publishing Director Europe. Brady Webb, Reprint Editor. Angela Gray, Designer. Office of publication: Brockbourne House, 77 Mount Ephraim, Tunbridge Wells, Kent TN4 8BS.

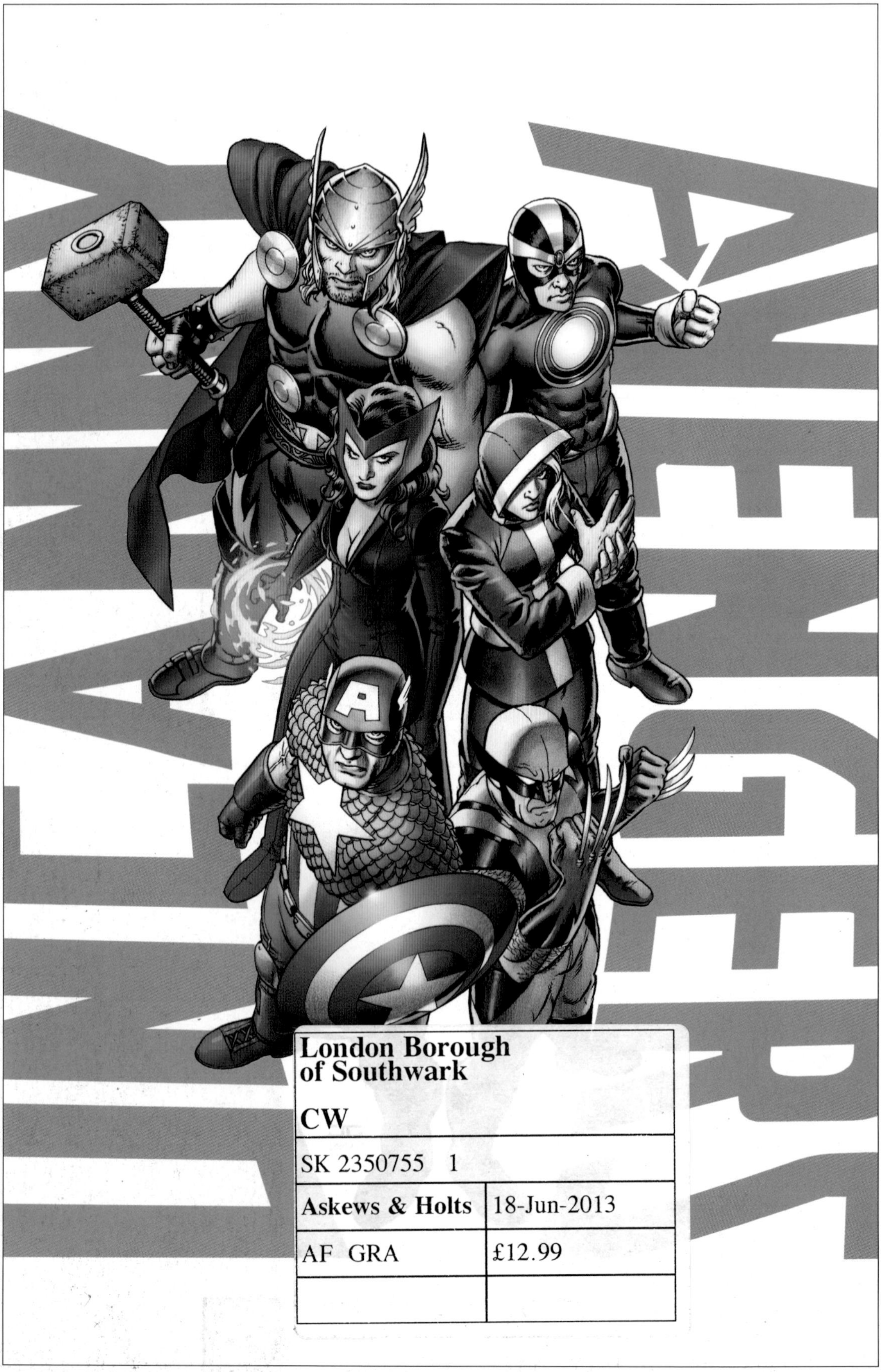
UNCANNY
AVENGERS

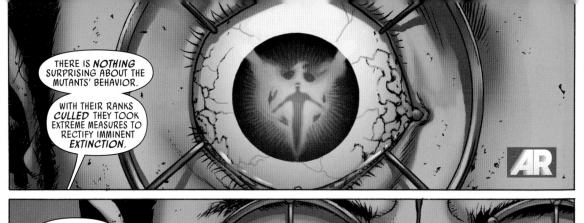

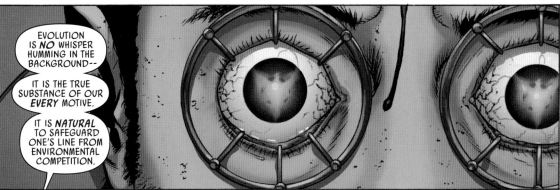

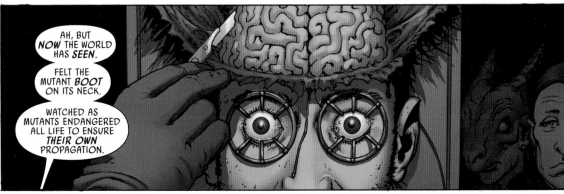

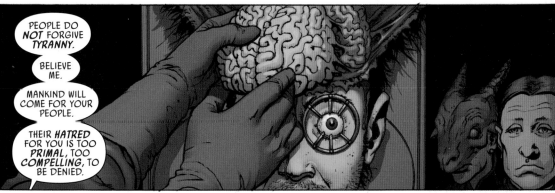

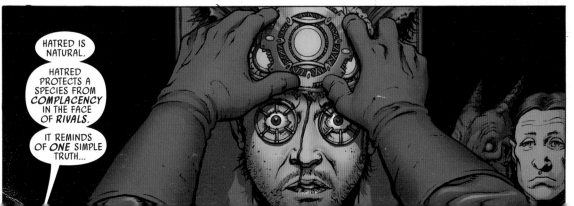

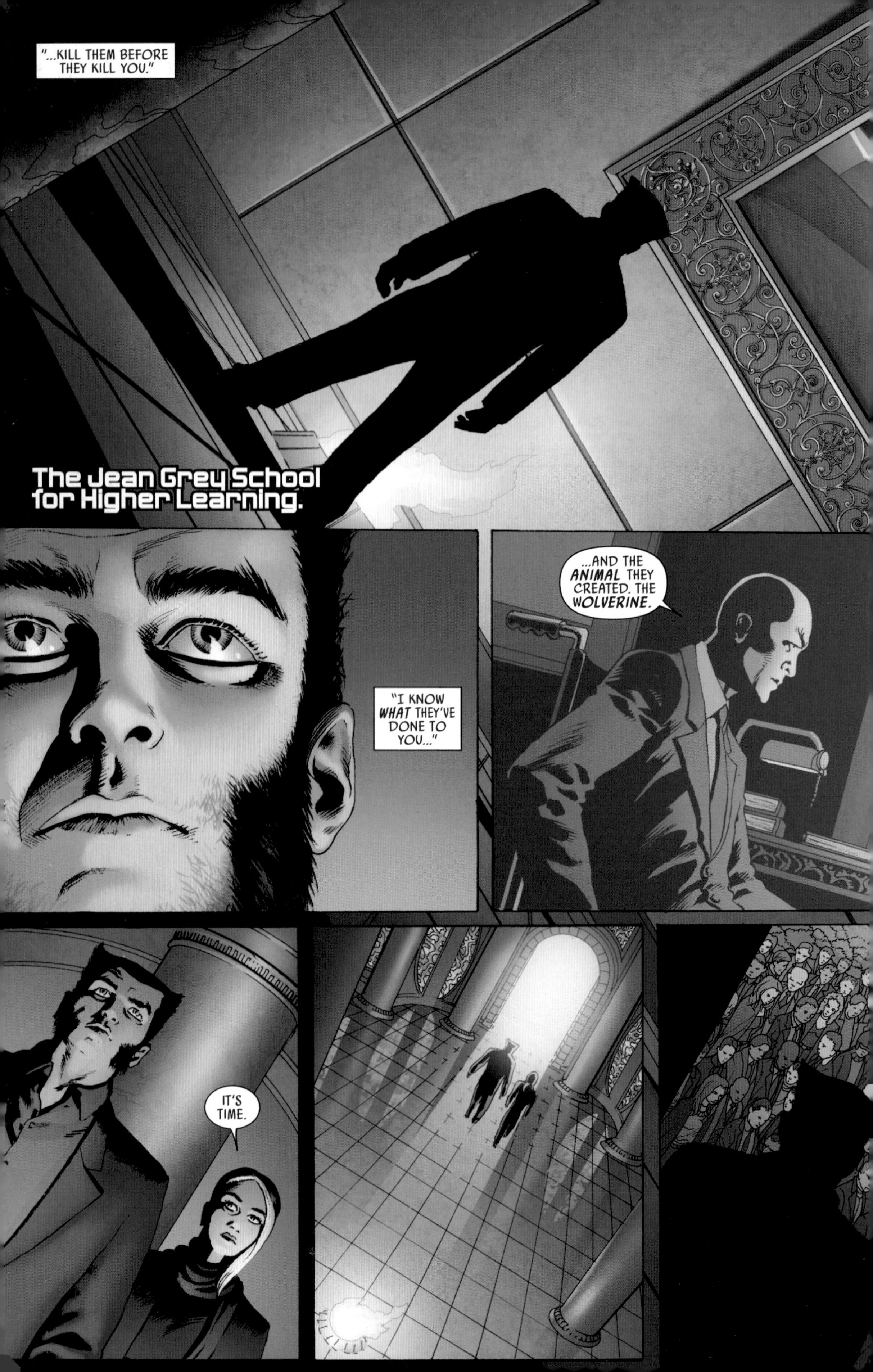
"...KILL THEM BEFORE THEY KILL YOU."
The Jean Grey School for Higher Learning.
"I KNOW WHAT THEY'VE DONE TO YOU..."
...AND THE ANIMAL THEY CREATED. THE WOLVERINE.
IT'S TIME.

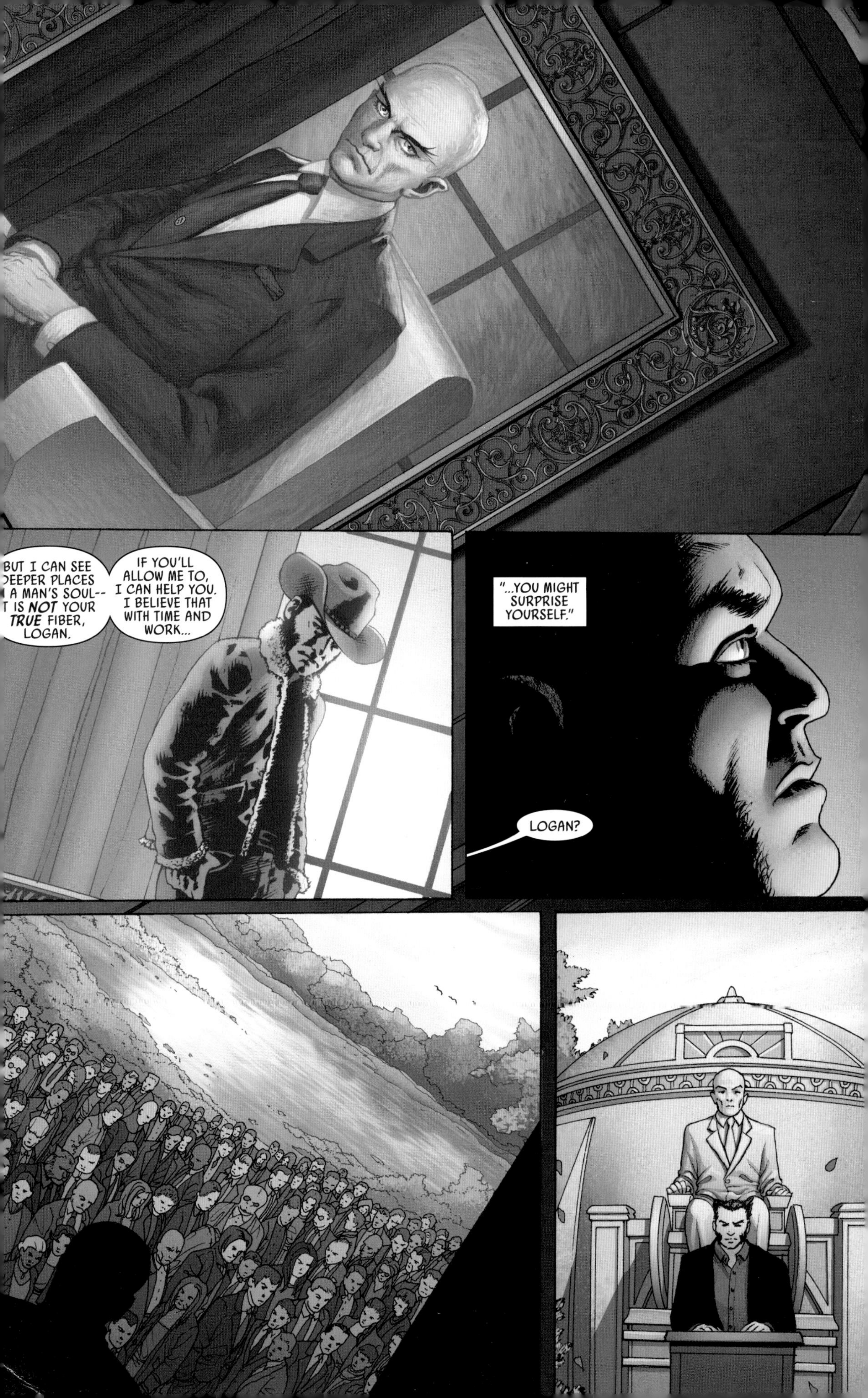
BUT I CAN SEE
DEEPER PLACES
A MAN'S SOUL--
T IS NOT YOUR
TRUE FIBER,
LOGAN.
IF YOU'LL ALLOW ME TO, I CAN HELP YOU. I BELIEVE THAT WITH TIME AND WORK...
"...YOU MIGHT SURPRISE YOURSELF."
LOGAN?

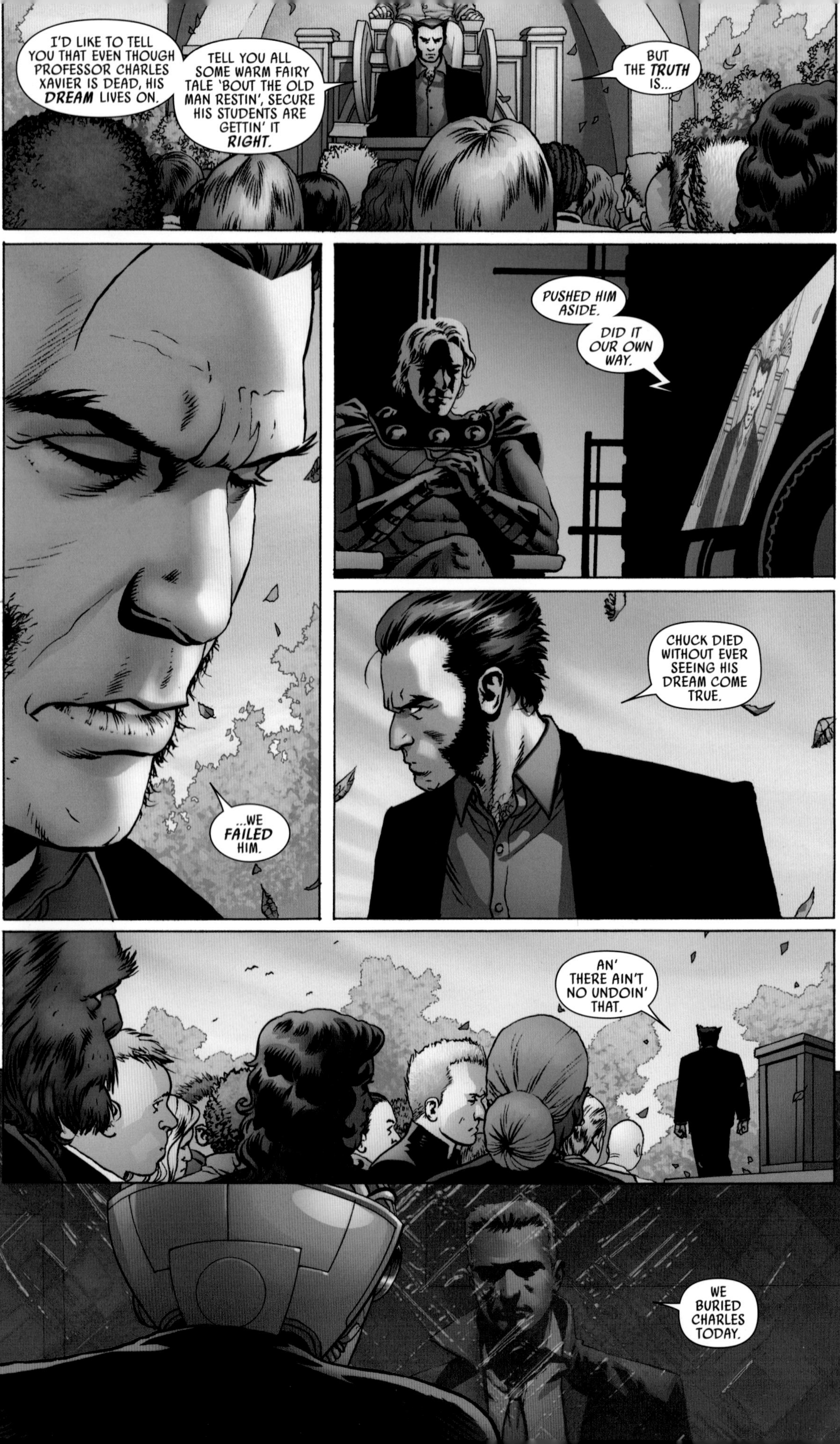
I'D LIKE TO TELL YOU THAT EVEN THOUGH PROFESSOR CHARLES XAVIER IS DEAD, HIS DREAM LIVES ON.
TELL YOU ALL SOME WARM FAIRY TALE 'BOUT THE OLD MAN RESTIN', SECURE HIS STUDENTS ARE GETTIN' IT RIGHT.
BUT THE TRUTH IS...
...WE FAILED HIM.
PUSHED HIM ASIDE.
DID IT OUR OWN WAY.
CHUCK DIED WITHOUT EVER SEEING HIS DREAM COME TRUE.
AN' THERE AIN'T NO UNDOIN' THAT.
WE BURIED CHARLES TODAY.

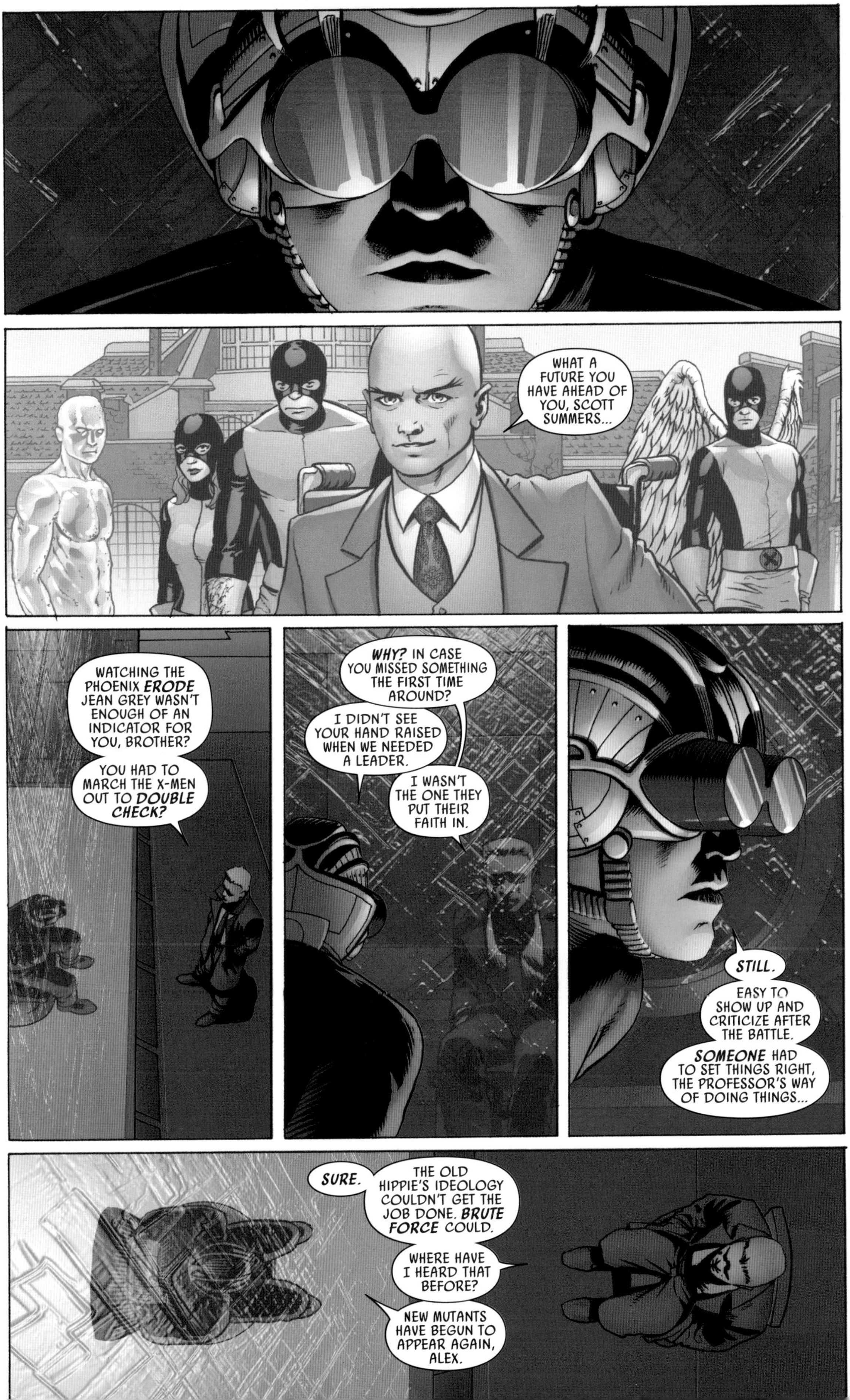
WHAT A FUTURE YOU HAVE AHEAD OF YOU, SCOTT SUMMERS...
WATCHING THE PHOENIX ERODE JEAN GREY WASN'T ENOUGH OF AN INDICATOR FOR YOU, BROTHER?
YOU HAD TO MARCH THE X-MEN OUT TO DOUBLE CHECK?
WHY? IN CASE YOU MISSED SOMETHING THE FIRST TIME AROUND?
I DIDN'T SEE YOUR HAND RAISED WHEN WE NEEDED A LEADER.
I WASN'T THE ONE THEY PUT THEIR FAITH IN.
STILL.
EASY TO SHOW UP AND CRITICIZE AFTER THE BATTLE.
SOMEONE HAD TO SET THINGS RIGHT, THE PROFESSOR'S WAY OF DOING THINGS...
SURE.
THE OLD HIPPIE'S IDEOLOGY COULDN'T GET THE JOB DONE. BRUTE FORCE COULD.
WHERE HAVE I HEARD THAT BEFORE?
NEW MUTANTS HAVE BEGUN TO APPEAR AGAIN, ALEX.

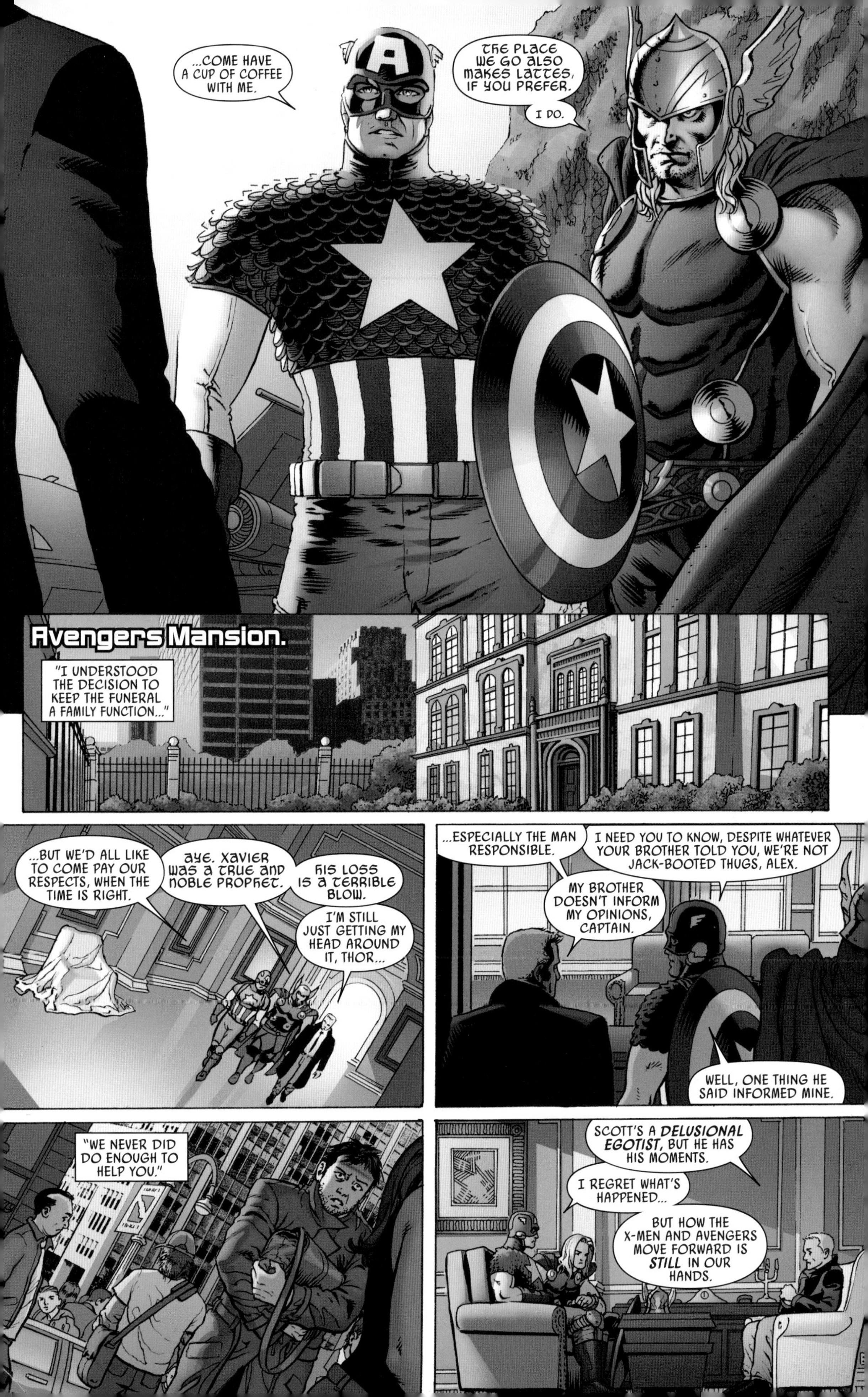
...COME HAVE A CUP OF COFFEE WITH ME.
THE PLACE WE GO ALSO MAKES LATTES, IF YOU PREFER.
I DO.
Avengers Mansion.
"I UNDERSTOOD THE DECISION TO KEEP THE FUNERAL A FAMILY FUNCTION..."
...BUT WE'D ALL LIKE TO COME PAY OUR RESPECTS, WHEN THE TIME IS RIGHT.
AYE. XAVIER WAS A TRUE AND NOBLE PROPHET.
HIS LOSS IS A TERRIBLE BLOW.
I'M STILL JUST GETTING MY HEAD AROUND IT, THOR...
...ESPECIALLY THE MAN RESPONSIBLE.
I NEED YOU TO KNOW, DESPITE WHATEVER YOUR BROTHER TOLD YOU, WE'RE NOT JACK-BOOTED THUGS, ALEX.
MY BROTHER DOESN'T INFORM MY OPINIONS, CAPTAIN.
WELL, ONE THING HE SAID INFORMED MINE.
"WE NEVER DID DO ENOUGH TO HELP YOU."
SCOTT'S A DELUSIONAL EGOTIST, BUT HE HAS HIS MOMENTS.
I REGRET WHAT'S HAPPENED...
BUT HOW THE X-MEN AND AVENGERS MOVE FORWARD IS STILL IN OUR HANDS.

I'D LIKE YOU TO JOIN US--TO BECOME AN AVENGER.

MORE THAN JOIN, I WANT YOU TO LEAD A SQUAD OF OUR VERY BEST.

X-MEN AND AVENGERS WORKING TOGETHER, SETTING AN EXAMPLE OF COOPERATION.

WITH XAVIER GONE, AND CYCLOPS LOCKED AWAY, SOMEONE HAS TO STAND UP AND REPRESENT THE MUTANTS.

"LOGAN IS TRYING, AND HE'S DOING GOOD WORK AT THE SCHOOL...

"...BUT WITH HIS CHECKERED PAST HE CAN'T BE THE FACE OF THIS."

BEEP-BEEP!

HONK!

HEY! WHADDAYA, ON DRUGS?! MOVE YER ASS!

SOMEBODY CALL THE COPS--

"YOU'RE A GOVERNMENT MAN, DEGREE IN GEOPHYSICS, A STUDENT OF XAVIER'S WITH A CLEAN HISTORY.

"PEOPLE WILL LISTEN TO YOU.

"THEY'LL FOLLOW YOU."

HEY, MAN... Y-YOU ALL RIGHT?

NEVER BETTER.

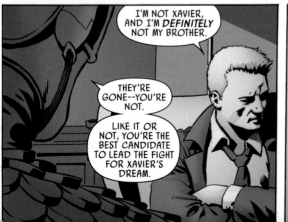

I'M NOT XAVIER, AND I'M DEFINITELY NOT MY BROTHER.

THEY'RE GONE--YOU'RE NOT.

LIKE IT OR NOT, YOU'RE THE BEST CANDIDATE TO LEAD THE FIGHT FOR XAVIER'S DREAM.

NO. NOT ME.

SOMEONE HAS TO STAND UP AND FILL THEIR SHOES, ALEX.

RIGHT...

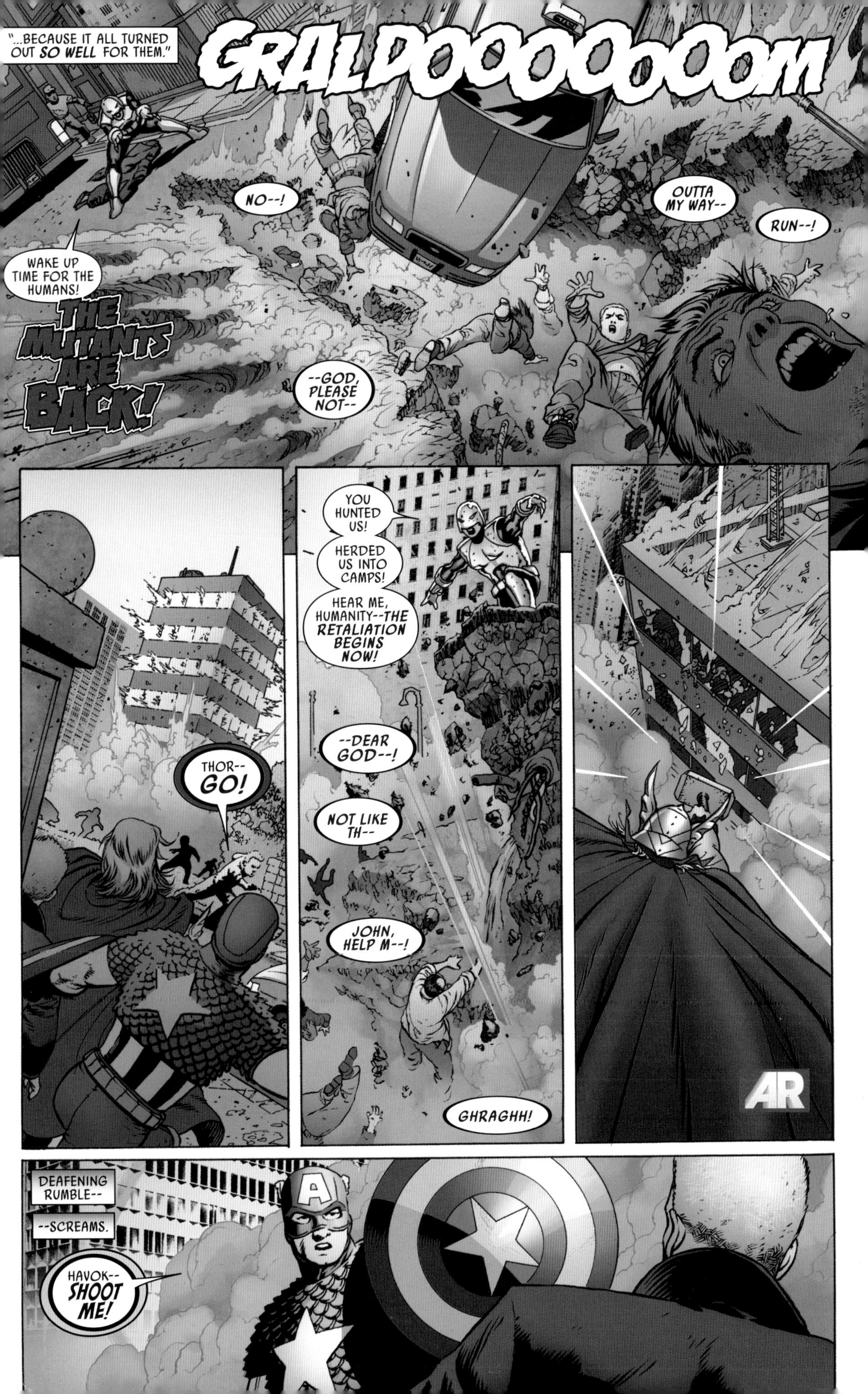
"...BECAUSE IT ALL TURNED OUT SO WELL FOR THEM."
GRALDOOOOOOOOM
WAKE UP TIME FOR THE HUMANS!
THE MUTANTS ARE BACK!
NO--!
--GOD, PLEASE NOT--
OUTTA MY WAY--
RUN--!
THOR-- GO!
YOU HUNTED US!
HERDED US INTO CAMPS!
HEAR ME, HUMANITY--THE RETALIATION BEGINS NOW!
--DEAR GOD--!
NOT LIKE TH--
JOHN, HELP M--!
GHRAGHH!
AR
DEAFENING RUMBLE--
--SCREAMS.
HAVOK-- SHOOT ME!

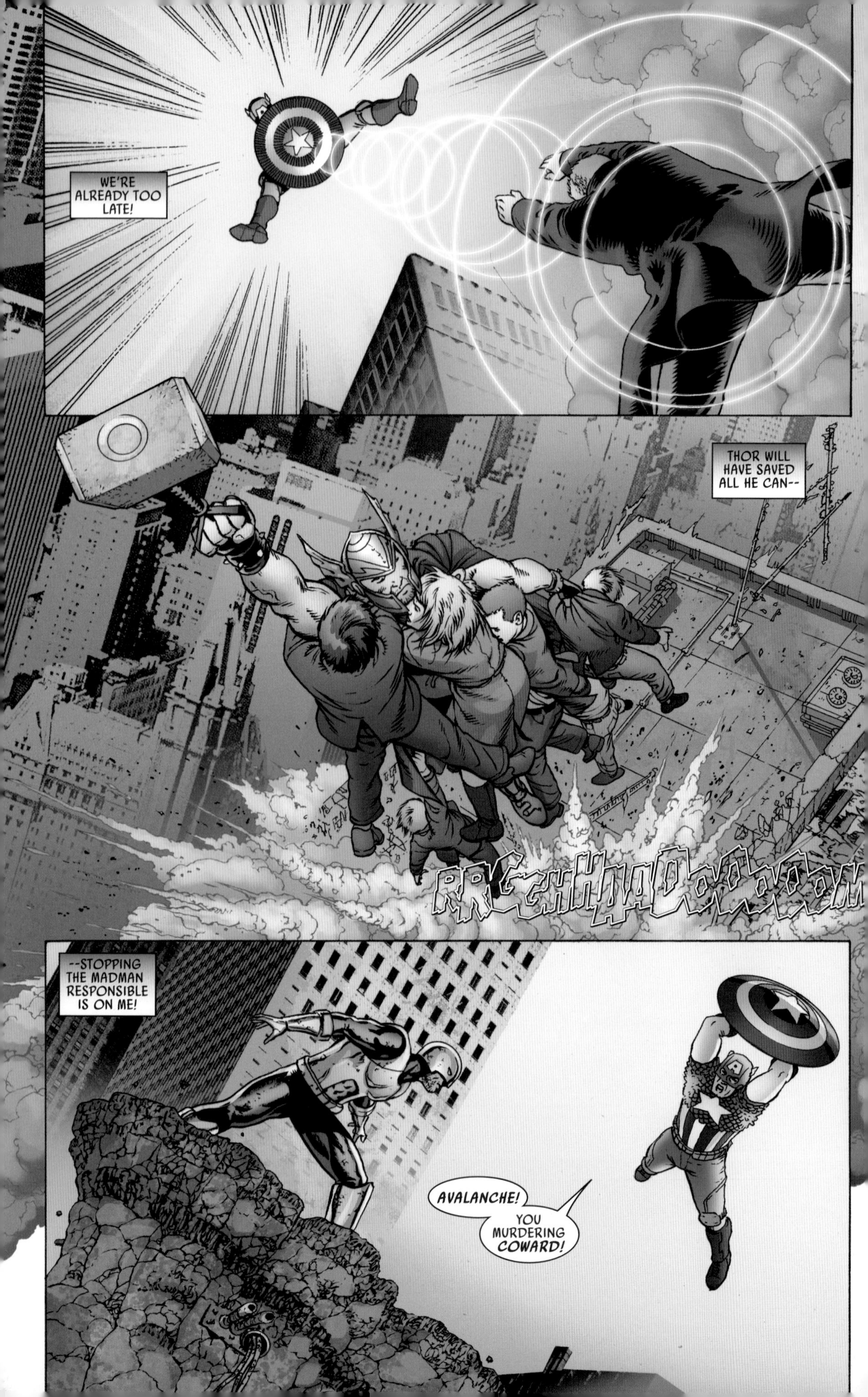
WE'RE ALREADY TOO LATE!
THOR WILL HAVE SAVED ALL HE CAN--
--STOPPING THE MADMAN RESPONSIBLE IS ON ME!
AVALANCHE!
YOU MURDERING COWARD!

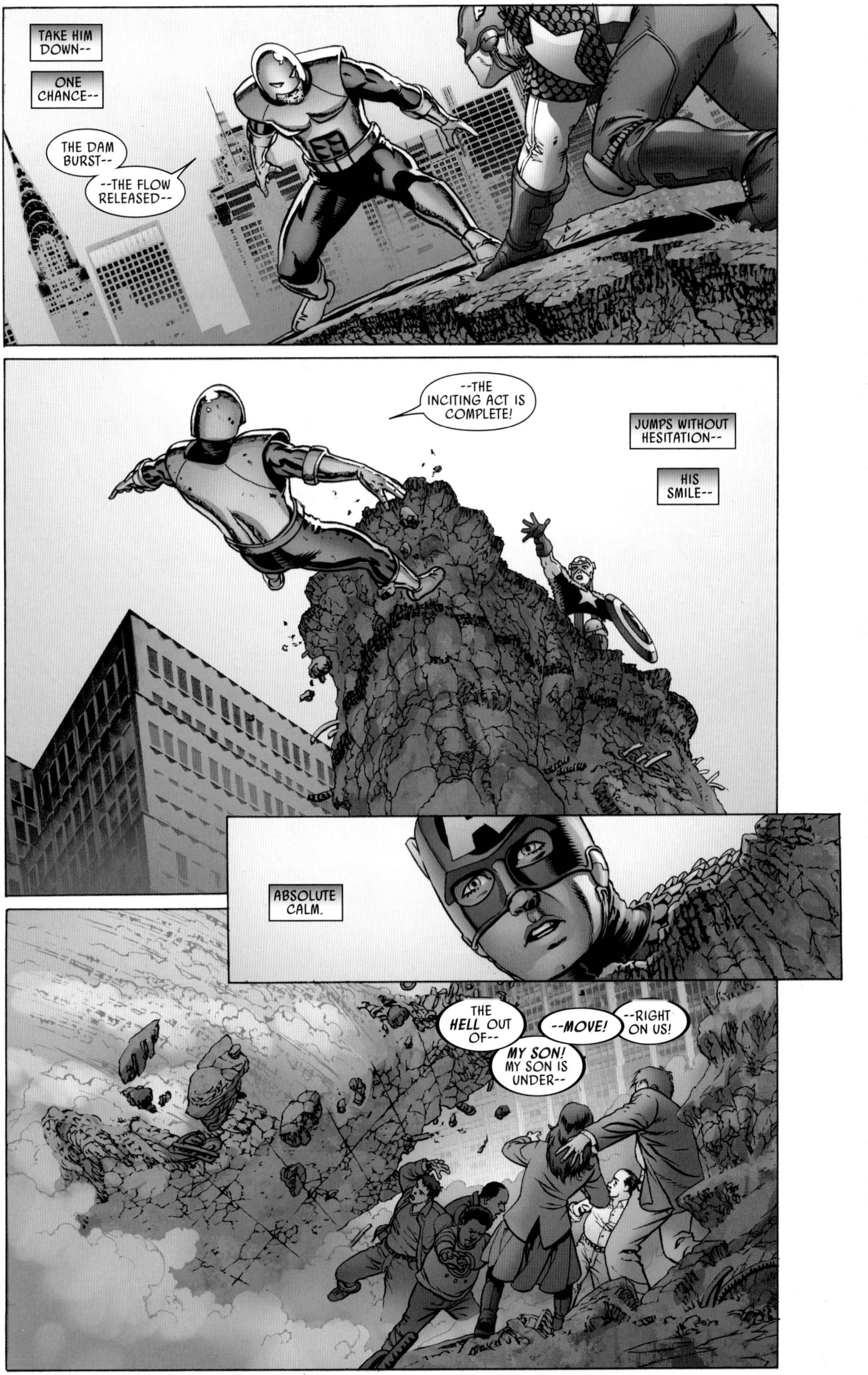
TAKE HIM DOWN--
ONE CHANCE--
THE DAM BURST--
--THE FLOW RELEASED--
--THE INCITING ACT IS COMPLETE!
JUMPS WITHOUT HESITATION--
HIS SMILE--
ABSOLUTE CALM.
THE HELL OUT OF--
--MOVE!
--RIGHT ON US!
MY SON! MY SON IS UNDER--

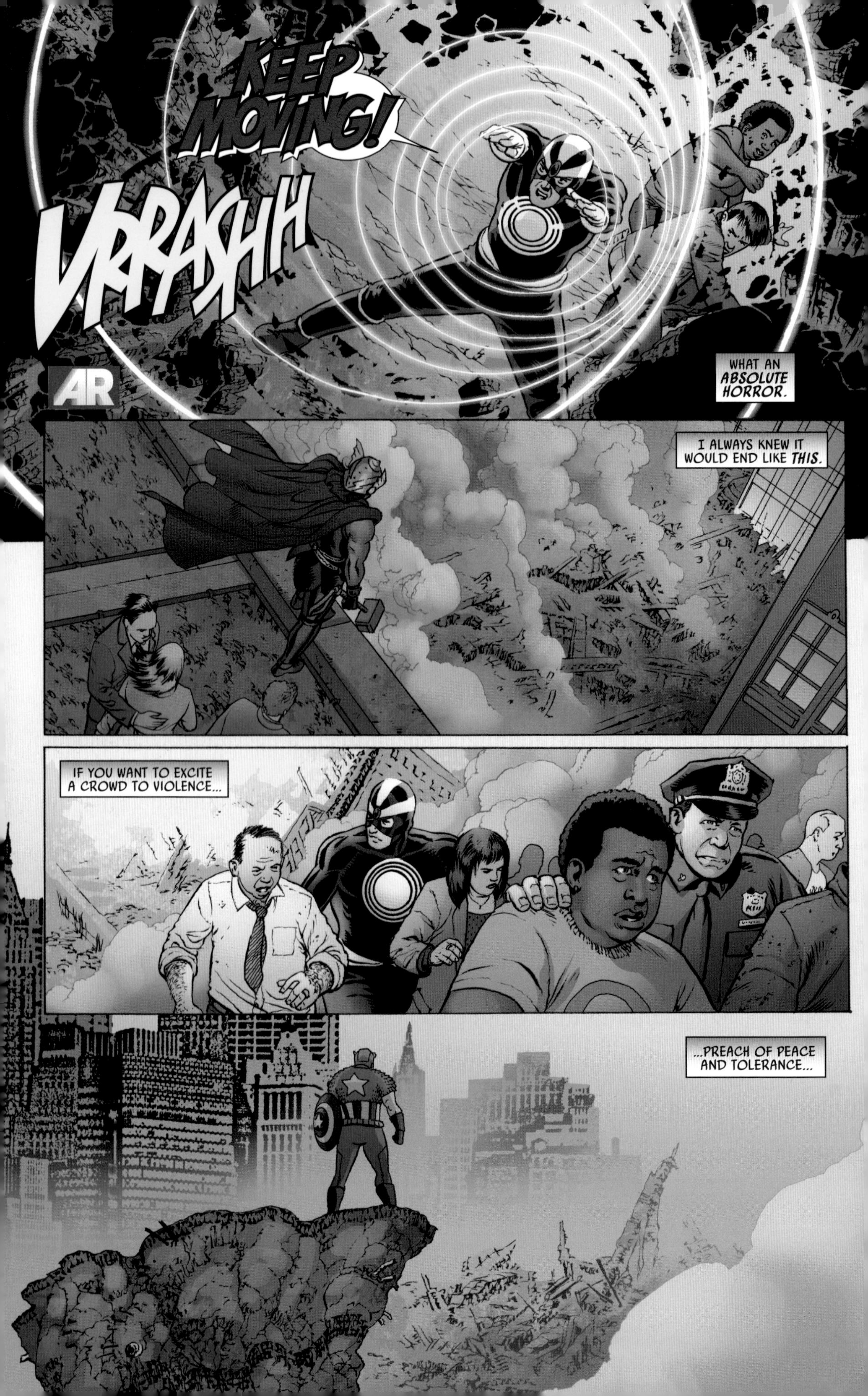
KEEP MOVING!
VRRASHH
AR
WHAT AN ABSOLUTE HORROR.
I ALWAYS KNEW IT WOULD END LIKE THIS.
IF YOU WANT TO EXCITE A CROWD TO VIOLENCE...
...PREACH OF PEACE AND TOLERANCE...

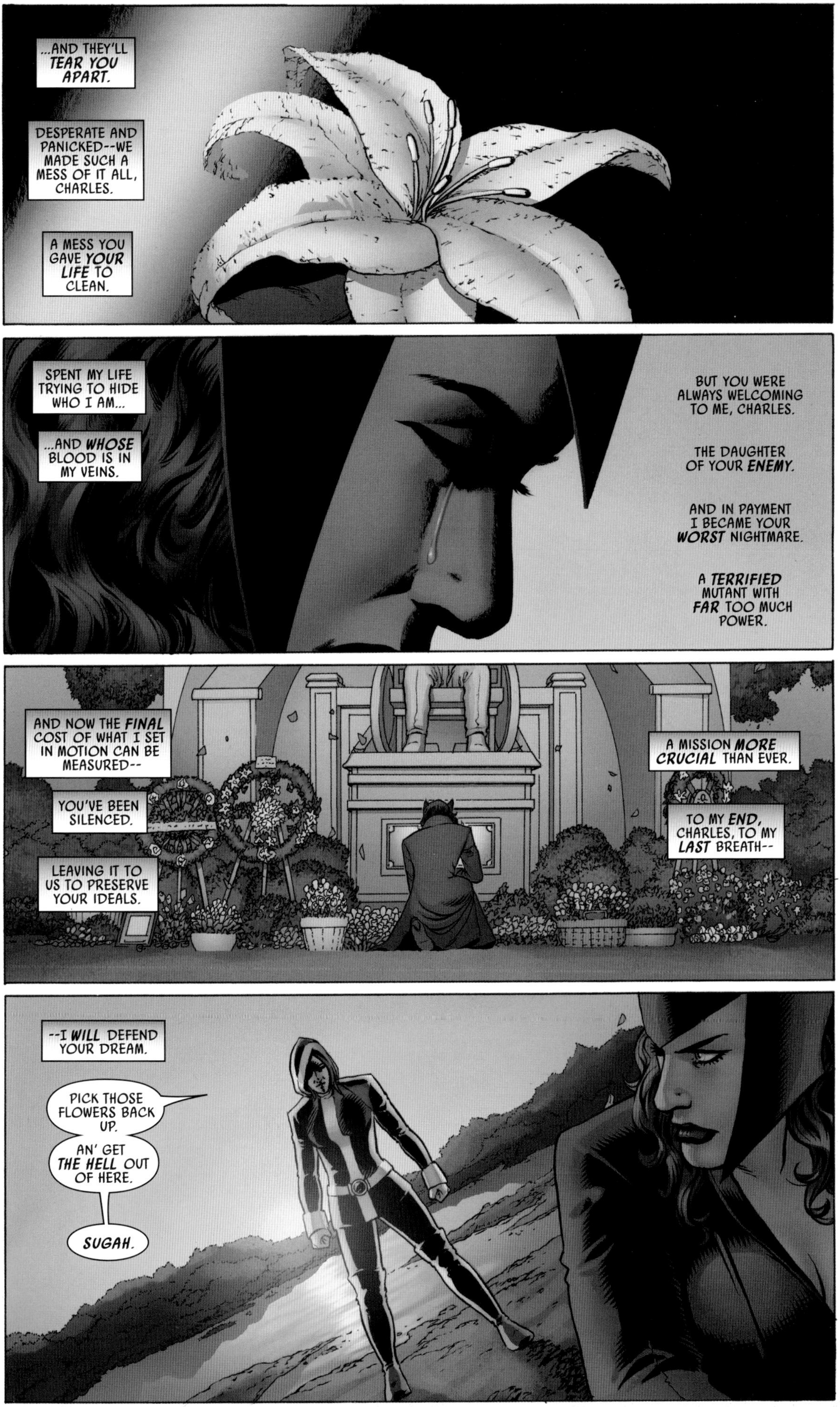
...AND THEY'LL TEAR YOU APART.
DESPERATE AND PANICKED--WE MADE SUCH A MESS OF IT ALL, CHARLES.
A MESS YOU GAVE YOUR LIFE TO CLEAN.
SPENT MY LIFE TRYING TO HIDE WHO I AM...
...AND WHOSE BLOOD IS IN MY VEINS.
BUT YOU WERE ALWAYS WELCOMING TO ME, CHARLES.
THE DAUGHTER OF YOUR ENEMY.
AND IN PAYMENT I BECAME YOUR WORST NIGHTMARE.
A TERRIFIED MUTANT WITH FAR TOO MUCH POWER.
AND NOW THE FINAL COST OF WHAT I SET IN MOTION CAN BE MEASURED--
YOU'VE BEEN SILENCED.
LEAVING IT TO US TO PRESERVE YOUR IDEALS.
A MISSION MORE CRUCIAL THAN EVER.
TO MY END, CHARLES, TO MY LAST BREATH--
--I WILL DEFEND YOUR DREAM.
PICK THOSE FLOWERS BACK UP.
AN' GET THE HELL OUT OF HERE.
SUGAH.

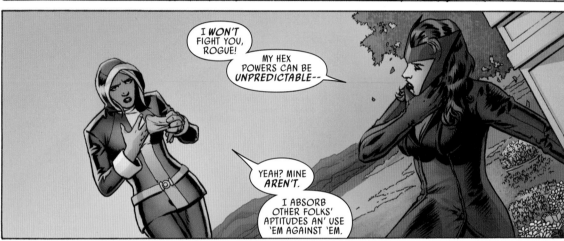

I **WON'T** FIGHT YOU, ROGUE!

MY HEX POWERS CAN BE **UNPREDICTABLE--**

YEAH? MINE **AREN'T.**

I ABSORB OTHER FOLKS' APTITUDES AN' USE 'EM AGAINST 'EM.

HERE.

LET ME **SHOW** YOU--

NOT WORKING...

WHAT THE **HELL** DID YOU DO TO MY--

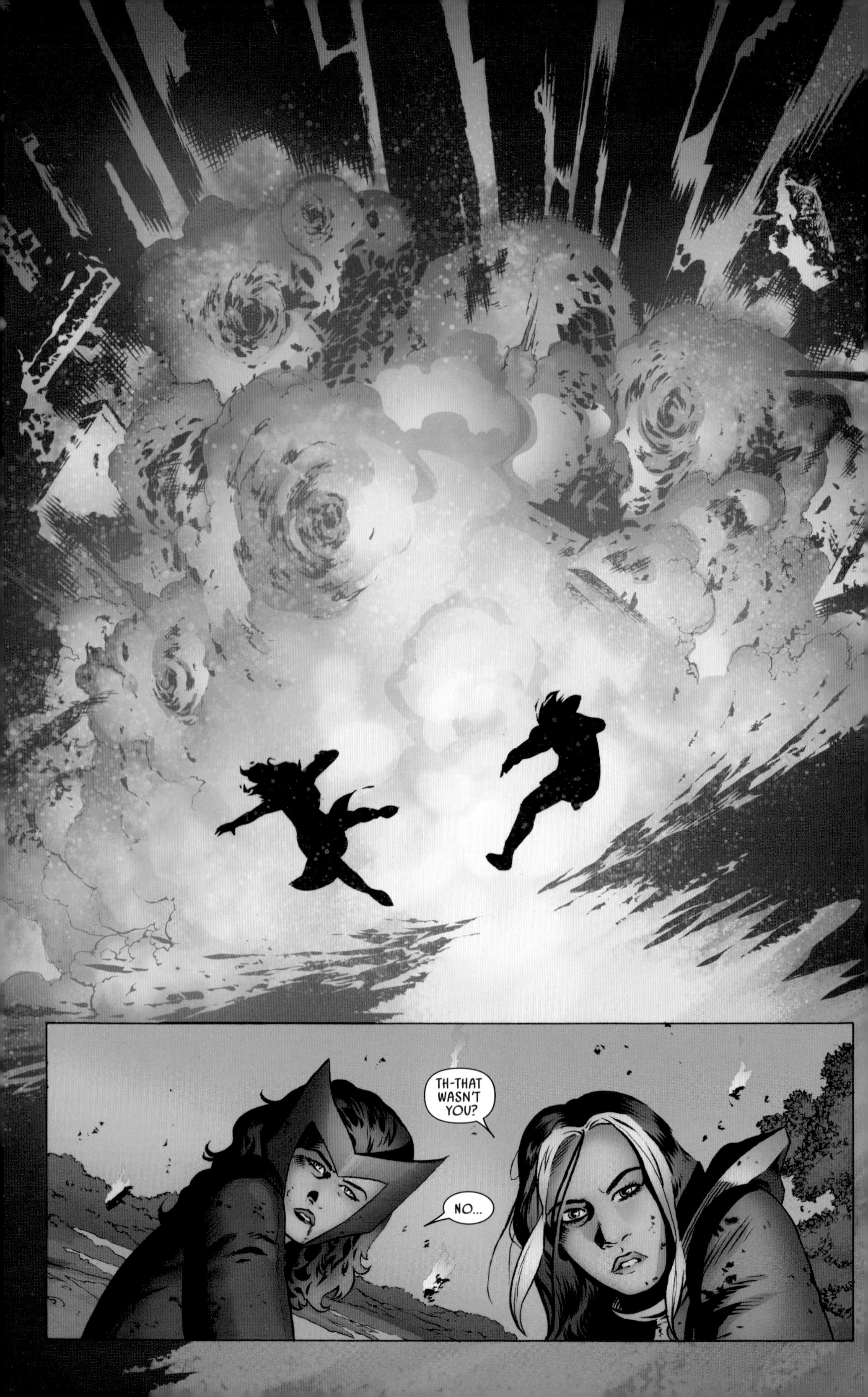
TH-THAT WASN'T YOU?
NO...

"...IT WAS *THEM*."

YOUR FOUL "*GIFTS*" FAIL AS YOU SUFFER THE GAZE OF *THE GOAT-FACED GIRL*!

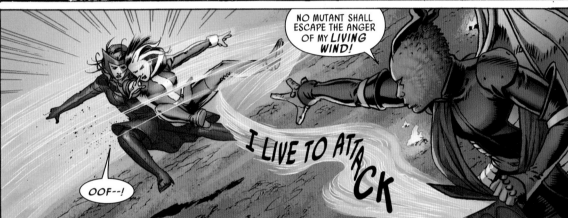

NO MUTANT SHALL ESCAPE THE ANGER OF MY *LIVING WIND*!

I LIVE TO ATTACK

OOF--!

I SUFFER *THE INSECT* UNTO MYSELF--

--FOR THE GOOD OF ALL *MAN*.

MY *CASSANDRA TOXIN* WILL END THE THREAT *THEY* REFUSE TO SEE!

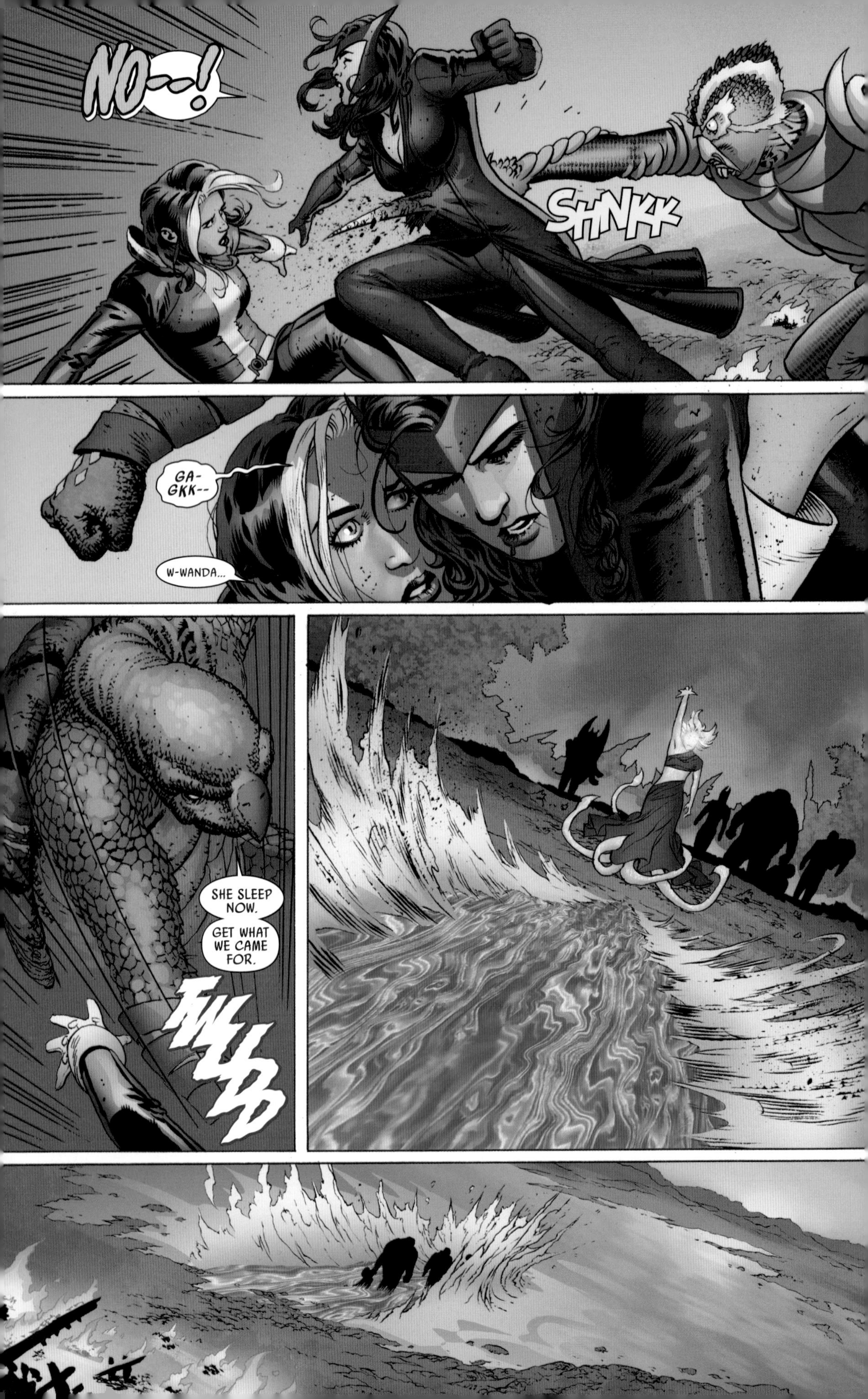
NO--!
SHNKK
GA-GKK--
W-WANDA...
SHE SLEEP NOW.
GET WHAT WE CAME FOR.
FWUDD

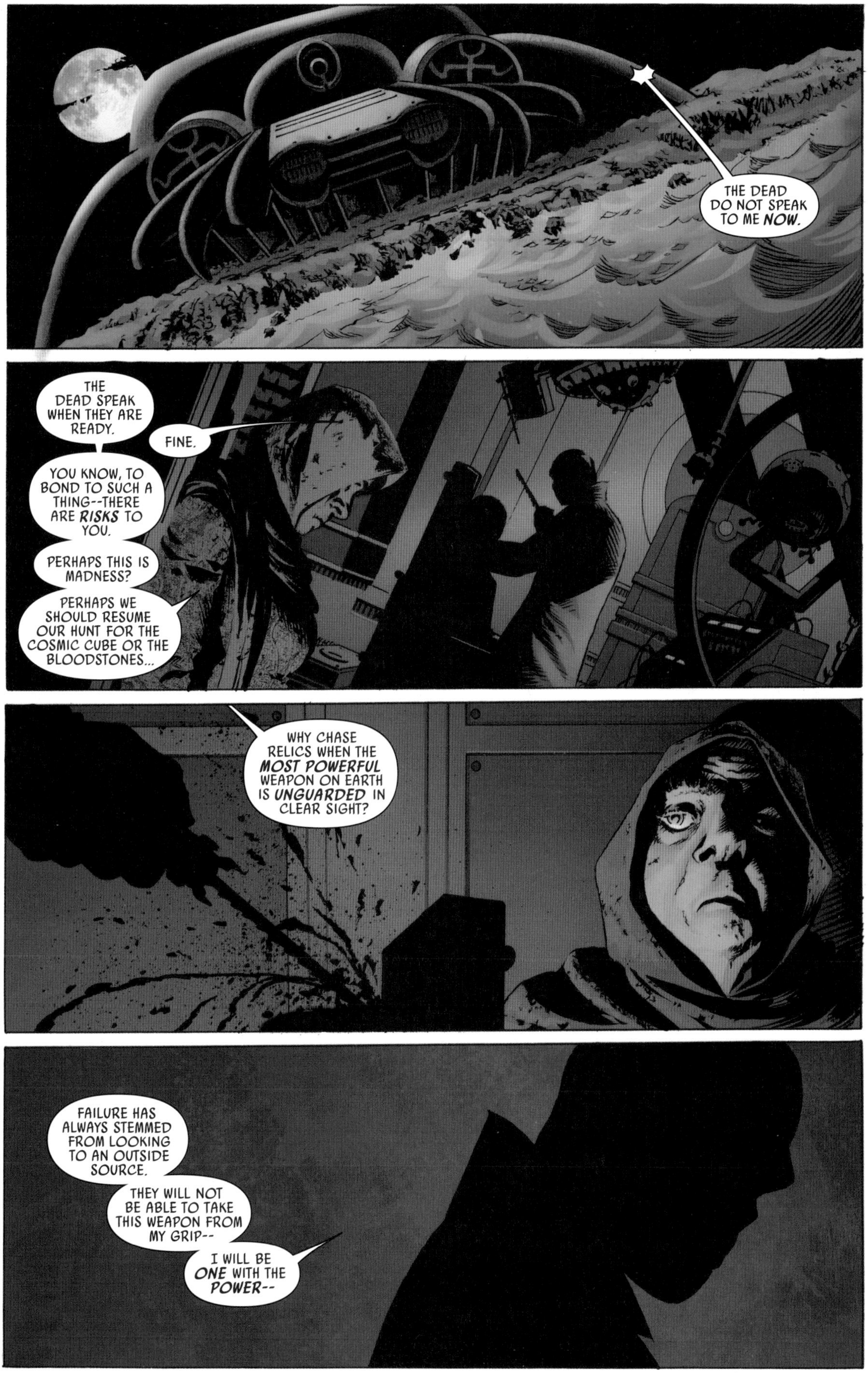
THE DEAD DO NOT SPEAK TO ME NOW.
THE DEAD SPEAK WHEN THEY ARE READY.
FINE.
YOU KNOW, TO BOND TO SUCH A THING--THERE ARE RISKS TO YOU.
PERHAPS THIS IS MADNESS?
PERHAPS WE SHOULD RESUME OUR HUNT FOR THE COSMIC CUBE OR THE BLOODSTONES...
WHY CHASE RELICS WHEN THE MOST POWERFUL WEAPON ON EARTH IS UNGUARDED IN CLEAR SIGHT?
FAILURE HAS ALWAYS STEMMED FROM LOOKING TO AN OUTSIDE SOURCE.
THEY WILL NOT BE ABLE TO TAKE THIS WEAPON FROM MY GRIP--
I WILL BE ONE WITH THE POWER--

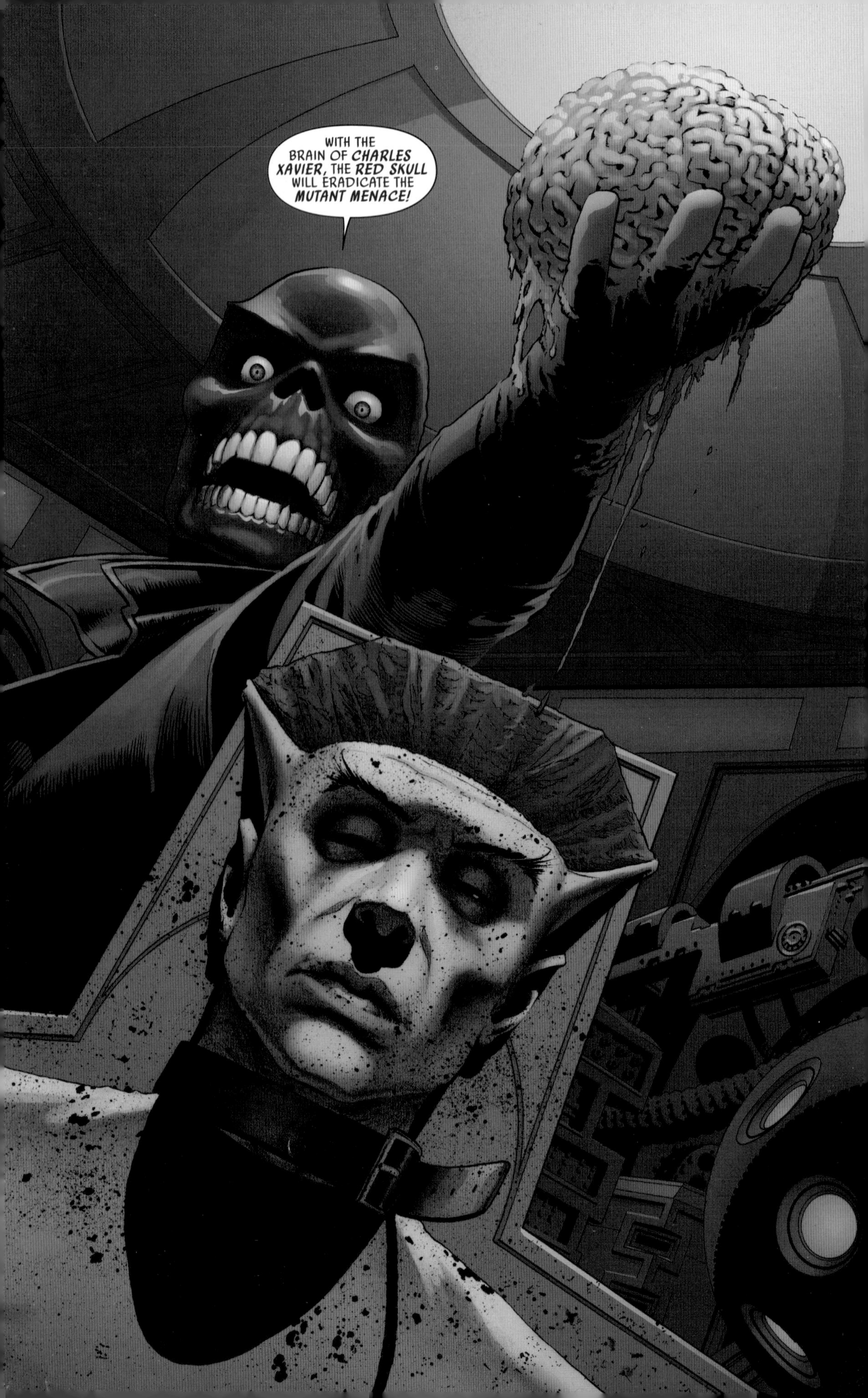
WITH THE BRAIN OF CHARLES XAVIER, THE RED SKULL WILL ERADICATE THE MUTANT MENACE!

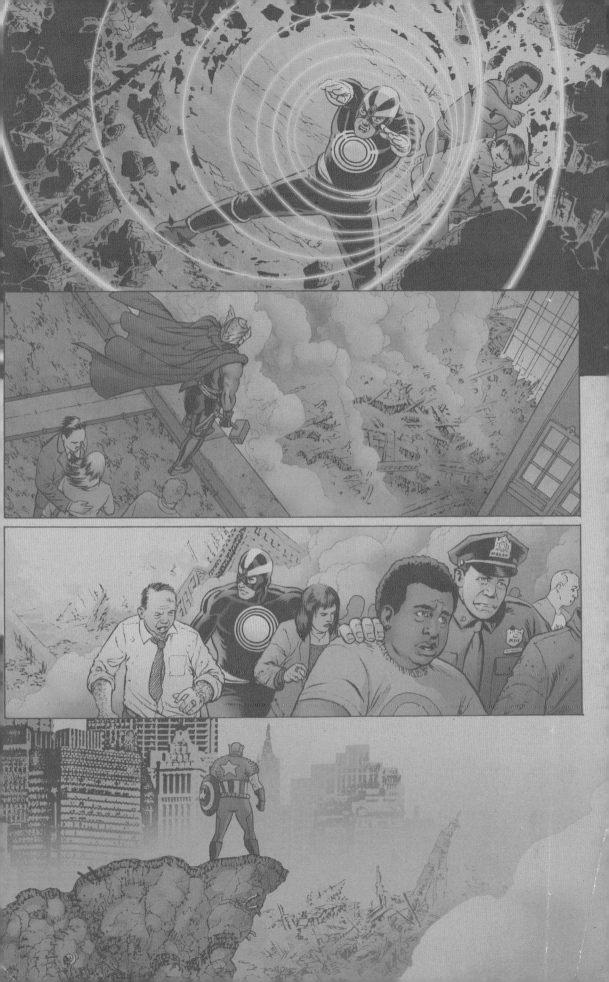

UNCANNY AVENGERS #2

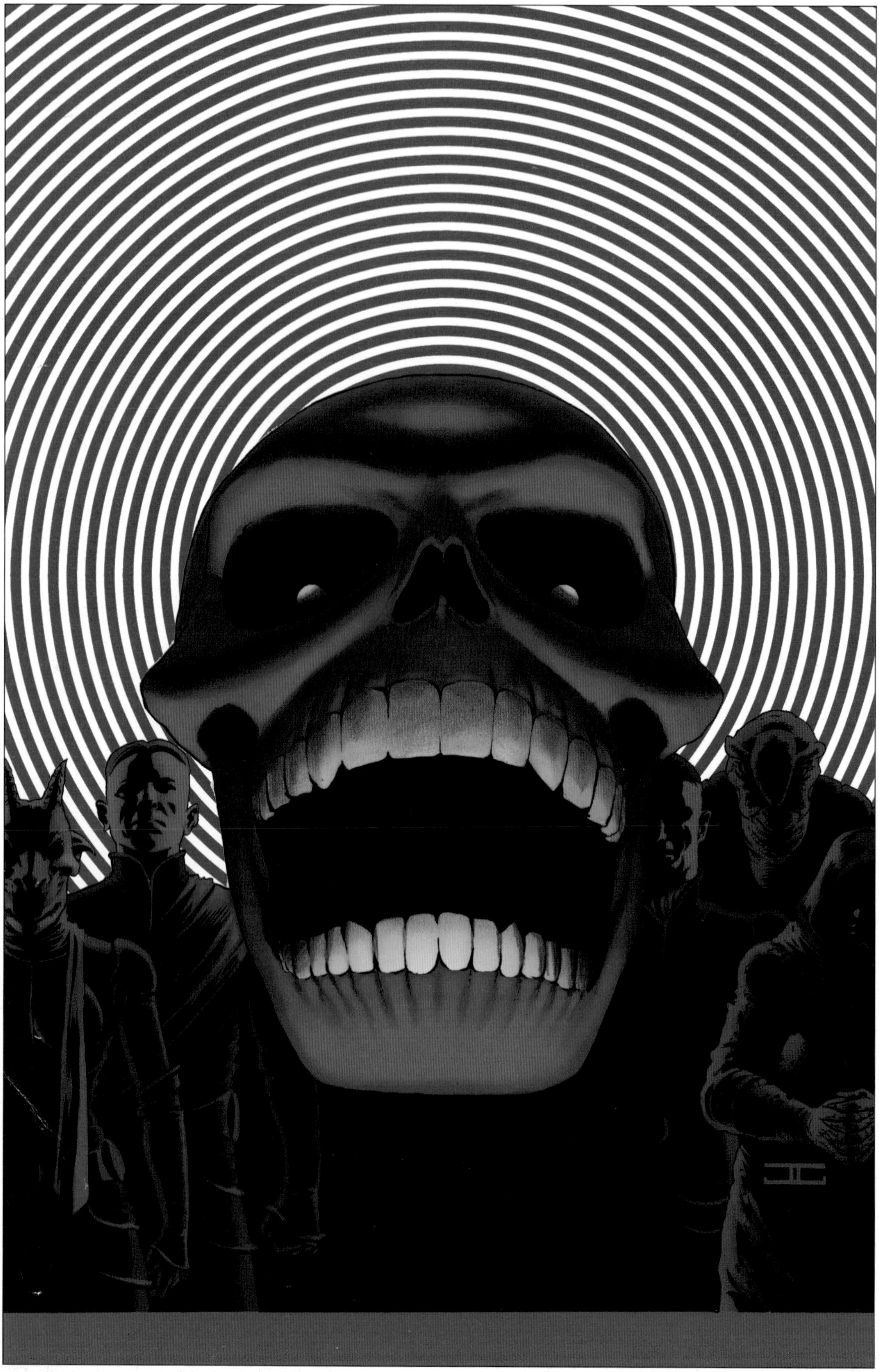

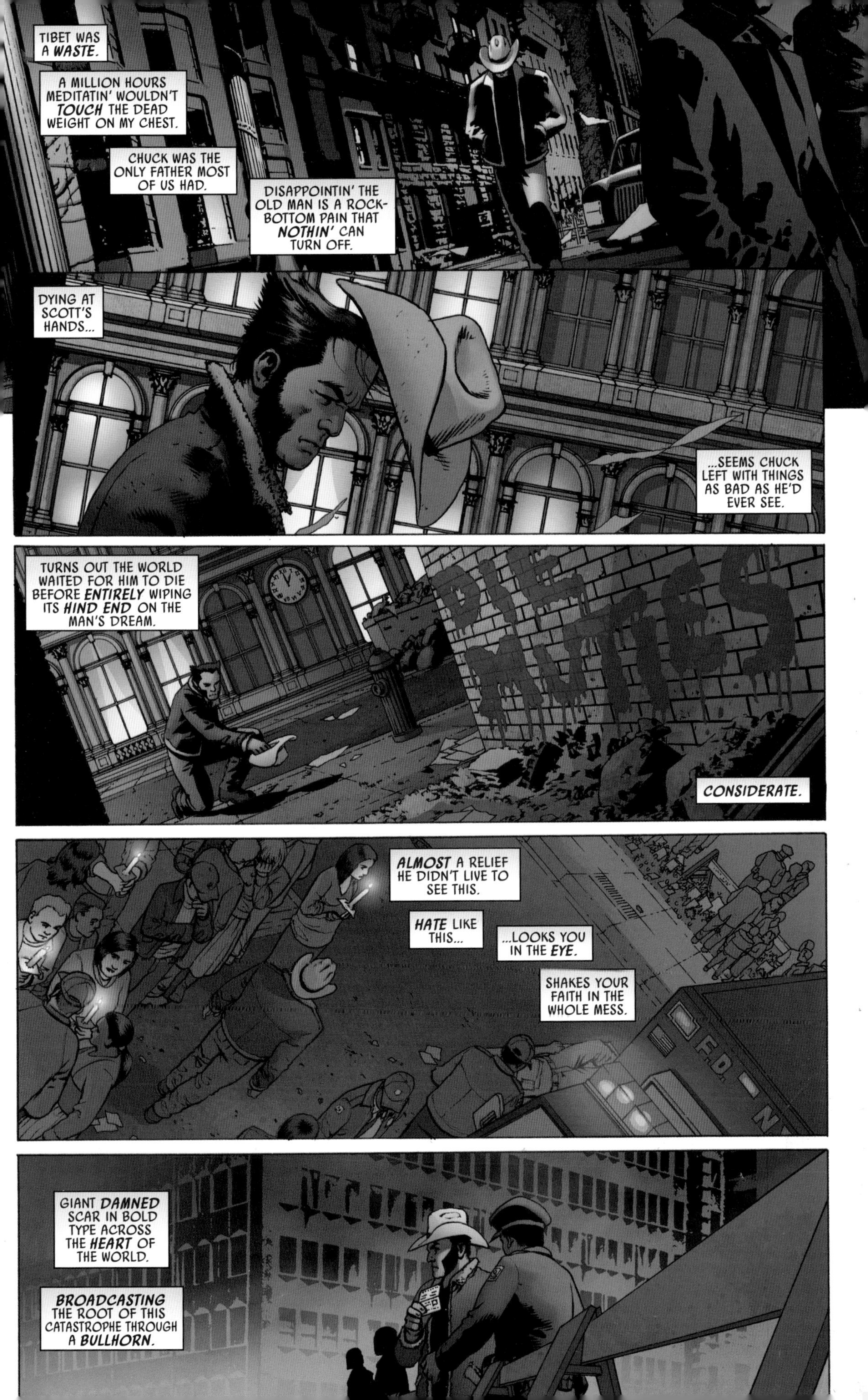
TIBET WAS A WASTE.
A MILLION HOURS MEDITATIN' WOULDN'T TOUCH THE DEAD WEIGHT ON MY CHEST.
CHUCK WAS THE ONLY FATHER MOST OF US HAD.
DISAPPOINTIN' THE OLD MAN IS A ROCK-BOTTOM PAIN THAT NOTHIN' CAN TURN OFF.
DYING AT SCOTT'S HANDS...
...SEEMS CHUCK LEFT WITH THINGS AS BAD AS HE'D EVER SEE.
TURNS OUT THE WORLD WAITED FOR HIM TO DIE BEFORE ENTIRELY WIPING ITS HIND END ON THE MAN'S DREAM.
DIE MUTIES
CONSIDERATE.
ALMOST A RELIEF HE DIDN'T LIVE TO SEE THIS.
HATE LIKE THIS...
...LOOKS YOU IN THE EYE.
SHAKES YOUR FAITH IN THE WHOLE MESS.
GIANT DAMNED SCAR IN BOLD TYPE ACROSS THE HEART OF THE WORLD.
BROADCASTING THE ROOT OF THIS CATASTROPHE THROUGH A BULLHORN.

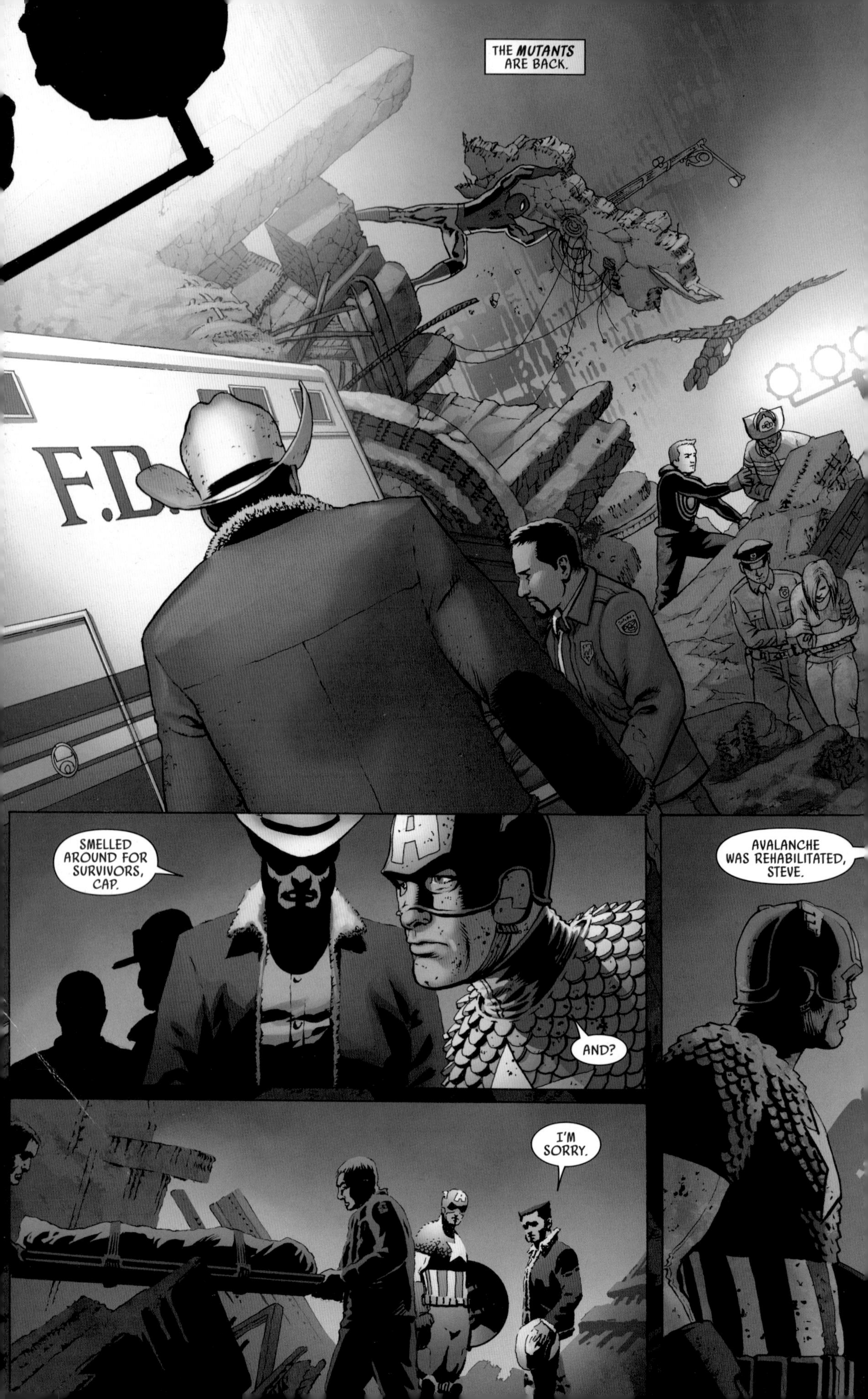
THE MUTANTS ARE BACK.
F.D.
SMELLED AROUND FOR SURVIVORS, CAP.
AND?
AVALANCHE WAS REHABILITATED, STEVE.
I'M SORRY.

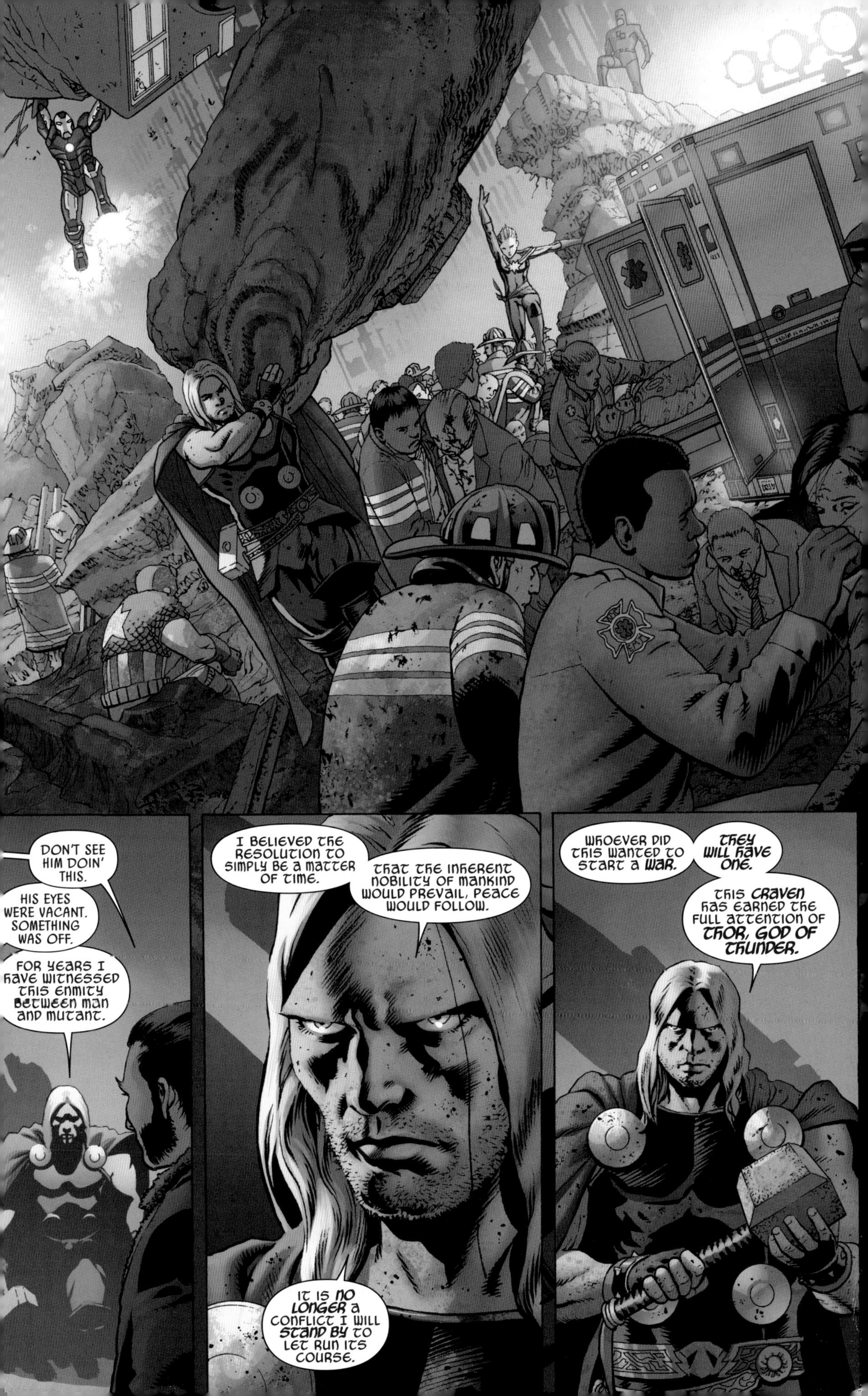
DON'T SEE HIM DOIN' THIS.
HIS EYES WERE VACANT. SOMETHING WAS OFF.
FOR YEARS I HAVE WITNESSED THIS ENMITY BETWEEN MAN AND MUTANT.
I BELIEVED THE RESOLUTION TO SIMPLY BE A MATTER OF TIME.
THAT THE INHERENT NOBILITY OF MANKIND WOULD PREVAIL, PEACE WOULD FOLLOW.
IT IS NO LONGER A CONFLICT I WILL STAND BY TO LET RUN ITS COURSE.
WHOEVER DID THIS WANTED TO START A WAR.
THEY WILL HAVE ONE.
THIS CRAVEN HAS EARNED THE FULL ATTENTION OF THOR, GOD OF THUNDER.

WE **WILL** FIND WHO WAS BEHIND THIS, AND WE **WILL** AVENGE OUR FALLEN, THOR.

BUT, NOW-- **RIGHT NOW**--OUR FIRST PRIORITY IS TO **PREVENT** MORE BLOODSHED.

TO ENSURE **NO ONE** USES THIS CATASTROPHE TO FURTHER AN AGENDA OF HATRED.

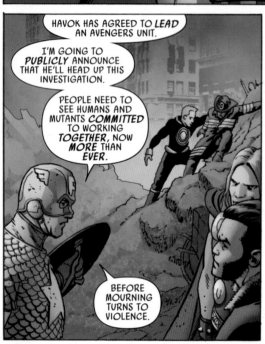

HAVOK HAS AGREED TO **LEAD** AN AVENGERS UNIT.

I'M GOING TO **PUBLICLY** ANNOUNCE THAT HE'LL HEAD UP THIS INVESTIGATION.

PEOPLE NEED TO SEE HUMANS AND MUTANTS **COMMITTED** TO WORKING **TOGETHER**, NOW **MORE** THAN **EVER**.

BEFORE MOURNING TURNS TO VIOLENCE.

LOT OF PEOPLE **DEAD** AT THE HANDS OF A **MUTANT** AND YOU WANT THE **BROTHER** OF A MUTANT NEARLY **TOOK OVER THE PLANET** TO HEAD UP **THE AVENGERS'** RESPONSE TO **THIS**?

GONNA **PISS** FOLKS OFF, STEVE.

GONNA GET MUTANTS **KILLED**.

I THOUGHT YOU'D BE **SUPPORTIVE** OF THIS, LOGAN.

COULDN'T'VE THOUGHT I'D BE **TOO** SUPPORTIVE GIVEN YOU **DIDN'T** BRING IT UP WITH ME FIRST.

LOGAN, **THIS** IS WHY CHARLES PUT HIS STUDENTS IN **UNIFORMS** AND SENT THEM OUT INTO THE WORLD. TO **PROTECT** AND **SERVE**--

--TO WIN **HEARTS AND MINDS**.

ALEX SUMMERS IS A **STRONG** AND **ETHICAL** MAN, A **PROVEN** LEADER.

A MAN WHO NORMAL PEOPLE CAN **IDENTIFY** WITH, AS WE NAVIGATE THIS.

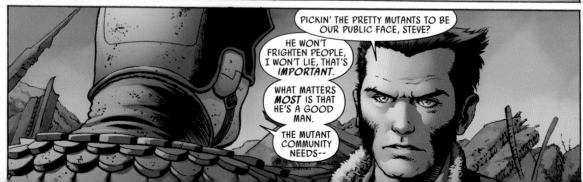

PICKIN' THE PRETTY MUTANTS TO BE OUR PUBLIC FACE, STEVE?

HE WON'T FRIGHTEN PEOPLE, I WON'T LIE, THAT'S **IMPORTANT**.

WHAT MATTERS **MOST** IS THAT HE'S A GOOD MAN.

THE MUTANT COMMUNITY NEEDS--

LISTEN TO YOU. "MUTANT COMMUNITY."

THERE AIN'T NO SUCH THING, CAP.

IT'S A LOAD O' *DRUNKEN SINCERITY*, FEEDING AN ILLUSION THAT WE ALL BELONG TO SOMETHIN' BIGGER.

IT'S JUST MORE O' THE CULT *KOOL-AID* SCOTT WAS SELLING.

HE INSISTED ON THANKING YOU PERSONALLY.

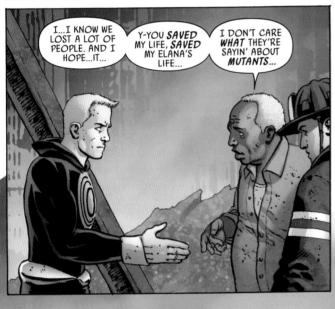

I...I KNOW WE LOST A LOT OF PEOPLE. AND I HOPE...IT...

Y-YOU *SAVED* MY LIFE, *SAVED* MY ELANA'S LIFE...

I DON'T CARE *WHAT* THEY'RE SAYIN' ABOUT *MUTANTS*...

THERE AIN'T ENOUGH HEROES IN THE WORLD.

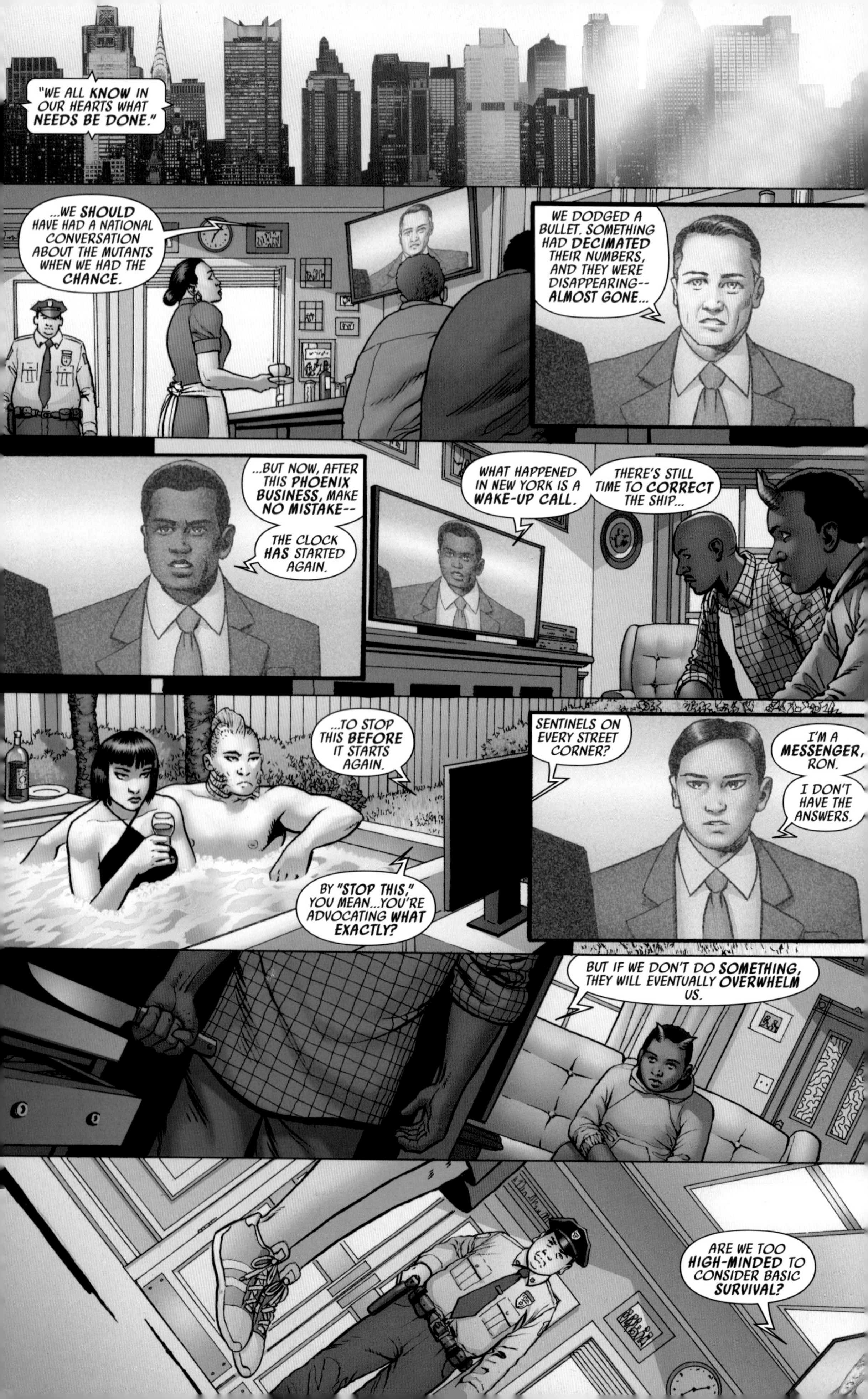
"WE ALL KNOW IN OUR HEARTS WHAT NEEDS BE DONE."
...WE SHOULD HAVE HAD A NATIONAL CONVERSATION ABOUT THE MUTANTS WHEN WE HAD THE CHANCE.
WE DODGED A BULLET. SOMETHING HAD DECIMATED THEIR NUMBERS, AND THEY WERE DISAPPEARING-- ALMOST GONE...
...BUT NOW, AFTER THIS PHOENIX BUSINESS, MAKE NO MISTAKE--
THE CLOCK HAS STARTED AGAIN.
WHAT HAPPENED IN NEW YORK IS A WAKE-UP CALL.
THERE'S STILL TIME TO CORRECT THE SHIP...
...TO STOP THIS BEFORE IT STARTS AGAIN.
BY "STOP THIS," YOU MEAN...YOU'RE ADVOCATING WHAT EXACTLY?
SENTINELS ON EVERY STREET CORNER?
I'M A MESSENGER, RON.
I DON'T HAVE THE ANSWERS.
BUT IF WE DON'T DO SOMETHING, THEY WILL EVENTUALLY OVERWHELM US.
ARE WE TOO HIGH-MINDED TO CONSIDER BASIC SURVIVAL?

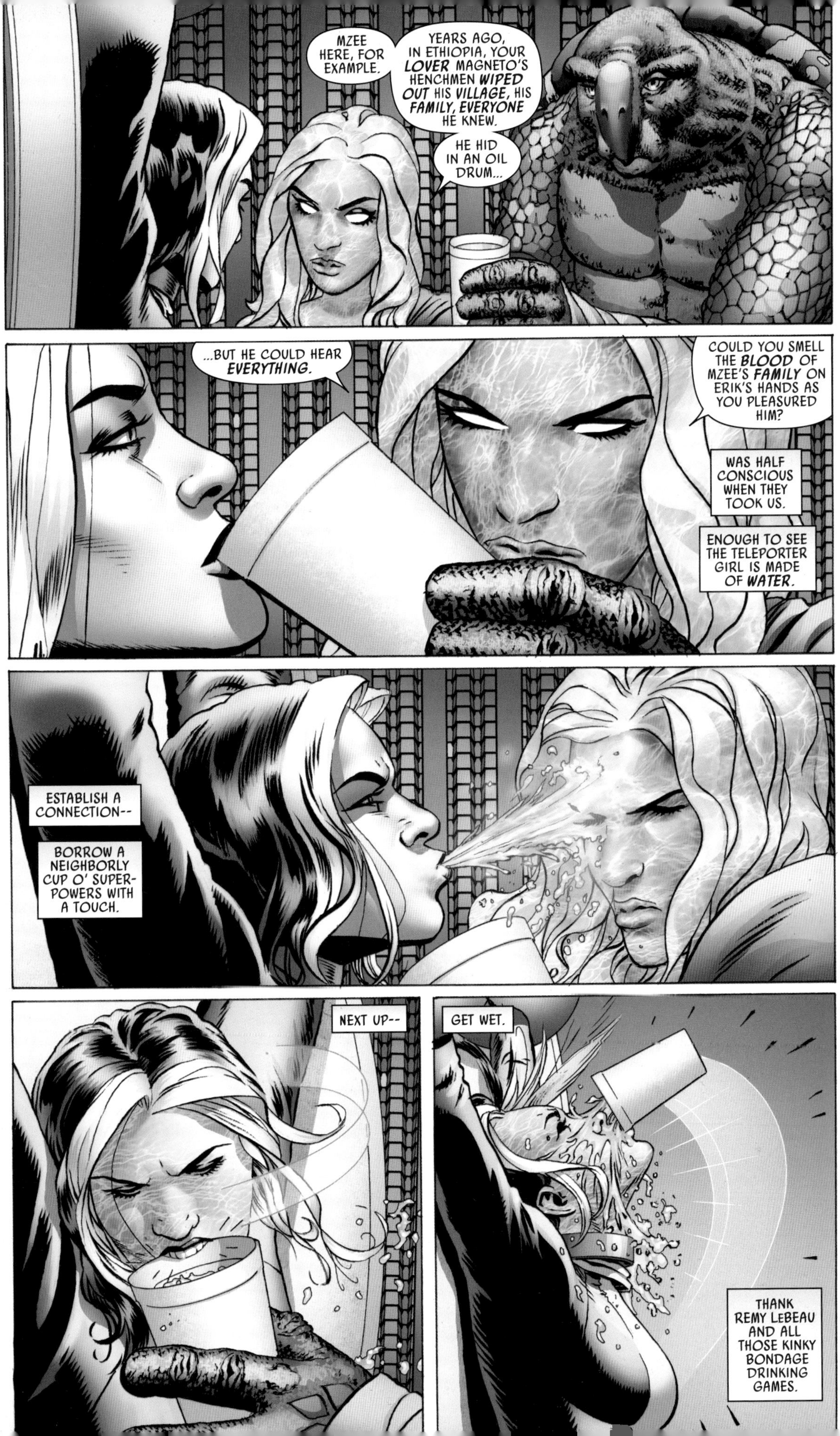
MZEE HERE, FOR EXAMPLE.
YEARS AGO, IN ETHIOPIA, YOUR LOVER MAGNETO'S HENCHMEN WIPED OUT HIS VILLAGE, HIS FAMILY, EVERYONE HE KNEW.
HE HID IN AN OIL DRUM...
...BUT HE COULD HEAR EVERYTHING.
COULD YOU SMELL THE BLOOD OF MZEE'S FAMILY ON ERIK'S HANDS AS YOU PLEASURED HIM?
WAS HALF CONSCIOUS WHEN THEY TOOK US.
ENOUGH TO SEE THE TELEPORTER GIRL IS MADE OF WATER.
ESTABLISH A CONNECTION--
BORROW A NEIGHBORLY CUP O' SUPER-POWERS WITH A TOUCH.
NEXT UP--
GET WET.
THANK REMY LEBEAU AND ALL THOSE KINKY BONDAGE DRINKING GAMES.

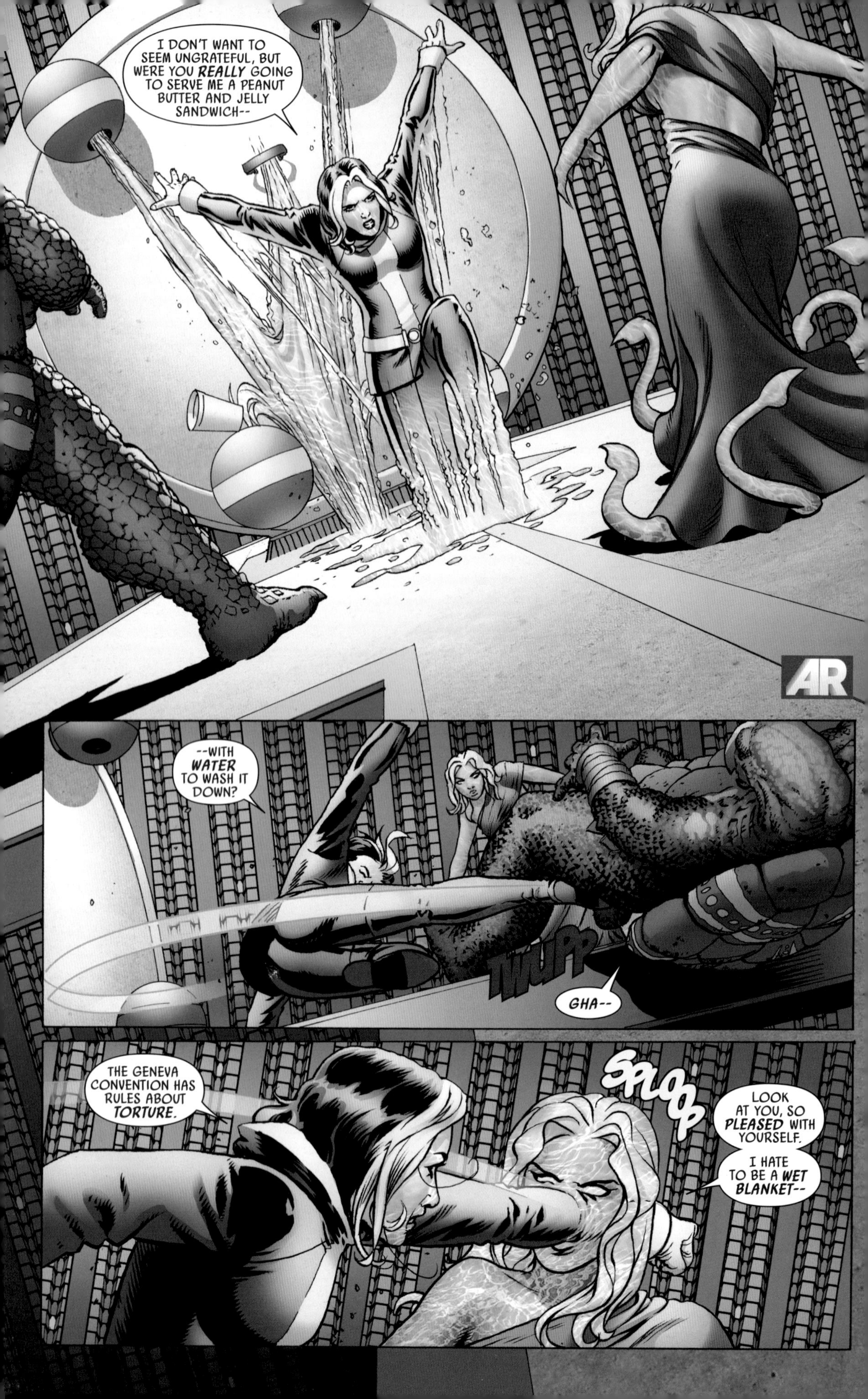
I DON'T WANT TO SEEM UNGRATEFUL, BUT WERE YOU REALLY GOING TO SERVE ME A PEANUT BUTTER AND JELLY SANDWICH--
--WITH WATER TO WASH IT DOWN?
TWUPP
GHA--
THE GENEVA CONVENTION HAS RULES ABOUT TORTURE.
SPLOOP
LOOK AT YOU, SO PLEASED WITH YOURSELF.
I HATE TO BE A WET BLANKET--

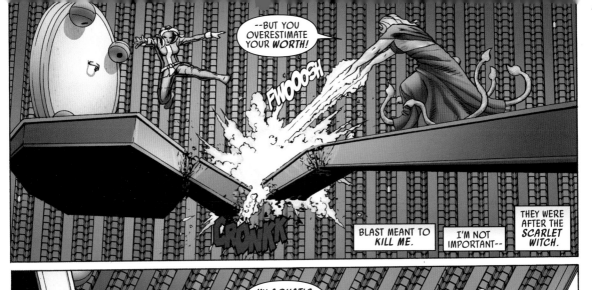

--BUT YOU OVERESTIMATE YOUR *WORTH!*

FWOOOOSH

KROWKK

BLAST MEANT TO *KILL ME.*

I'M NOT *IMPORTANT--*

THEY WERE AFTER THE *SCARLET WITCH.*

MY *AQUATIC TELEPORTATION* CANNOT SAVE YOU FROM THIS *FALL,* X-MAN!

MEANS I'M JUST A *TOKEN* TO BE HELD IN CASE A USE IS *FOUND--*

A *TOKEN* TO BE *KILLED* SHOULD SHE PROVE *DIFFICULT.*

I AM *MOST DEFINITELY* THAT.

WANDA NEARLY DIED *PROTECTING* ME--

DOESN'T *MATTER--*

--SHE'S TOO DAMNED *UNPREDICTABLE* TO BE LEFT IN *ANYONE'S* HANDS.

THE MISSION IS *CLEAR...*

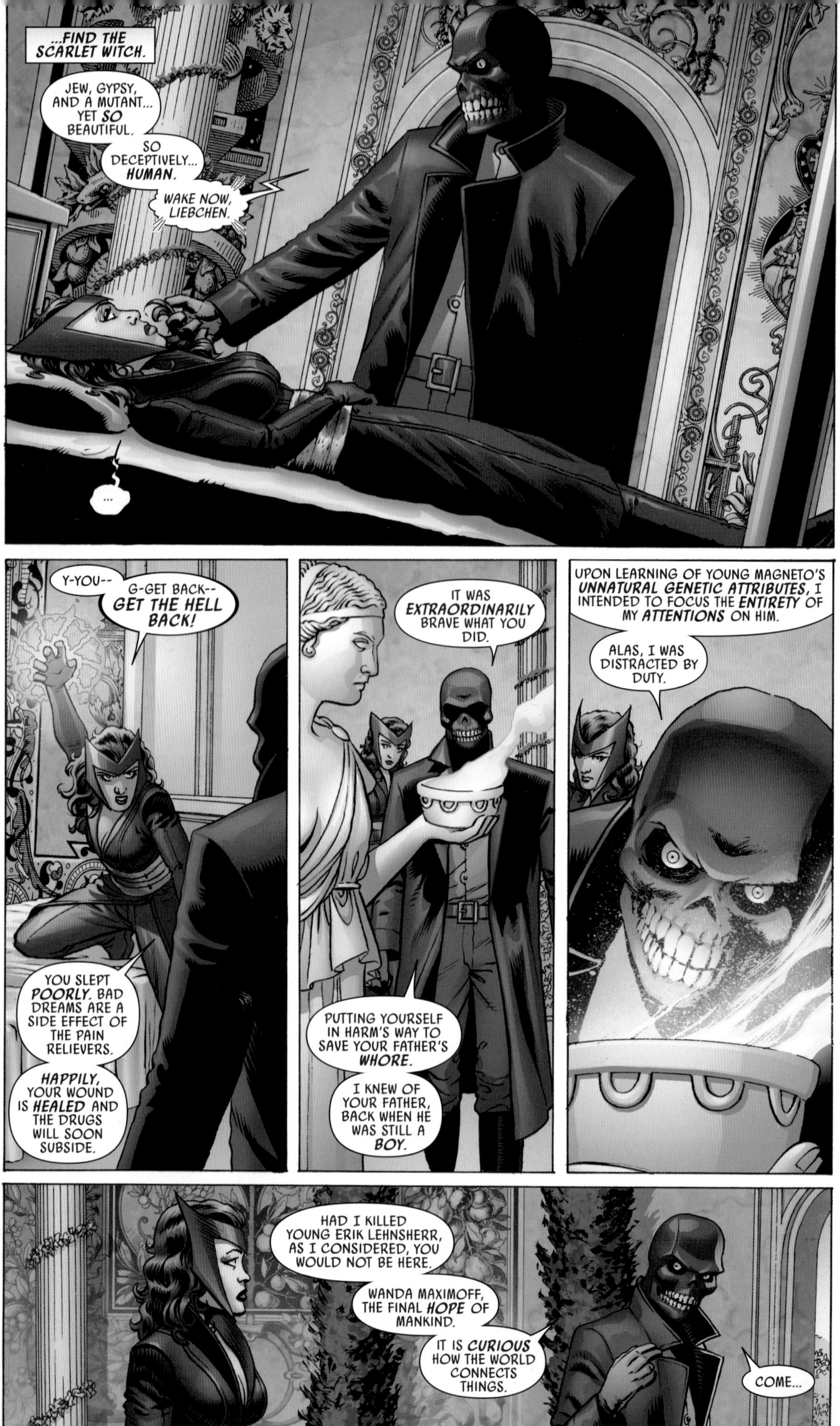
...FIND THE SCARLET WITCH.
JEW, GYPSY, AND A MUTANT... YET SO BEAUTIFUL.
SO DECEPTIVELY... HUMAN.
WAKE NOW, LIEBCHEN.
...
Y-YOU--
G-GET BACK-- GET THE HELL BACK!
YOU SLEPT POORLY. BAD DREAMS ARE A SIDE EFFECT OF THE PAIN RELIEVERS.
HAPPILY, YOUR WOUND IS HEALED AND THE DRUGS WILL SOON SUBSIDE.
IT WAS EXTRAORDINARILY BRAVE WHAT YOU DID.
PUTTING YOURSELF IN HARM'S WAY TO SAVE YOUR FATHER'S WHORE.
I KNEW OF YOUR FATHER, BACK WHEN HE WAS STILL A BOY.
UPON LEARNING OF YOUNG MAGNETO'S UNNATURAL GENETIC ATTRIBUTES, I INTENDED TO FOCUS THE ENTIRETY OF MY ATTENTIONS ON HIM.
ALAS, I WAS DISTRACTED BY DUTY.
HAD I KILLED YOUNG ERIK LEHNSHERR, AS I CONSIDERED, YOU WOULD NOT BE HERE.
WANDA MAXIMOFF, THE FINAL HOPE OF MANKIND.
IT IS CURIOUS HOW THE WORLD CONNECTS THINGS.
COME...

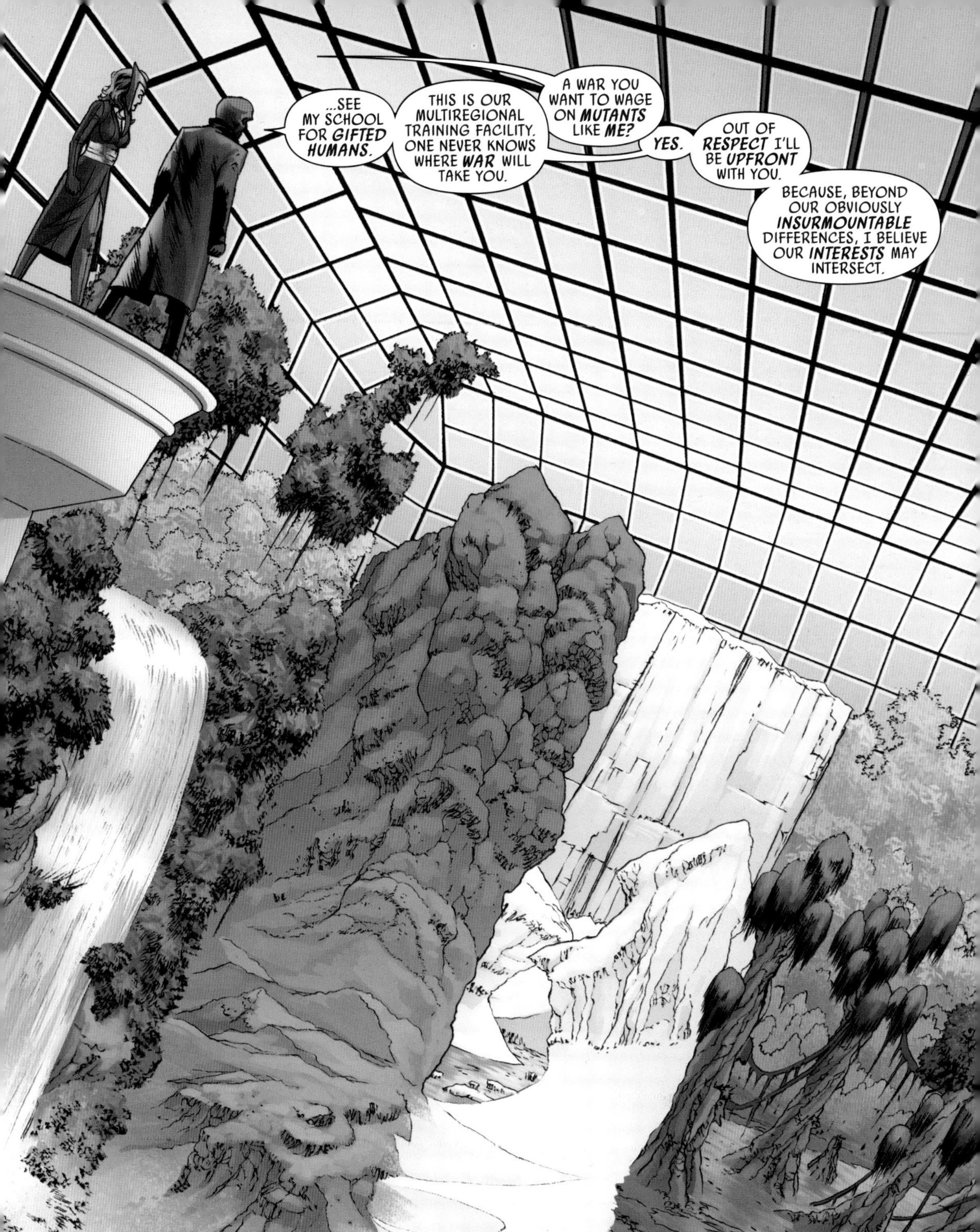
...SEE MY SCHOOL FOR GIFTED HUMANS.
THIS IS OUR MULTIREGIONAL TRAINING FACILITY. ONE NEVER KNOWS WHERE WAR WILL TAKE YOU.
A WAR YOU WANT TO WAGE ON MUTANTS LIKE ME?
YES.
OUT OF RESPECT I'LL BE UPFRONT WITH YOU.
BECAUSE, BEYOND OUR OBVIOUSLY INSURMOUNTABLE DIFFERENCES, I BELIEVE OUR INTERESTS MAY INTERSECT.

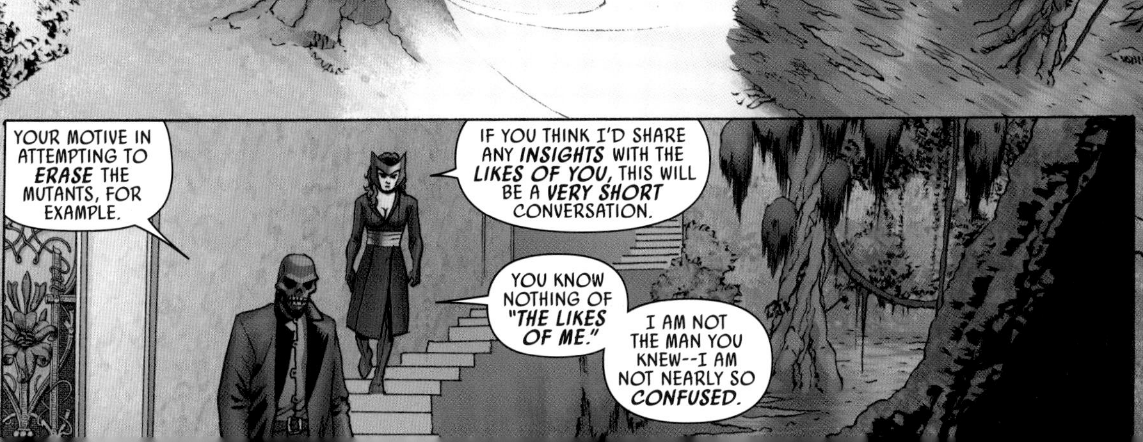
YOUR MOTIVE IN ATTEMPTING TO ERASE THE MUTANTS, FOR EXAMPLE.
IF YOU THINK I'D SHARE ANY INSIGHTS WITH THE LIKES OF YOU, THIS WILL BE A VERY SHORT CONVERSATION.
YOU KNOW NOTHING OF "THE LIKES OF ME."
I AM NOT THE MAN YOU KNEW--I AM NOT NEARLY SO CONFUSED.

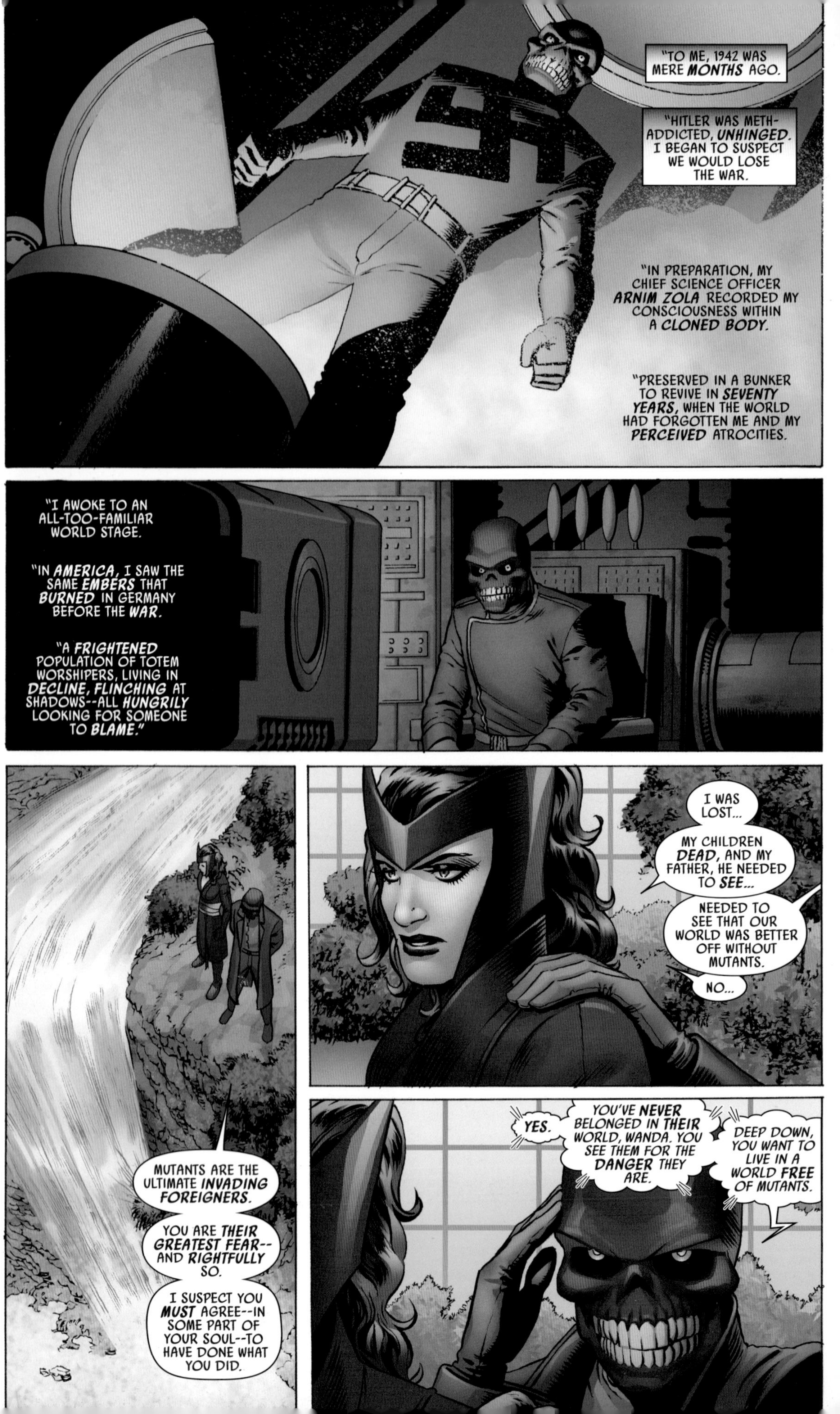
"TO ME, 1942 WAS MERE MONTHS AGO.
"HITLER WAS METH-ADDICTED, UNHINGED. I BEGAN TO SUSPECT WE WOULD LOSE THE WAR.
"IN PREPARATION, MY CHIEF SCIENCE OFFICER ARNIM ZOLA RECORDED MY CONSCIOUSNESS WITHIN A CLONED BODY.
"PRESERVED IN A BUNKER TO REVIVE IN SEVENTY YEARS, WHEN THE WORLD HAD FORGOTTEN ME AND MY PERCEIVED ATROCITIES.
"I AWOKE TO AN ALL-TOO-FAMILIAR WORLD STAGE.
"IN AMERICA, I SAW THE SAME EMBERS THAT BURNED IN GERMANY BEFORE THE WAR.
"A FRIGHTENED POPULATION OF TOTEM WORSHIPERS, LIVING IN DECLINE, FLINCHING AT SHADOWS--ALL HUNGRILY LOOKING FOR SOMEONE TO BLAME."
I WAS LOST...
MY CHILDREN DEAD, AND MY FATHER, HE NEEDED TO SEE...
NEEDED TO SEE THAT OUR WORLD WAS BETTER OFF WITHOUT MUTANTS.
NO...
MUTANTS ARE THE ULTIMATE INVADING FOREIGNERS.
YOU ARE THEIR GREATEST FEAR--AND RIGHTFULLY SO.
I SUSPECT YOU MUST AGREE--IN SOME PART OF YOUR SOUL--TO HAVE DONE WHAT YOU DID.
YES.
YOU'VE NEVER BELONGED IN THEIR WORLD, WANDA. YOU SEE THEM FOR THE DANGER THEY ARE.
DEEP DOWN, YOU WANT TO LIVE IN A WORLD FREE OF MUTANTS.

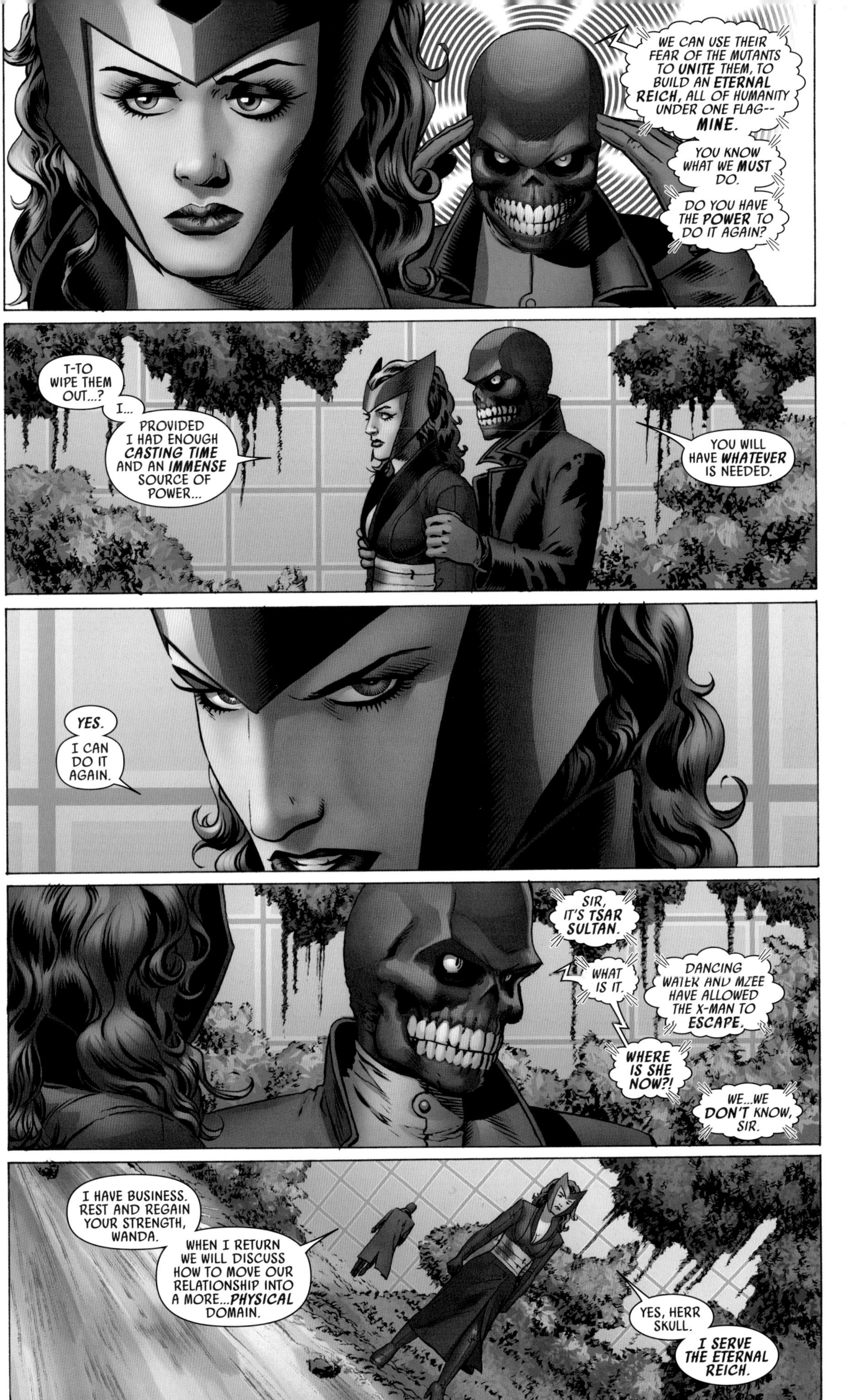
WE CAN USE THEIR FEAR OF THE MUTANTS TO UNITE THEM, TO BUILD AN ETERNAL REICH, ALL OF HUMANITY UNDER ONE FLAG-- MINE.
YOU KNOW WHAT WE MUST DO.
DO YOU HAVE THE POWER TO DO IT AGAIN?
T-TO WIPE THEM OUT...?
I...
PROVIDED I HAD ENOUGH CASTING TIME AND AN IMMENSE SOURCE OF POWER...
YOU WILL HAVE WHATEVER IS NEEDED.
YES.
I CAN DO IT AGAIN.
SIR, IT'S TSAR SULTAN.
WHAT IS IT.
DANCING WATER AND MZEE HAVE ALLOWED THE X-MAN TO ESCAPE.
WHERE IS SHE NOW?!
WE...WE DON'T KNOW, SIR.
I HAVE BUSINESS. REST AND REGAIN YOUR STRENGTH, WANDA.
WHEN I RETURN WE WILL DISCUSS HOW TO MOVE OUR RELATIONSHIP INTO A MORE...PHYSICAL DOMAIN.
YES, HERR SKULL.
I SERVE THE ETERNAL REICH.

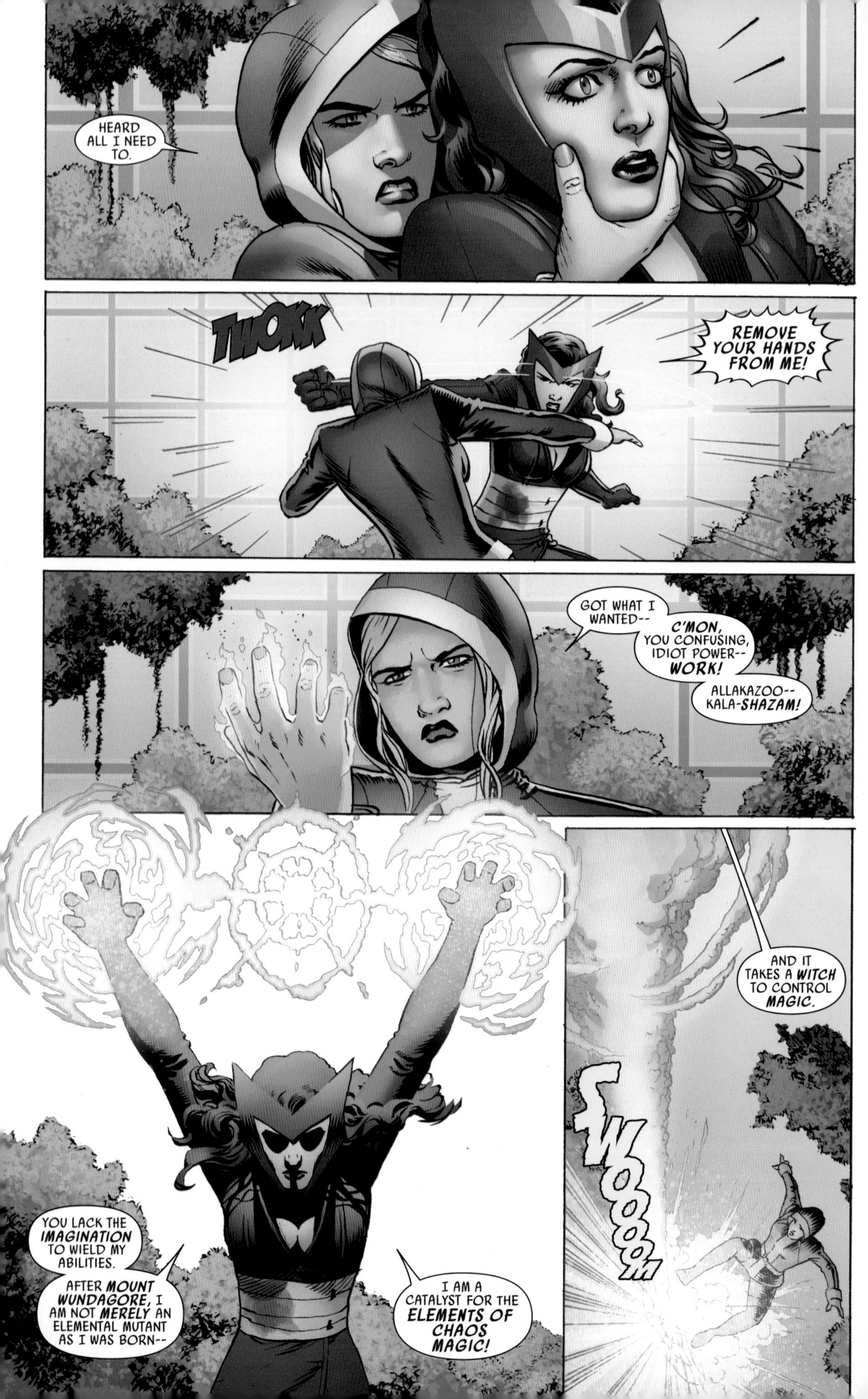

HEARD ALL I NEED TO.
TWOKK
REMOVE YOUR HANDS FROM ME!
GOT WHAT I WANTED-- C'MON, YOU CONFUSING, IDIOT POWER-- WORK!
ALLAKAZOO-- KALA-SHAZAM!
YOU LACK THE IMAGINATION TO WIELD MY ABILITIES.
AFTER MOUNT WUNDAGORE, I AM NOT MERELY AN ELEMENTAL MUTANT AS I WAS BORN--
I AM A CATALYST FOR THE ELEMENTS OF CHAOS MAGIC!
AND IT TAKES A WITCH TO CONTROL MAGIC.
SWOOOOM

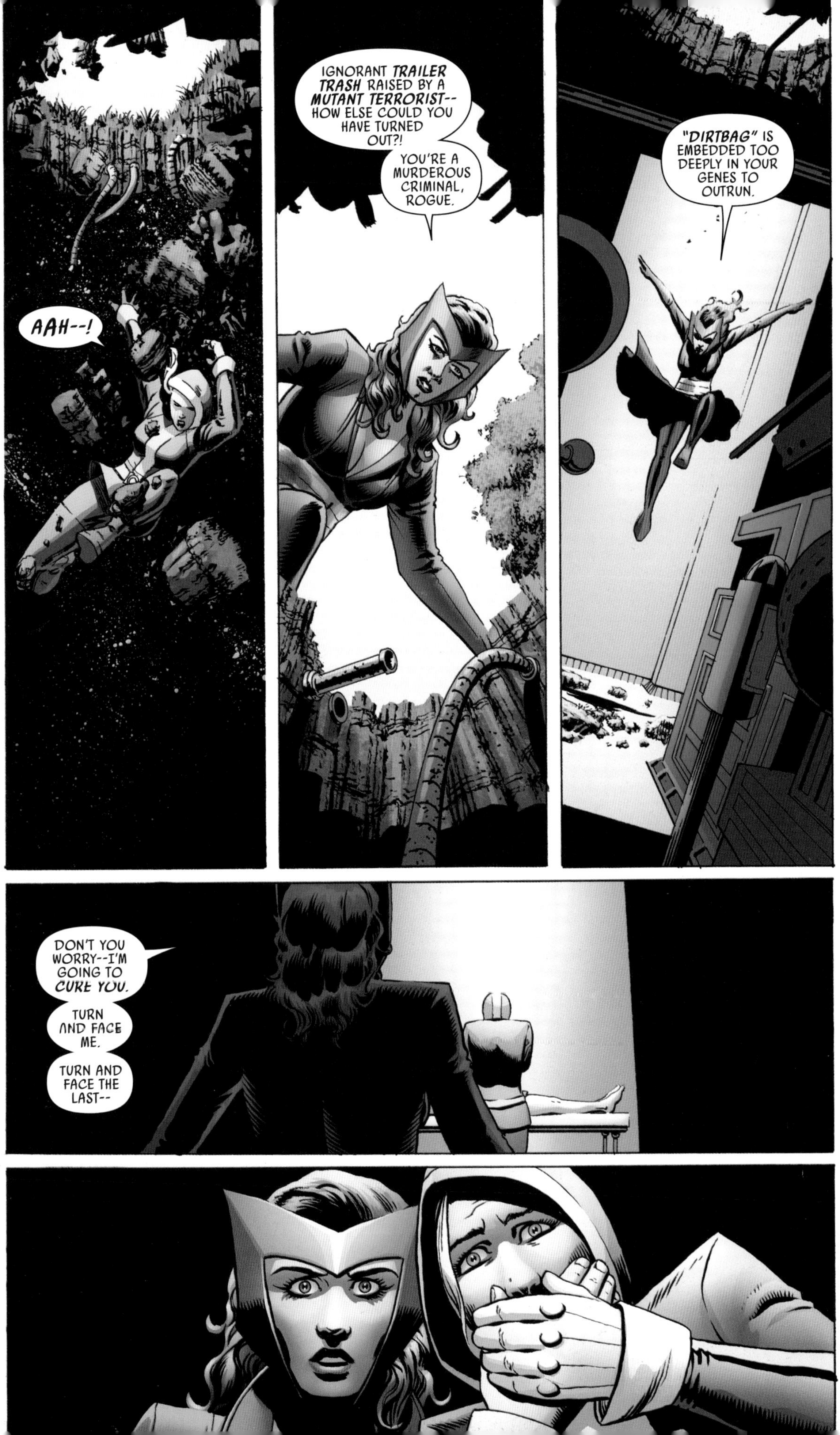
AAH--!
IGNORANT TRAILER TRASH RAISED BY A MUTANT TERRORIST--HOW ELSE COULD YOU HAVE TURNED OUT?!
YOU'RE A MURDEROUS CRIMINAL, ROGUE.
"DIRTBAG" IS EMBEDDED TOO DEEPLY IN YOUR GENES TO OUTRUN.
DON'T YOU WORRY--I'M GOING TO CURE YOU.
TURN AND FACE ME.
TURN AND FACE THE LAST--

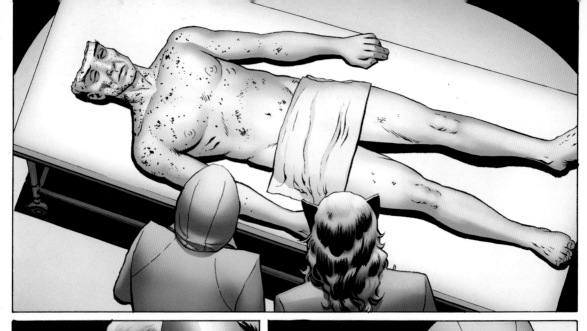

HE...DID *THIS*...

TOOK CHARLES APART...

I...I WAS GOING TO HELP HIM...

DEAR GOD.

YOU *KNOW* ROGUE'S HISTORY.

ARE WE EXPECTED TO FIGHT BESIDE SOMEONE WE DO NOT-- *DARE NOT*-- TRUST...

NO. THE X-MEN WILL DISBAND IF ROGUE IS ACCEPTED, PROFESSOR.

DO AS YOU MUST, STORM.

I WILL *NOT* ABANDON THIS CHILD.

ALL MUTANTS LEAD *EXTRAORDINARILY* DIFFICULT LIVES, MOST MAKE MISTAKES AND DESERVE A *CHANCE FOR REDEMPTION*.

EVEN IF IT MEANS SHE WILL BE MY *SOLE* REMAINING STUDENT...

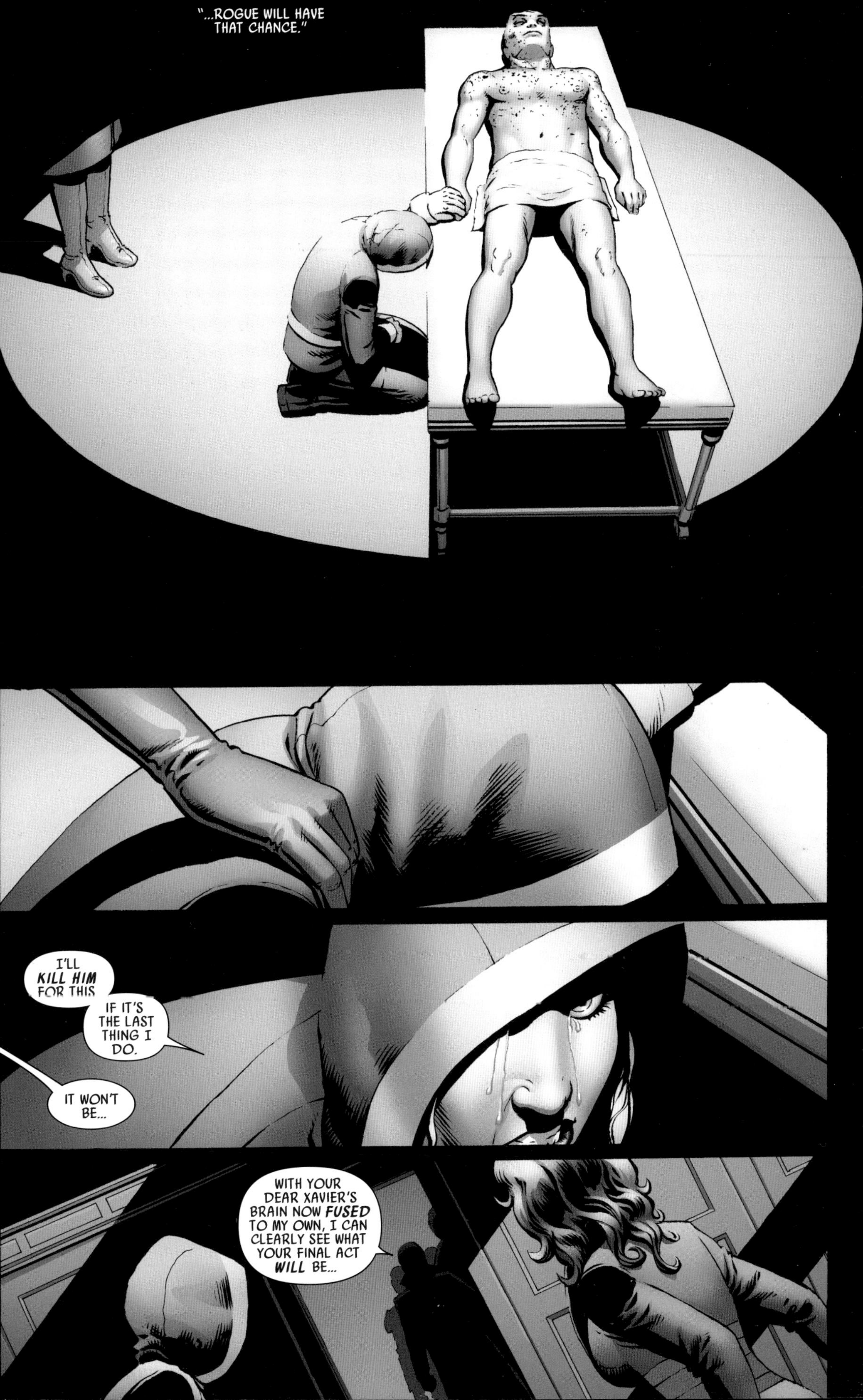
"...ROGUE WILL HAVE THAT CHANCE."
I'LL KILL HIM FOR THIS
IF IT'S THE LAST THING I DO.
IT WON'T BE...
WITH YOUR DEAR XAVIER'S BRAIN NOW FUSED TO MY OWN, I CAN CLEARLY SEE WHAT YOUR FINAL ACT WILL BE...

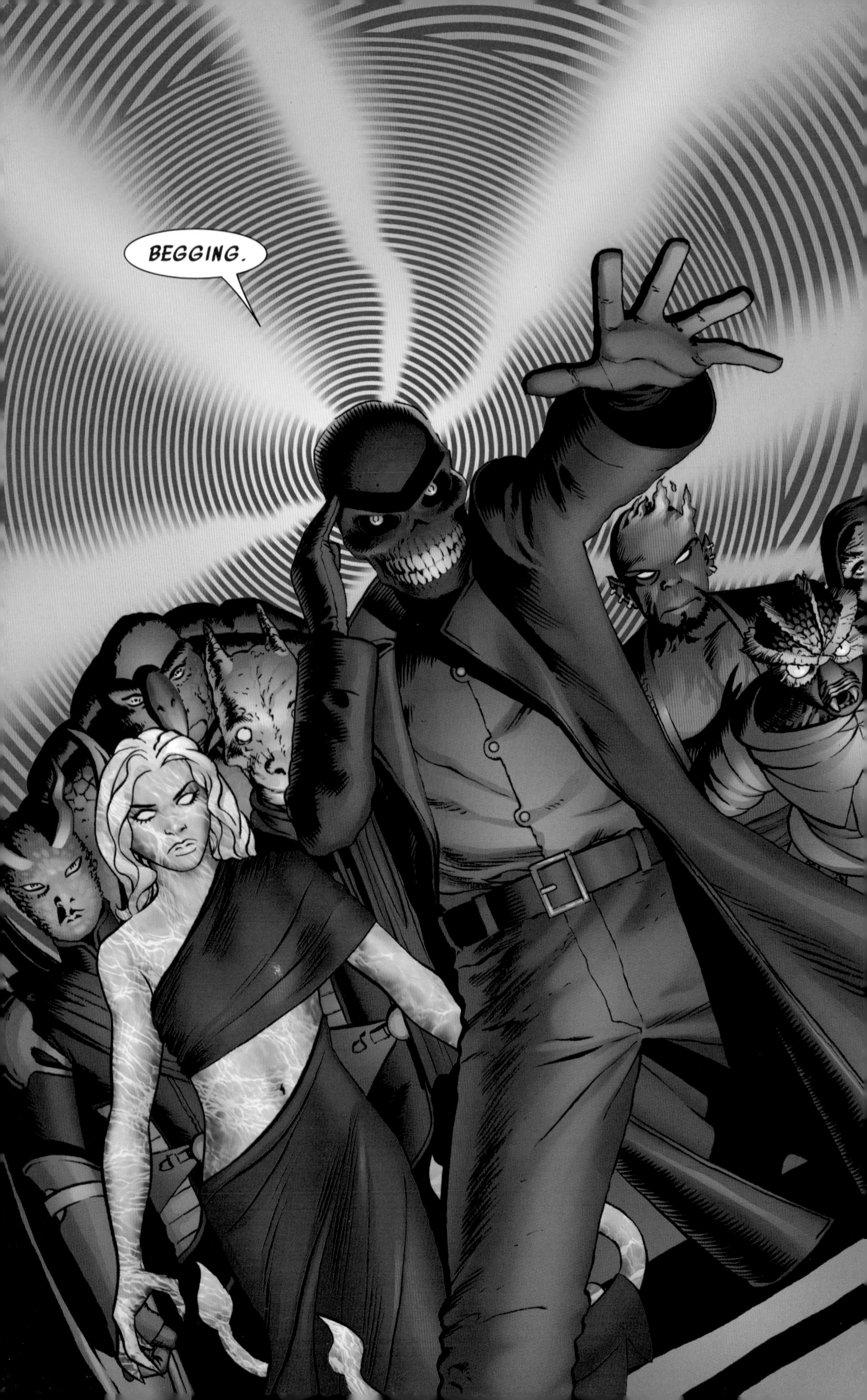
BEGGING.

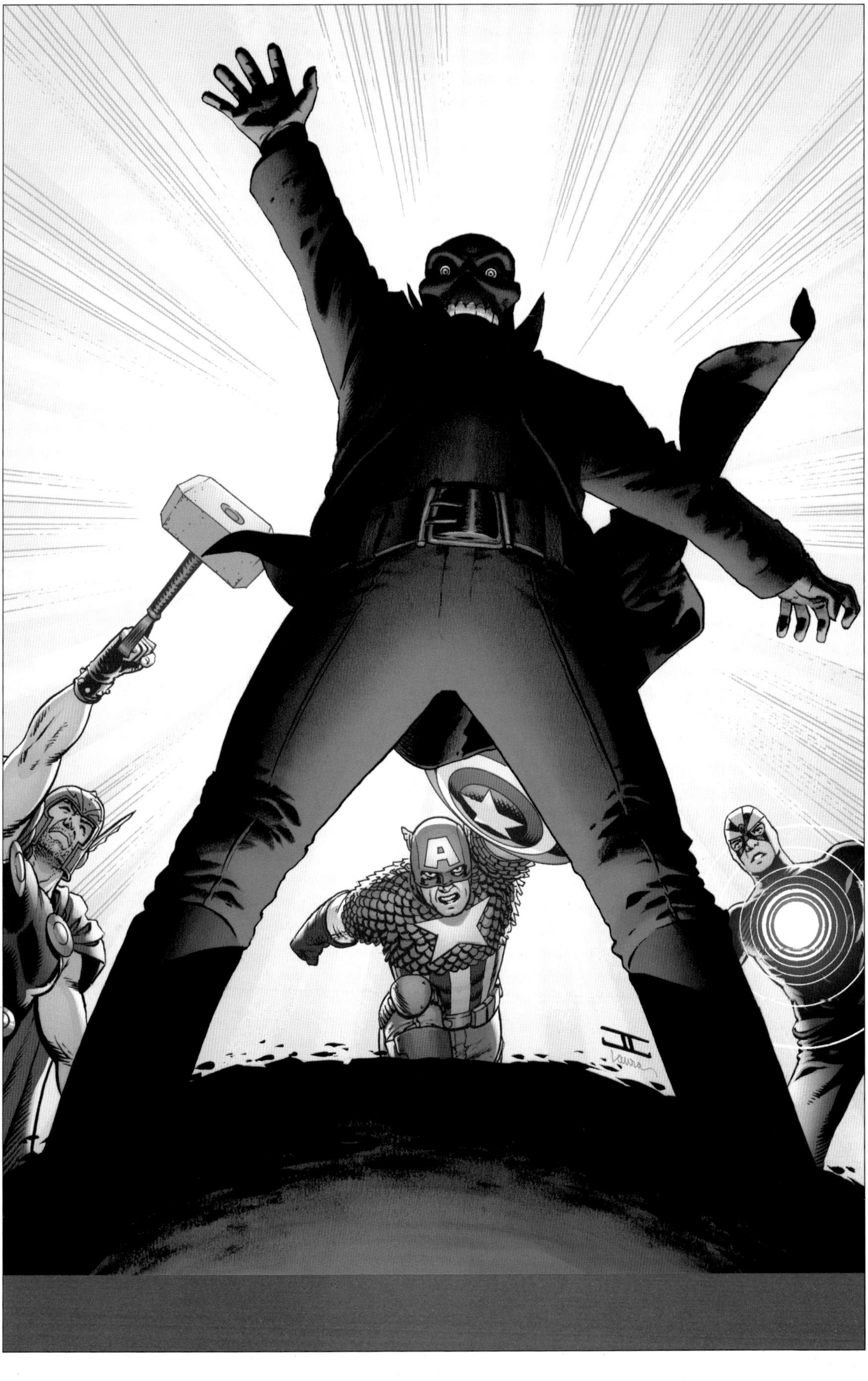

THE TIME IS LATE IN THE AFTERNOON.

THE **CENTURY** IS NOT HIS OWN.

BUT SOON THE **WORLD** WOULD BE.

HE MOVES FORWARD IN **TOTAL** CONFIDENCE OF THAT **ONE TRUTH**.

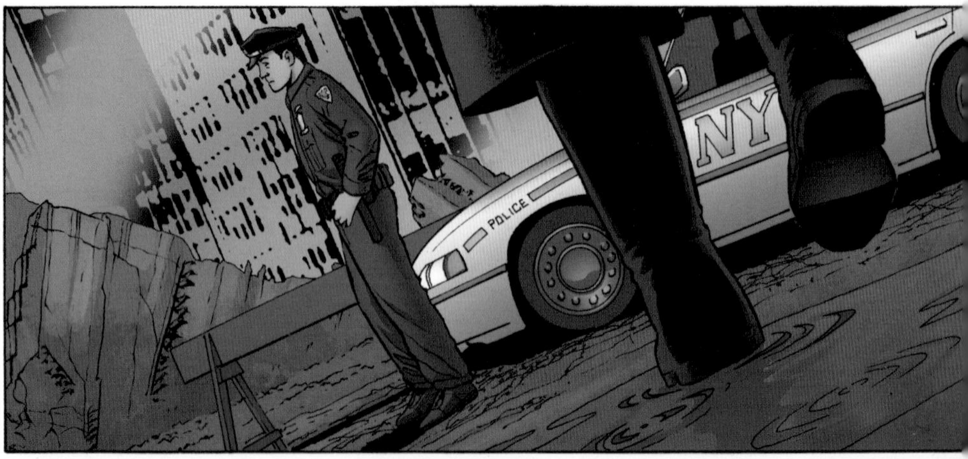
NY
POLICE

HE IS A **WEAPON**, THE LAST NAZI BOMB, LAUNCHED FROM THE PAST TO WIN A WAR **LONG** MISTAKEN TO BE OVER.

ONLY NOW HE WIELDS THE ABILITIES OF THE MOST POWERFUL TELEPATH IN HISTORY.

A WONDERFUL GIFT HE WILL PUT TO GRAND PURPOSE...

TOTAL DOMINATION.

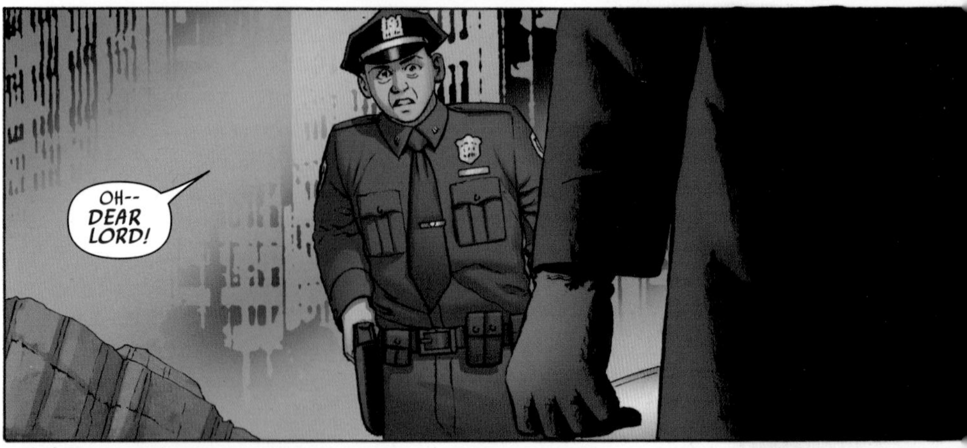
OH-- DEAR LORD!

HIS TIME AT WAR HAD TAUGHT HIM THAT A PEOPLE TAKEN BY **FORCE** WOULD **NEVER** STOP FIGHTING THEIR OPPRESSORS.

TO ACHIEVE A LASTING CHANGE THE SQUALID MASSES MUST BELIEVE A MOVEMENT IS OF **THEIR** CHOOSING.

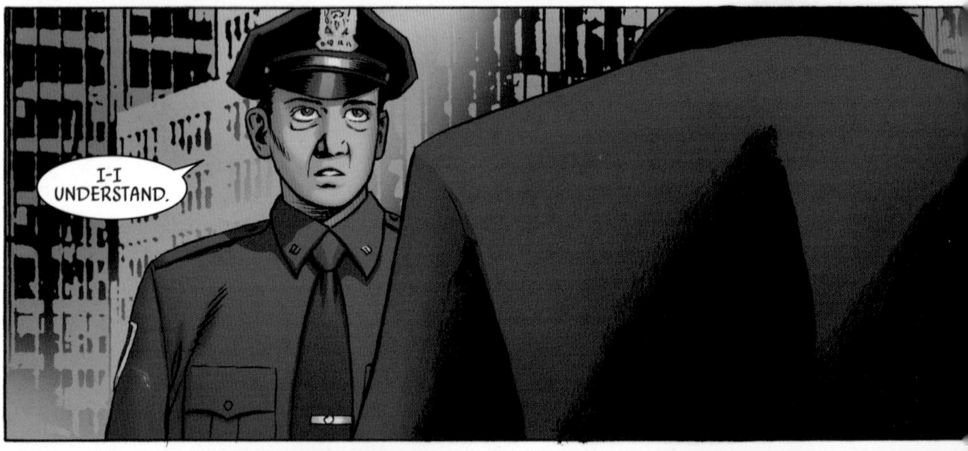
I-I UNDERSTAND.

AND TO STIR A FRIGHTENED PEOPLE TO ACTION, ONE NEED ONLY **JUSTIFY**, WITH **GREAT PASSION**, THEIR **HATE** AND **BIGOTRY** AS **JUST**.

"ONE FOOT AT A TIME," HE REMINDS HIMSELF.

"THERE ARE MANY STEPS YET TO TAKE...

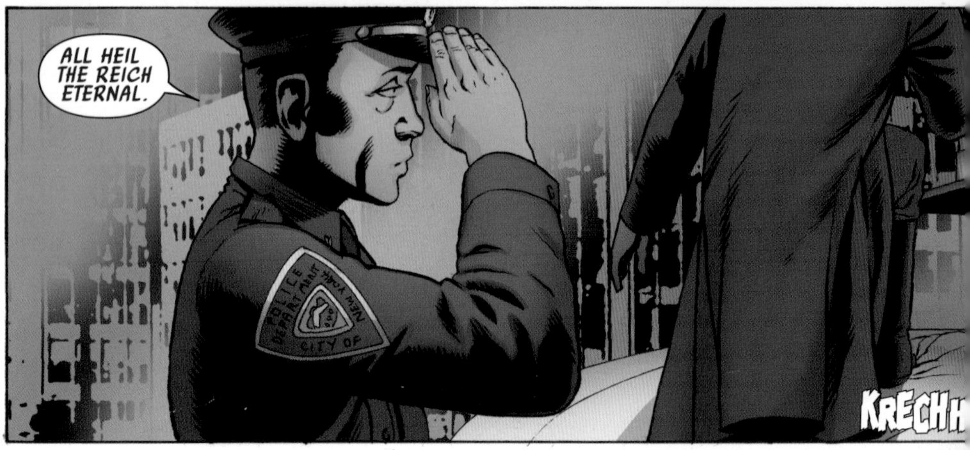
ALL HEIL THE REICH ETERNAL.
KRECHH

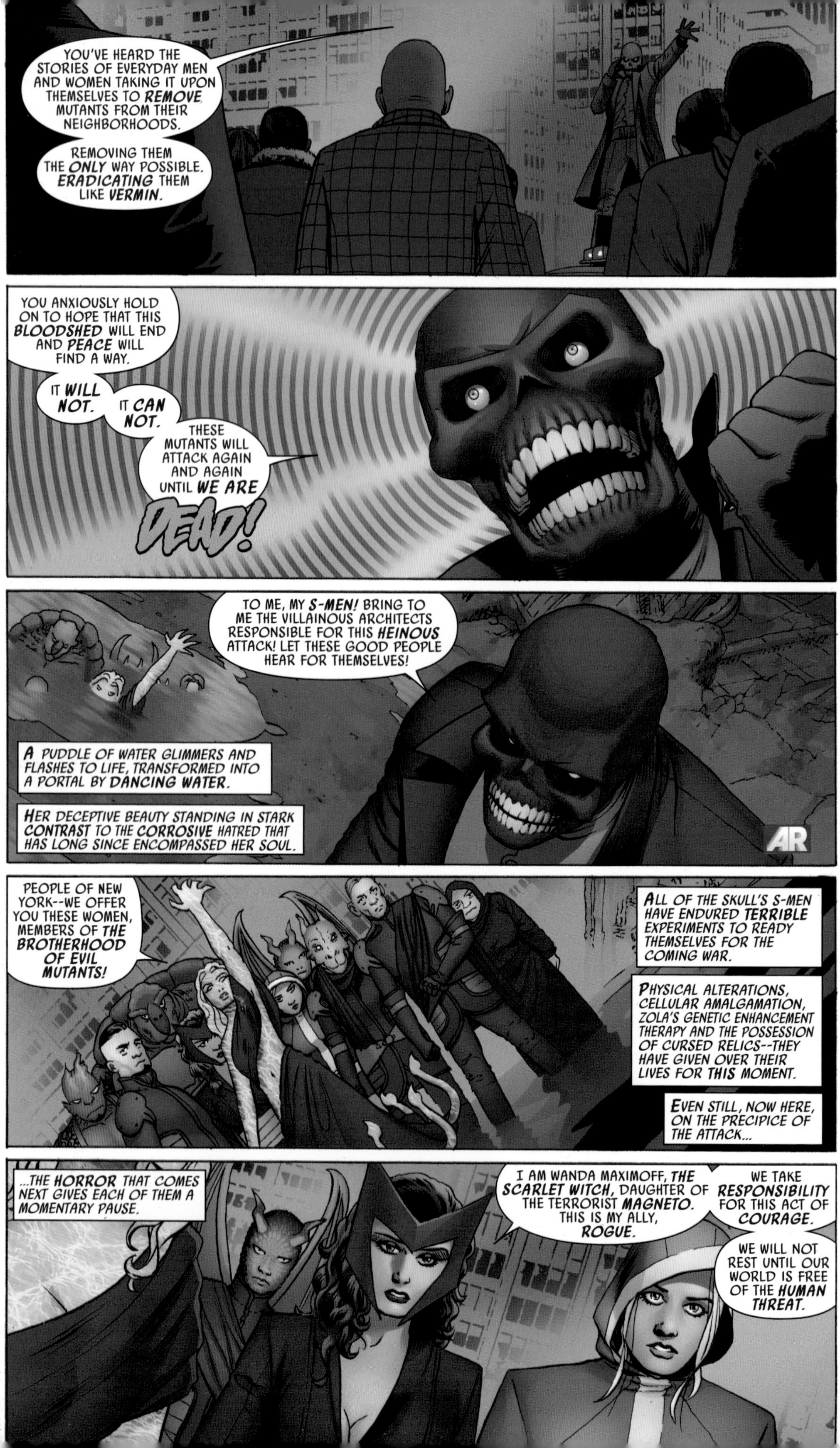
YOU'VE HEARD THE STORIES OF EVERYDAY MEN AND WOMEN TAKING IT UPON THEMSELVES TO REMOVE MUTANTS FROM THEIR NEIGHBORHOODS.
REMOVING THEM THE ONLY WAY POSSIBLE. ERADICATING THEM LIKE VERMIN.
YOU ANXIOUSLY HOLD ON TO HOPE THAT THIS BLOODSHED WILL END AND PEACE WILL FIND A WAY.
IT WILL NOT.
IT CAN NOT.
THESE MUTANTS WILL ATTACK AGAIN AND AGAIN UNTIL WE ARE DEAD!
TO ME, MY S-MEN! BRING TO ME THE VILLAINOUS ARCHITECTS RESPONSIBLE FOR THIS HEINOUS ATTACK! LET THESE GOOD PEOPLE HEAR FOR THEMSELVES!
A PUDDLE OF WATER GLIMMERS AND FLASHES TO LIFE, TRANSFORMED INTO A PORTAL BY DANCING WATER.
HER DECEPTIVE BEAUTY STANDING IN STARK CONTRAST TO THE CORROSIVE HATRED THAT HAS LONG SINCE ENCOMPASSED HER SOUL.
AR
PEOPLE OF NEW YORK--WE OFFER YOU THESE WOMEN, MEMBERS OF THE BROTHERHOOD OF EVIL MUTANTS!
ALL OF THE SKULL'S S-MEN HAVE ENDURED TERRIBLE EXPERIMENTS TO READY THEMSELVES FOR THE COMING WAR.
PHYSICAL ALTERATIONS, CELLULAR AMALGAMATION, ZOLA'S GENETIC ENHANCEMENT THERAPY AND THE POSSESSION OF CURSED RELICS--THEY HAVE GIVEN OVER THEIR LIVES FOR THIS MOMENT.
EVEN STILL, NOW HERE, ON THE PRECIPICE OF THE ATTACK...
...THE HORROR THAT COMES NEXT GIVES EACH OF THEM A MOMENTARY PAUSE.
I AM WANDA MAXIMOFF, THE SCARLET WITCH, DAUGHTER OF THE TERRORIST MAGNETO. THIS IS MY ALLY, ROGUE.
WE TAKE RESPONSIBILITY FOR THIS ACT OF COURAGE.
WE WILL NOT REST UNTIL OUR WORLD IS FREE OF THE HUMAN THREAT.

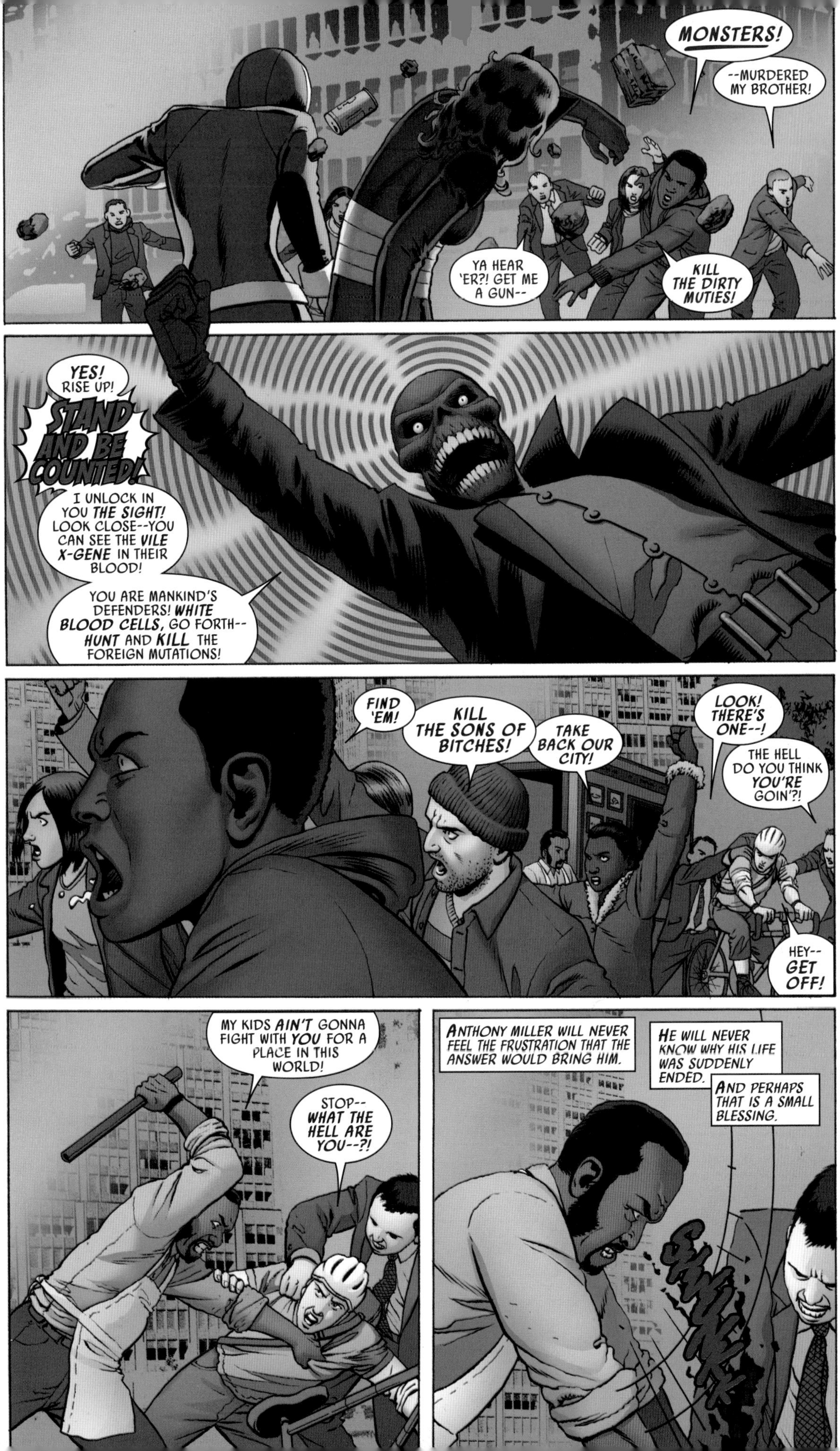
MONSTERS!
--MURDERED MY BROTHER!
YA HEAR 'ER?! GET ME A GUN--
KILL THE DIRTY MUTIES!
YES! RISE UP!
STAND AND BE COUNTED!
I UNLOCK IN YOU THE SIGHT! LOOK CLOSE--YOU CAN SEE THE VILE X-GENE IN THEIR BLOOD!
YOU ARE MANKIND'S DEFENDERS! WHITE BLOOD CELLS, GO FORTH--HUNT AND KILL THE FOREIGN MUTATIONS!
FIND 'EM!
KILL THE SONS OF BITCHES!
TAKE BACK OUR CITY!
LOOK! THERE'S ONE--!
THE HELL DO YOU THINK YOU'RE GOIN'?!
HEY--GET OFF!
MY KIDS AIN'T GONNA FIGHT WITH YOU FOR A PLACE IN THIS WORLD!
STOP--WHAT THE HELL ARE YOU--?!
ANTHONY MILLER WILL NEVER FEEL THE FRUSTRATION THAT THE ANSWER WOULD BRING HIM.
HE WILL NEVER KNOW WHY HIS LIFE WAS SUDDENLY ENDED.
AND PERHAPS THAT IS A SMALL BLESSING.

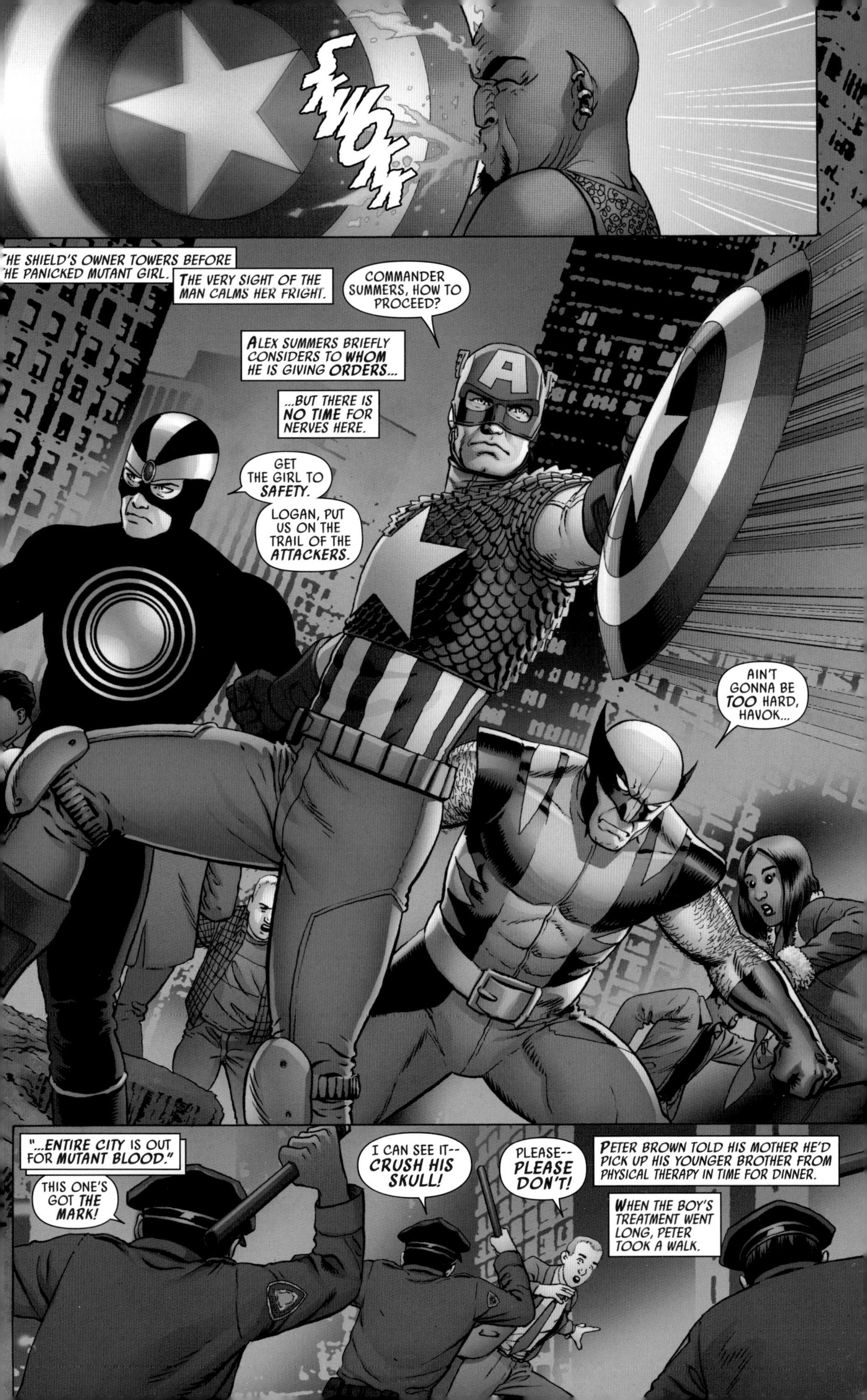

FWOK
HE SHIELD'S OWNER TOWERS BEFORE HE PANICKED MUTANT GIRL.
THE VERY SIGHT OF THE MAN CALMS HER FRIGHT.
COMMANDER SUMMERS, HOW TO PROCEED?
ALEX SUMMERS BRIEFLY CONSIDERS TO WHOM HE IS GIVING ORDERS...
...BUT THERE IS NO TIME FOR NERVES HERE.
GET THE GIRL TO SAFETY.
LOGAN, PUT US ON THE TRAIL OF THE ATTACKERS.
AIN'T GONNA BE TOO HARD, HAVOK...
"...ENTIRE CITY IS OUT FOR MUTANT BLOOD."
THIS ONE'S GOT THE MARK!
I CAN SEE IT-- CRUSH HIS SKULL!
PLEASE-- PLEASE DON'T!
PETER BROWN TOLD HIS MOTHER HE'D PICK UP HIS YOUNGER BROTHER FROM PHYSICAL THERAPY IN TIME FOR DINNER.
WHEN THE BOY'S TREATMENT WENT LONG, PETER TOOK A WALK.

AS THE BATON CRACKS HIS SKULL, HE'S GRATEFUL HIS BROTHER *WASN'T* READY.

GRATEFUL THE BOY WOULDN'T SEE HIM BEATEN TO DEATH.

HOWDYA LIKE THIS, YA MUTIE SCUM?!

SKROP

THE IMAGE OF THE FAMILY HE'LL NEVER AGAIN SEE OFFERS PETER SOME COMFORT...

...THE MEN WHO TROUNCE HIS ATTACKERS OFFER *MORE.*

THE HELL'S GOTTEN INTO YOU?!

TWONK

OOF--!

WE NEED TO FIND ANY MUTANTS WE CAN AND GET THEM TO *SAFETY.*

SPLIT UP--STAY IN CONTACT. WE'LL REGROUP WHEN MORE HELP ARRIVES TO--

SPLIT?!

ALEX, UNTIL WE KNOW MORE--

YOU WANTED ME LEADING-- I'M LEADING.

YOU WANT ME TO STEP DOWN, YOU JUST GIVE THE SAY-SO--

GO BE CAPTAIN AMERICA.

NO...I SHOULDN'T SECOND-GUESS YOU--IT'S YOUR CALL.

GOOD. NOW GET OUT THERE AND SAVE PEOPLE.

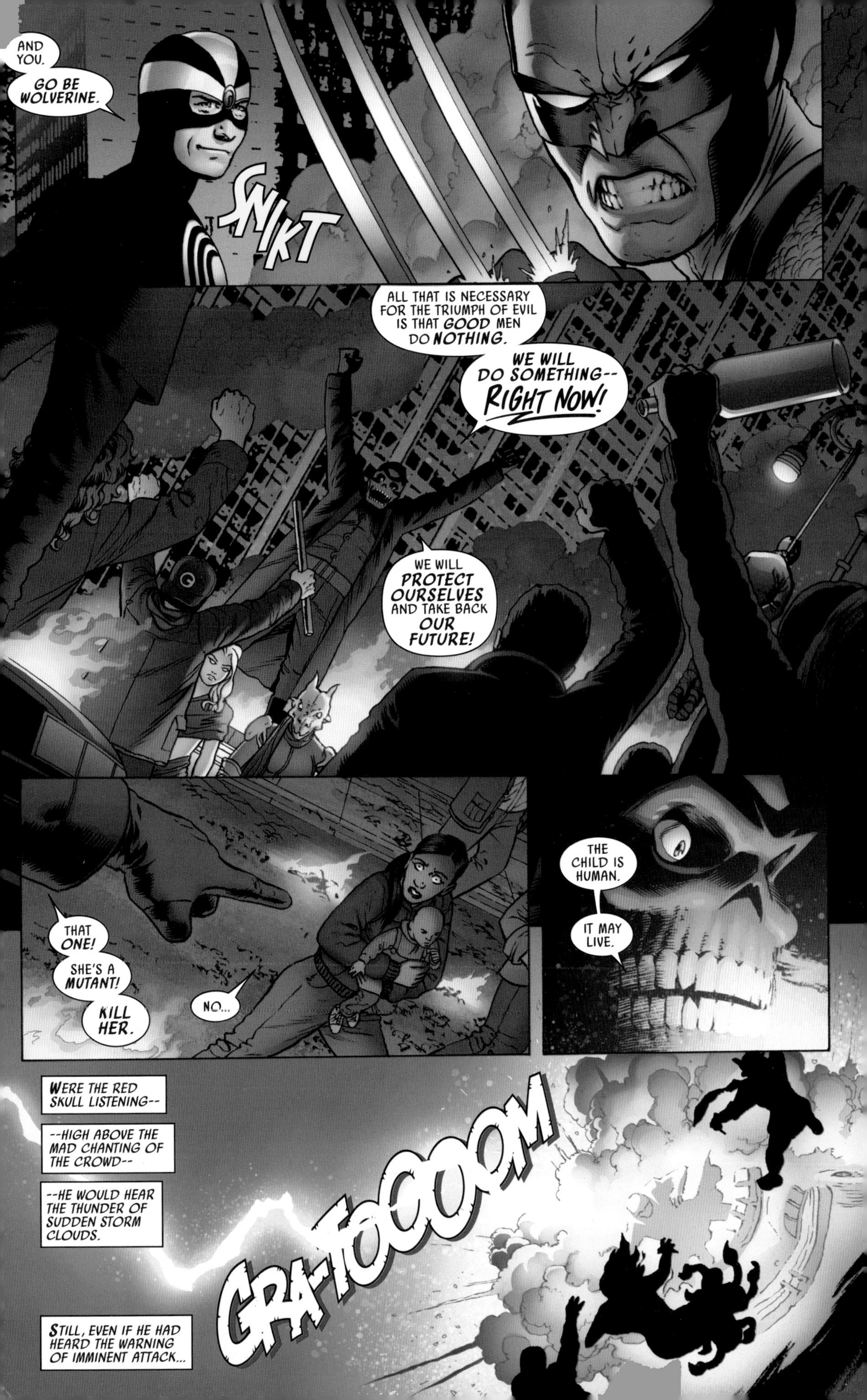
AND YOU.
GO BE WOLVERINE.
SNIKT
ALL THAT IS NECESSARY FOR THE TRIUMPH OF EVIL IS THAT GOOD MEN DO NOTHING.
WE WILL DO SOMETHING-- RIGHT NOW!
WE WILL PROTECT OURSELVES AND TAKE BACK OUR FUTURE!
THAT ONE!
SHE'S A MUTANT!
KILL HER.
NO...
THE CHILD IS HUMAN.
IT MAY LIVE.
WERE THE RED SKULL LISTENING--
--HIGH ABOVE THE MAD CHANTING OF THE CROWD--
--HE WOULD HEAR THE THUNDER OF SUDDEN STORM CLOUDS.
GRA-TOCOOOM
STILL, EVEN IF HE HAD HEARD THE WARNING OF IMMINENT ATTACK...

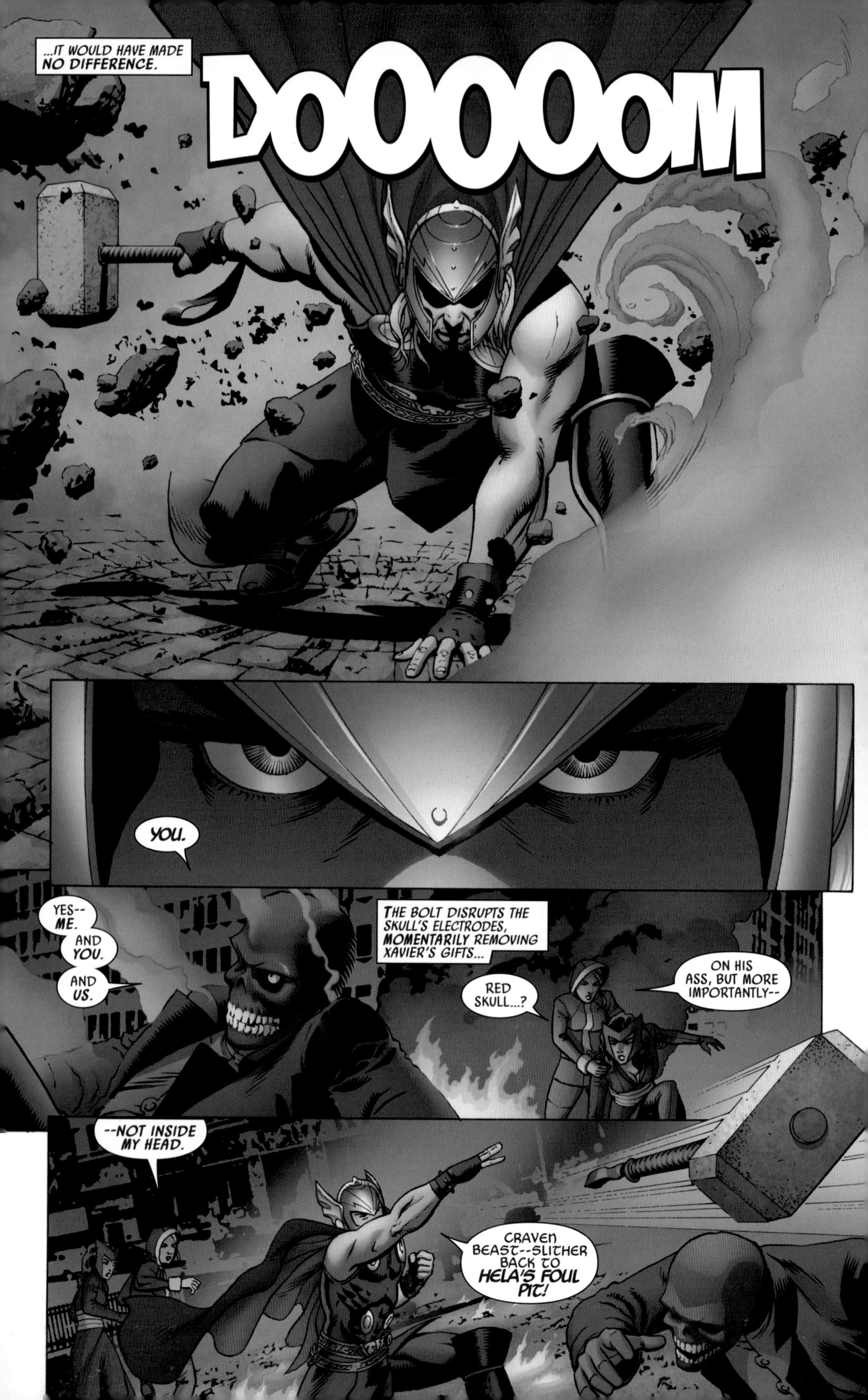
...IT WOULD HAVE MADE NO DIFFERENCE.
DOOOOOM
YOU.
YES-- ME.
AND YOU.
AND US.
THE BOLT DISRUPTS THE SKULL'S ELECTRODES, MOMENTARILY REMOVING XAVIER'S GIFTS...
RED SKULL...?
ON HIS ASS, BUT MORE IMPORTANTLY--
--NOT INSIDE MY HEAD.
CRAVEN BEAST--SLITHER BACK TO HELA'S FOUL PIT!

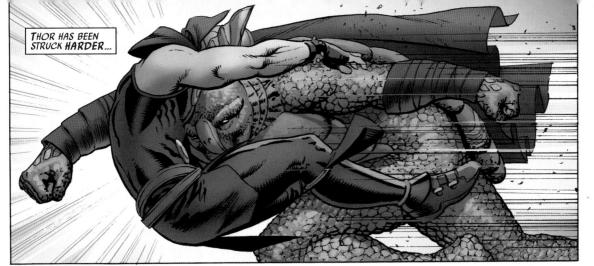

THOR HAS BEEN STRUCK *HARDER*...

...BUT *NOT* OFTEN.

MOTHER--

THE *CROOKED EMERALD* INSIDE THE TORTOISE MAN'S HEART POSSESSES THE PSYCHE OF A LONG-DEAD AFRICAN GOD, *MZEE*.

I HAVE NO FIGHT WITH YOU. I BATTLE ONLY THE MUTANTS WHO SLAUGHTERED MY FAMILY...

...BUT I WILL NOT BE HELD BACK.

WE WILL SEE.

I AM *MZEE!* MADE *INFLEXIBLE* BY THE *GRAVITY* OF THE *TRUE SOUL!*

I AM THE *IMPOSSIBLE STRENGTH!*

IT IS FACT: MZEE IS THE *LORD OF PHYSICAL WILL.*

UNSTOPPABLE BY ANY FORCE ON EARTH.

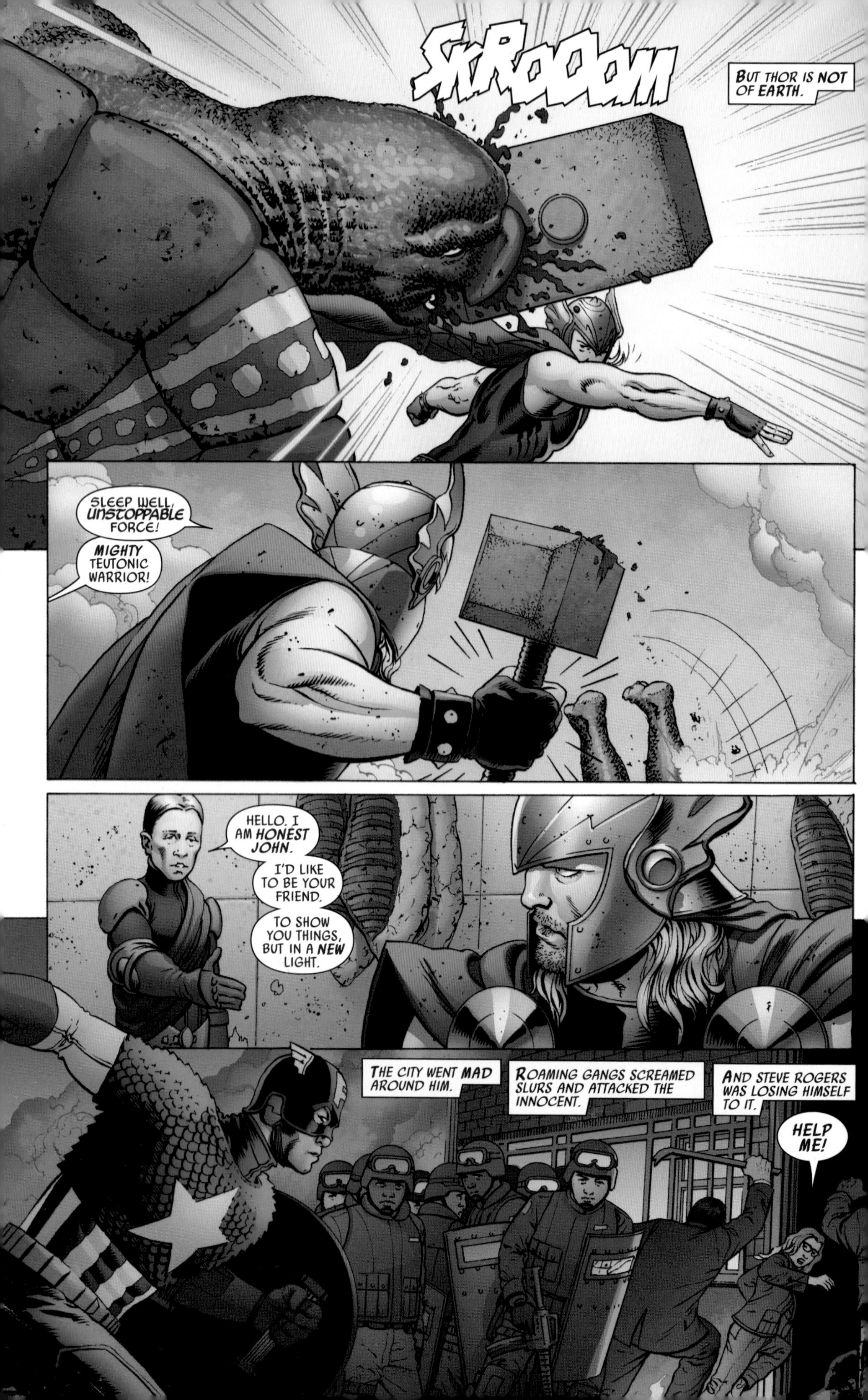
SKROOOM
BUT THOR IS NOT OF EARTH.
SLEEP WELL, UNSTOPPABLE FORCE!
MIGHTY TEUTONIC WARRIOR!
HELLO. I AM HONEST JOHN.
I'D LIKE TO BE YOUR FRIEND.
TO SHOW YOU THINGS, BUT IN A NEW LIGHT.
THE CITY WENT MAD AROUND HIM.
ROAMING GANGS SCREAMED SLURS AND ATTACKED THE INNOCENT.
AND STEVE ROGERS WAS LOSING HIMSELF TO IT.
HELP ME!

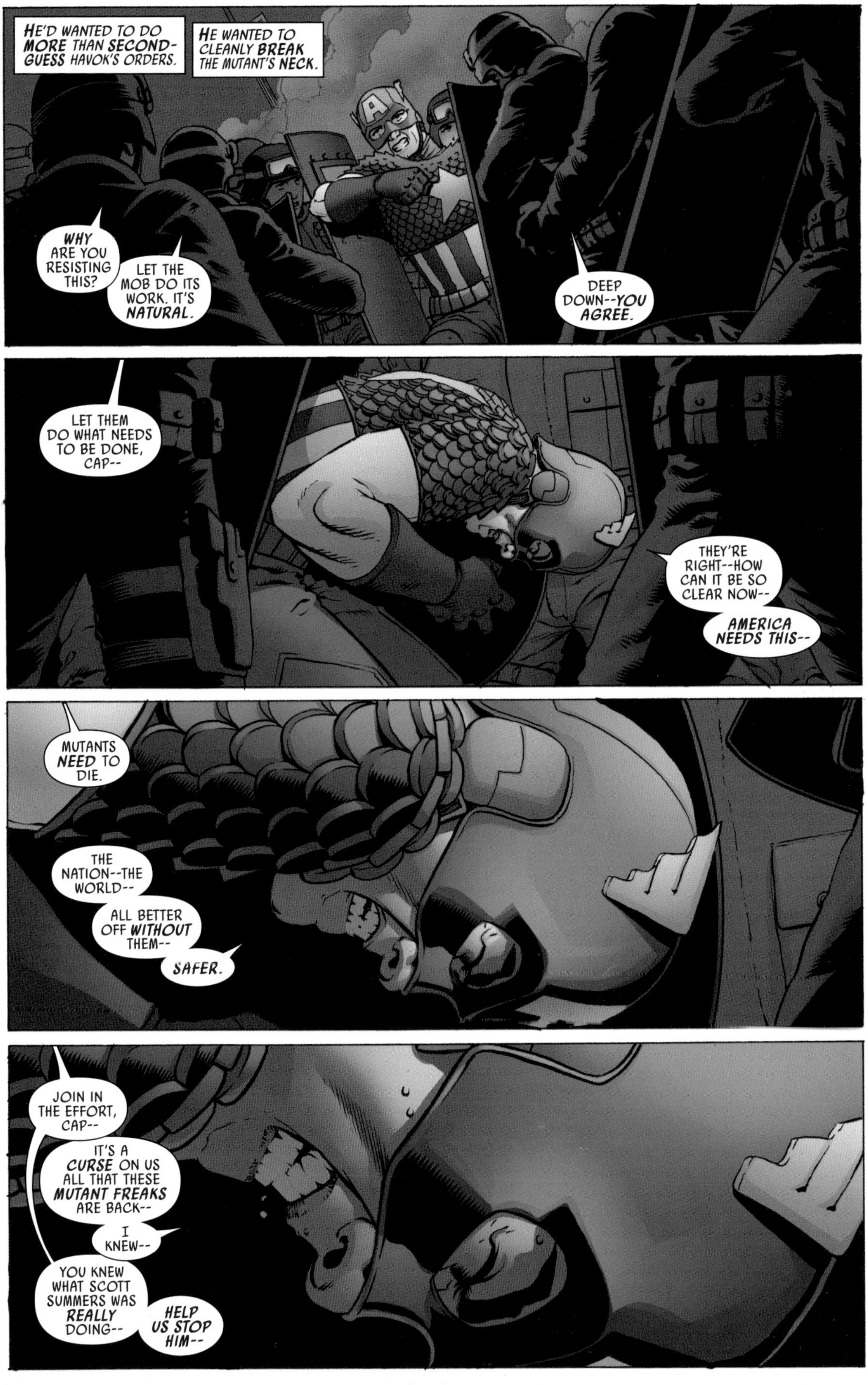
HE'D WANTED TO DO MORE THAN SECOND-GUESS HAVOK'S ORDERS.
HE WANTED TO CLEANLY BREAK THE MUTANT'S NECK.
WHY ARE YOU RESISTING THIS?
LET THE MOB DO ITS WORK. IT'S NATURAL.
DEEP DOWN--YOU AGREE.
LET THEM DO WHAT NEEDS TO BE DONE, CAP--
THEY'RE RIGHT--HOW CAN IT BE SO CLEAR NOW--
AMERICA NEEDS THIS--
MUTANTS NEED TO DIE.
THE NATION--THE WORLD--
ALL BETTER OFF WITHOUT THEM--
SAFER.
JOIN IN THE EFFORT, CAP--
IT'S A CURSE ON US ALL THAT THESE MUTANT FREAKS ARE BACK--
I KNEW--
YOU KNEW WHAT SCOTT SUMMERS WAS REALLY DOING--
HELP US STOP HIM--

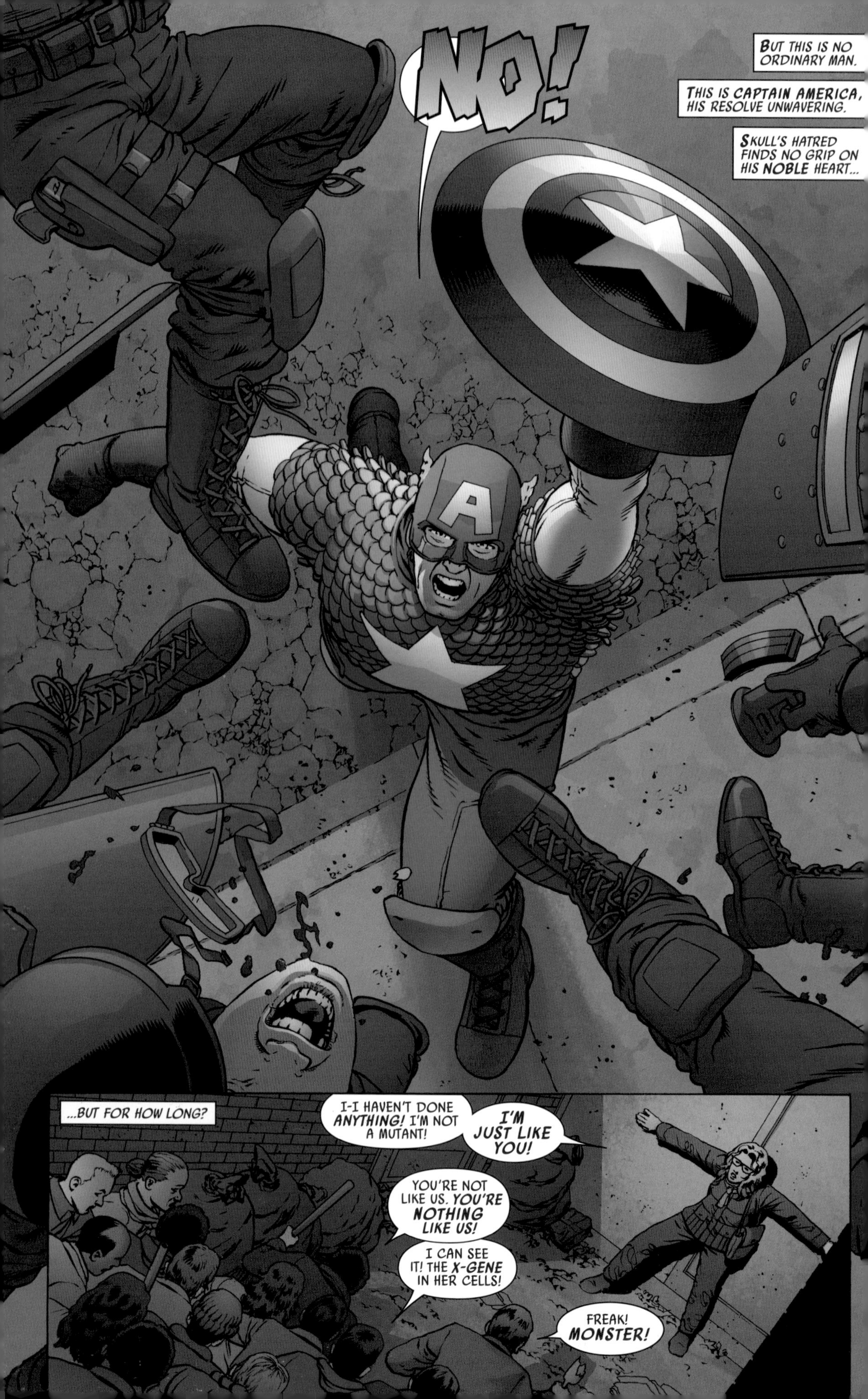
NO!
BUT THIS IS NO ORDINARY MAN.
THIS IS CAPTAIN AMERICA, HIS RESOLVE UNWAVERING.
SKULL'S HATRED FINDS NO GRIP ON HIS NOBLE HEART...
...BUT FOR HOW LONG?
I-I HAVEN'T DONE ANYTHING! I'M NOT A MUTANT!
I'M JUST LIKE YOU!
YOU'RE NOT LIKE US. YOU'RE NOTHING LIKE US!
I CAN SEE IT! THE X-GENE IN HER CELLS!
FREAK! MONSTER!

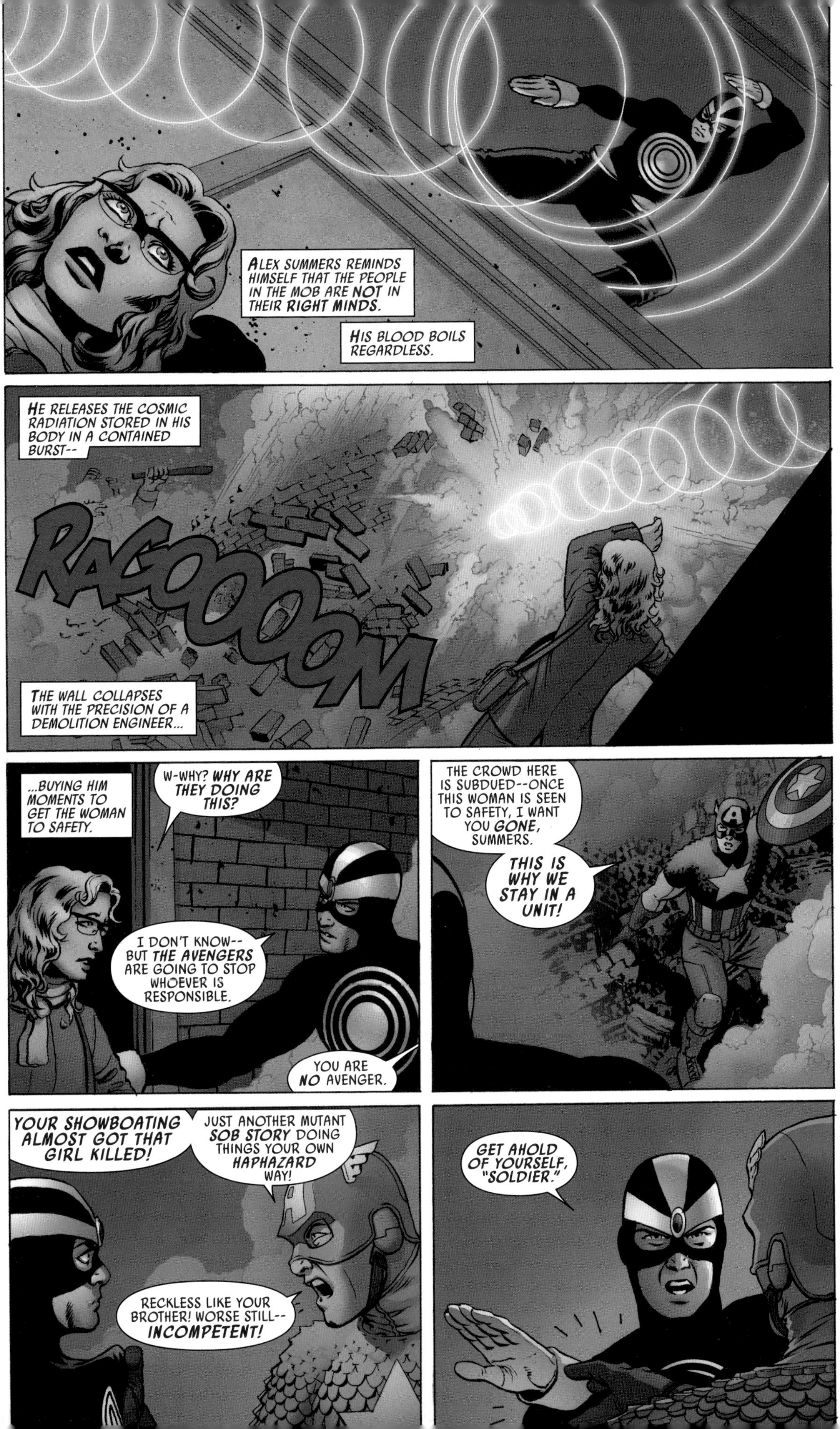
ALEX SUMMERS REMINDS HIMSELF THAT THE PEOPLE IN THE MOB ARE NOT IN THEIR RIGHT MINDS.
HIS BLOOD BOILS REGARDLESS.
HE RELEASES THE COSMIC RADIATION STORED IN HIS BODY IN A CONTAINED BURST--
RAGOOOOM
THE WALL COLLAPSES WITH THE PRECISION OF A DEMOLITION ENGINEER...
...BUYING HIM MOMENTS TO GET THE WOMAN TO SAFETY.
W-WHY? WHY ARE THEY DOING THIS?
I DON'T KNOW-- BUT THE AVENGERS ARE GOING TO STOP WHOEVER IS RESPONSIBLE.
YOU ARE NO AVENGER.
THE CROWD HERE IS SUBDUED--ONCE THIS WOMAN IS SEEN TO SAFETY, I WANT YOU GONE, SUMMERS.
THIS IS WHY WE STAY IN A UNIT!
YOUR SHOWBOATING ALMOST GOT THAT GIRL KILLED!
JUST ANOTHER MUTANT SOB STORY DOING THINGS YOUR OWN HAPHAZARD WAY!
RECKLESS LIKE YOUR BROTHER! WORSE STILL-- INCOMPETENT!
GET AHOLD OF YOURSELF, "SOLDIER."

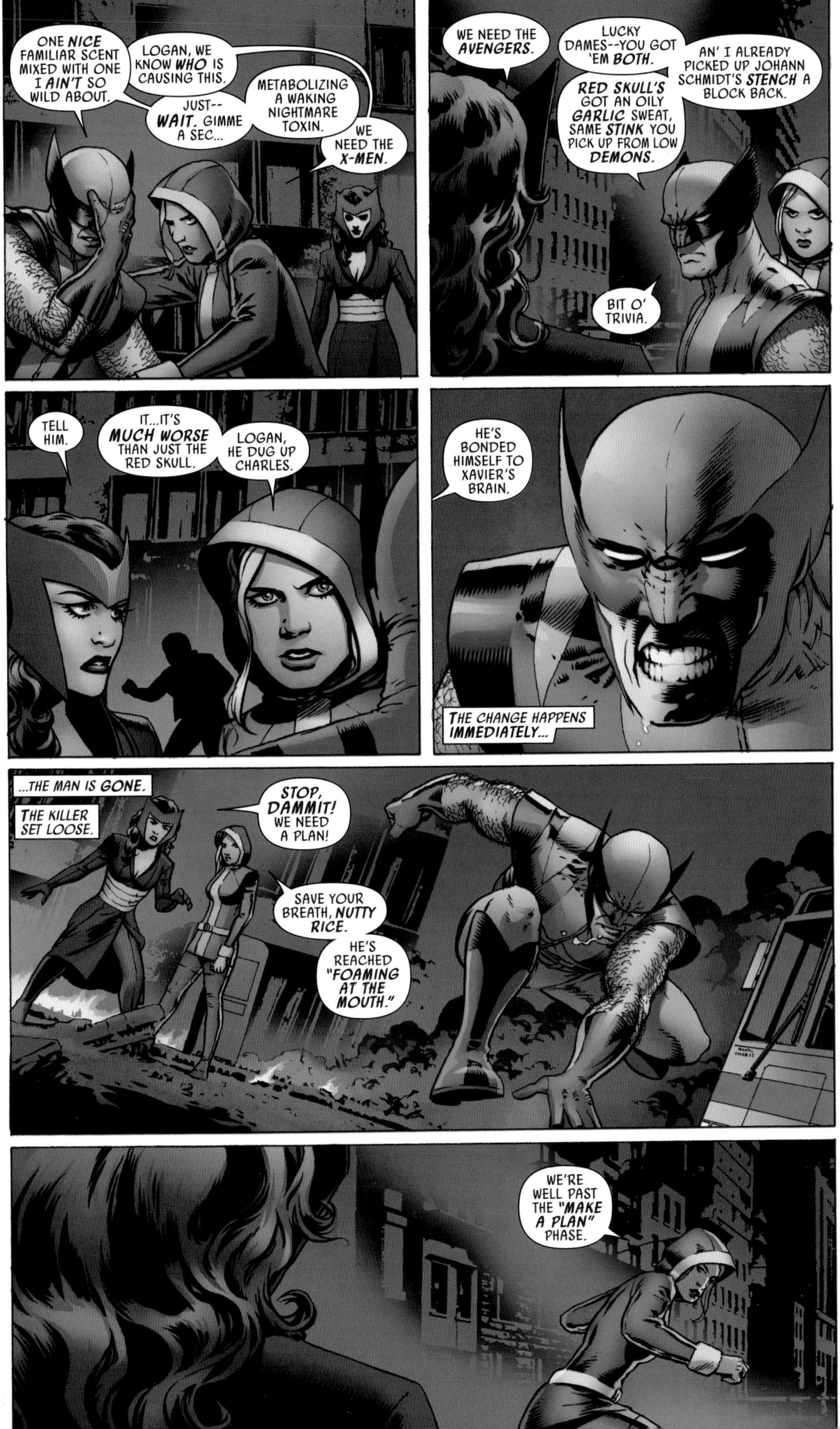
ONE NICE FAMILIAR SCENT MIXED WITH ONE I AIN'T SO WILD ABOUT.
LOGAN, WE KNOW WHO IS CAUSING THIS.
JUST-- WAIT. GIMME A SEC...
METABOLIZING A WAKING NIGHTMARE TOXIN.
WE NEED THE X-MEN.
WE NEED THE AVENGERS.
LUCKY DAMES--YOU GOT 'EM BOTH.
RED SKULL'S GOT AN OILY GARLIC SWEAT, SAME STINK YOU PICK UP FROM LOW DEMONS.
AN' I ALREADY PICKED UP JOHANN SCHMIDT'S STENCH A BLOCK BACK.
BIT O' TRIVIA.
TELL HIM.
IT...IT'S MUCH WORSE THAN JUST THE RED SKULL.
LOGAN, HE DUG UP CHARLES.
HE'S BONDED HIMSELF TO XAVIER'S BRAIN.
THE CHANGE HAPPENS IMMEDIATELY...
...THE MAN IS GONE.
THE KILLER SET LOOSE.
STOP, DAMMIT! WE NEED A PLAN!
SAVE YOUR BREATH, NUTTY RICE.
HE'S REACHED "FOAMING AT THE MOUTH."
WE'RE WELL PAST THE "MAKE A PLAN" PHASE.

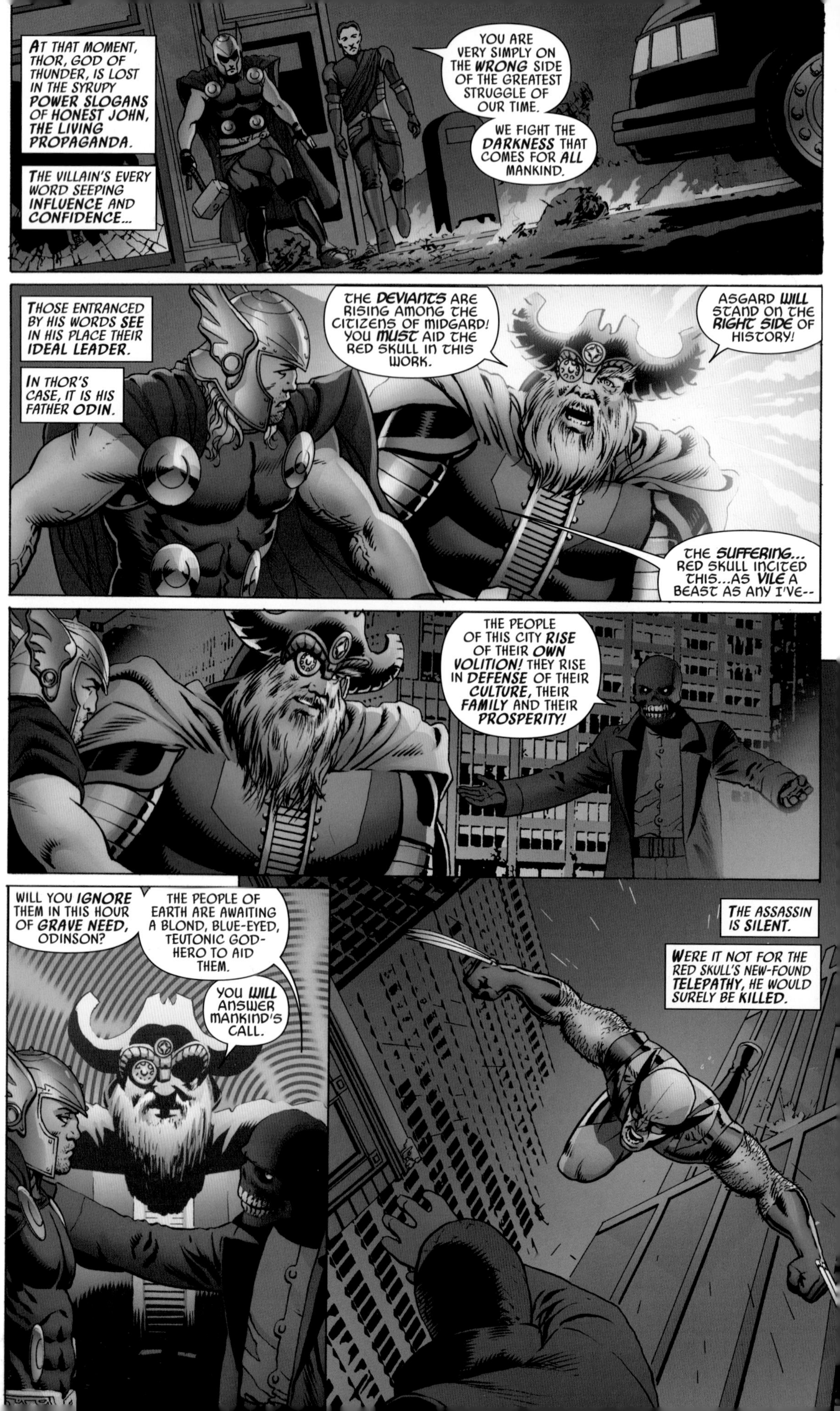
AT THAT MOMENT, THOR, GOD OF THUNDER, IS LOST IN THE SYRUPY POWER SLOGANS OF HONEST JOHN, THE LIVING PROPAGANDA.
THE VILLAIN'S EVERY WORD SEEPING INFLUENCE AND CONFIDENCE...
YOU ARE VERY SIMPLY ON THE WRONG SIDE OF THE GREATEST STRUGGLE OF OUR TIME.
WE FIGHT THE DARKNESS THAT COMES FOR ALL MANKIND.
THOSE ENTRANCED BY HIS WORDS SEE IN HIS PLACE THEIR IDEAL LEADER.
IN THOR'S CASE, IT IS HIS FATHER ODIN.
THE DEVIANTS ARE RISING AMONG THE CITIZENS OF MIDGARD! YOU MUST AID THE RED SKULL IN THIS WORK.
ASGARD WILL STAND ON THE RIGHT SIDE OF HISTORY!
THE SUFFERING... RED SKULL INCITED THIS...AS VILE A BEAST AS ANY I'VE--
THE PEOPLE OF THIS CITY RISE OF THEIR OWN VOLITION! THEY RISE IN DEFENSE OF THEIR CULTURE, THEIR FAMILY AND THEIR PROSPERITY!
WILL YOU IGNORE THEM IN THIS HOUR OF GRAVE NEED, ODINSON?
THE PEOPLE OF EARTH ARE AWAITING A BLOND, BLUE-EYED, TEUTONIC GOD-HERO TO AID THEM.
YOU WILL ANSWER MANKIND'S CALL.
THE ASSASSIN IS SILENT.
WERE IT NOT FOR THE RED SKULL'S NEW-FOUND TELEPATHY, HE WOULD SURELY BE KILLED.

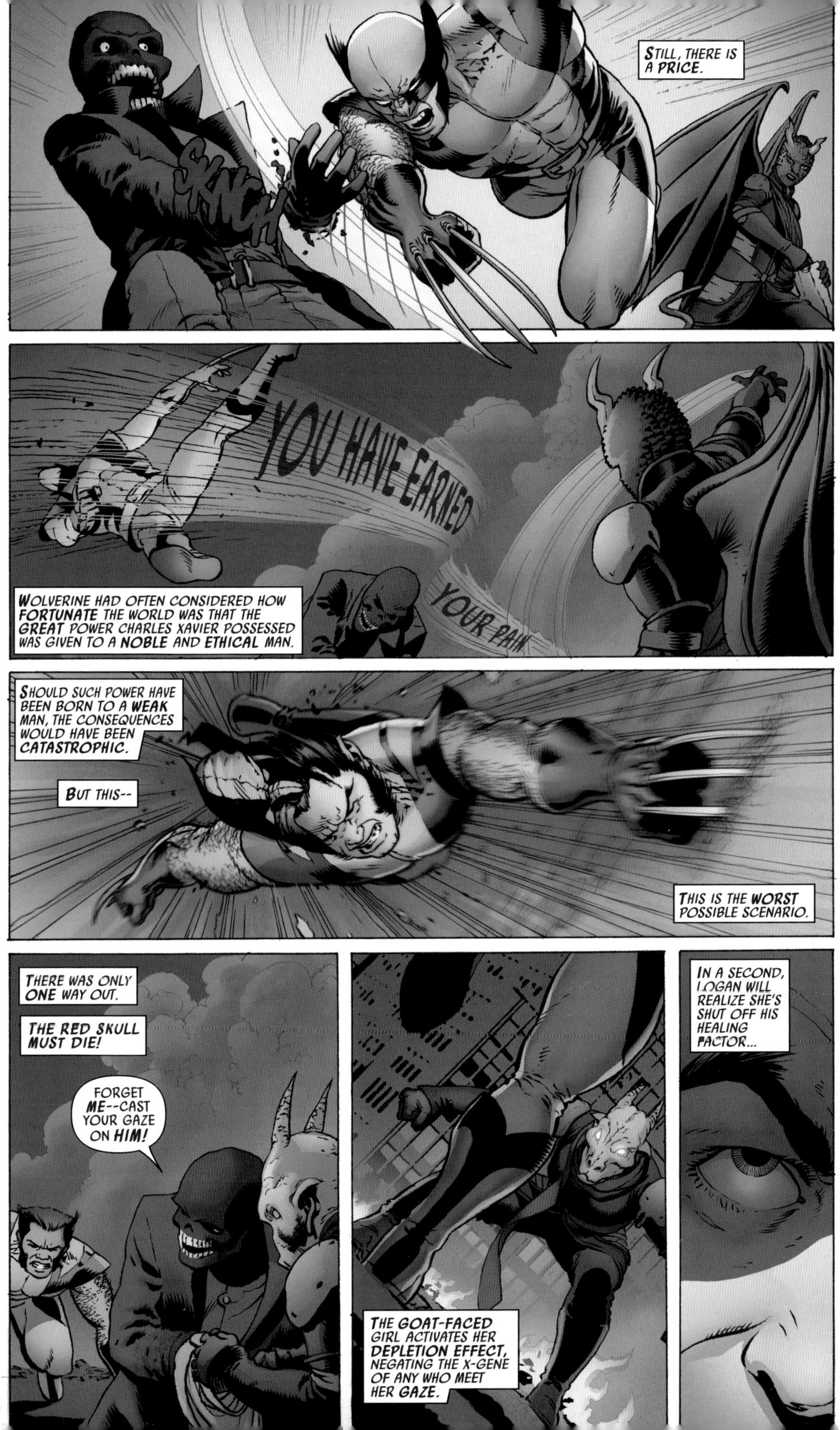

STILL, THERE IS A PRICE.
SKNCH!
YOU HAVE EARNED YOUR PAIN
WOLVERINE HAD OFTEN CONSIDERED HOW FORTUNATE THE WORLD WAS THAT THE GREAT POWER CHARLES XAVIER POSSESSED WAS GIVEN TO A NOBLE AND ETHICAL MAN.
SHOULD SUCH POWER HAVE BEEN BORN TO A WEAK MAN, THE CONSEQUENCES WOULD HAVE BEEN CATASTROPHIC.
BUT THIS--
THIS IS THE WORST POSSIBLE SCENARIO.
THERE WAS ONLY ONE WAY OUT.
THE RED SKULL MUST DIE!
FORGET ME--CAST YOUR GAZE ON HIM!
THE GOAT-FACED GIRL ACTIVATES HER DEPLETION EFFECT, NEGATING THE X-GENE OF ANY WHO MEET HER GAZE.
IN A SECOND, LOGAN WILL REALIZE SHE'S SHUT OFF HIS HEALING FACTOR...

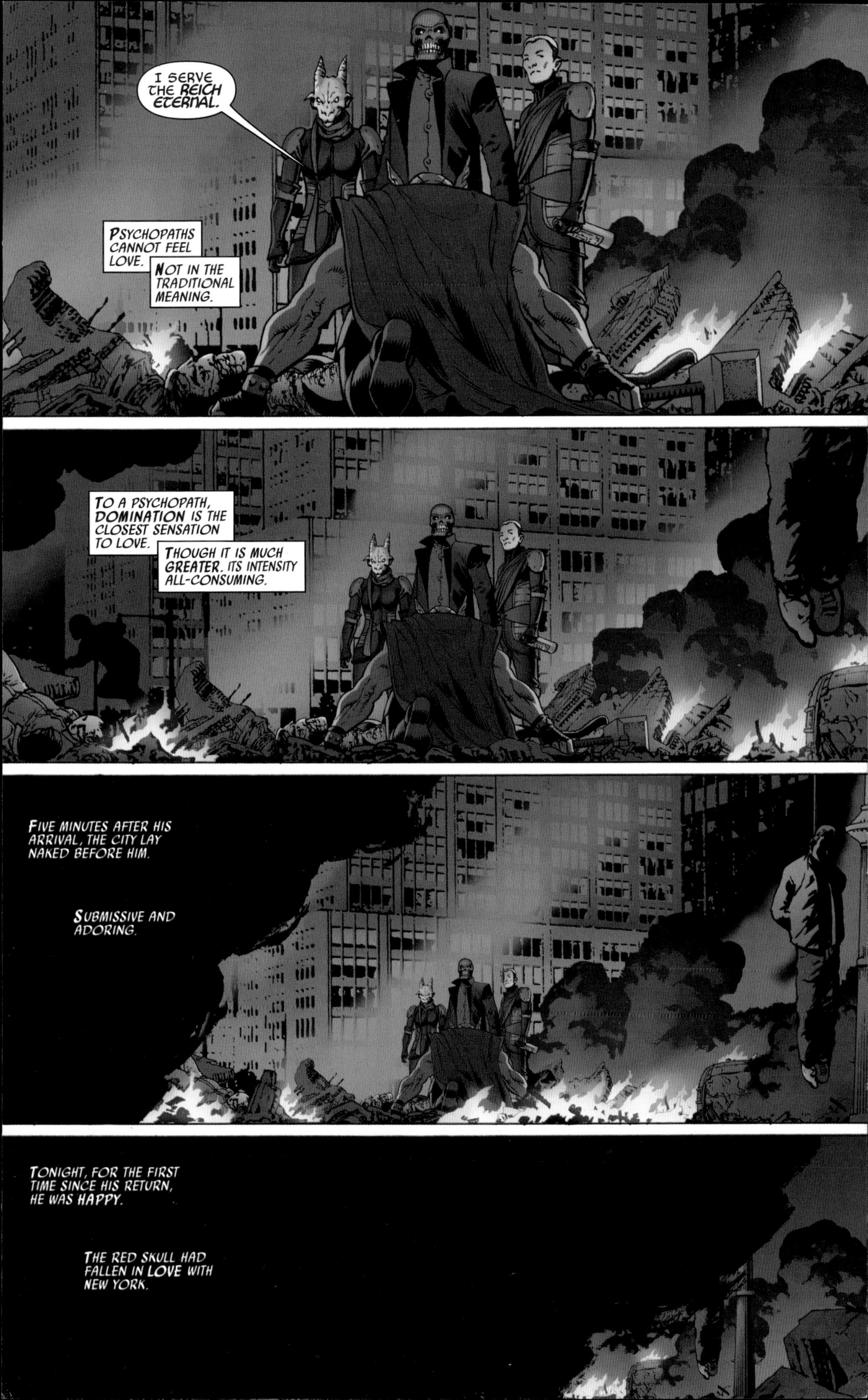
I SERVE THE REICH ETERNAL.
PSYCHOPATHS CANNOT FEEL LOVE.
NOT IN THE TRADITIONAL MEANING.
TO A PSYCHOPATH, DOMINATION IS THE CLOSEST SENSATION TO LOVE.
THOUGH IT IS MUCH GREATER. ITS INTENSITY ALL-CONSUMING.
FIVE MINUTES AFTER HIS ARRIVAL, THE CITY LAY NAKED BEFORE HIM.
SUBMISSIVE AND ADORING.
TONIGHT, FOR THE FIRST TIME SINCE HIS RETURN, HE WAS HAPPY.
THE RED SKULL HAD FALLEN IN LOVE WITH NEW YORK.

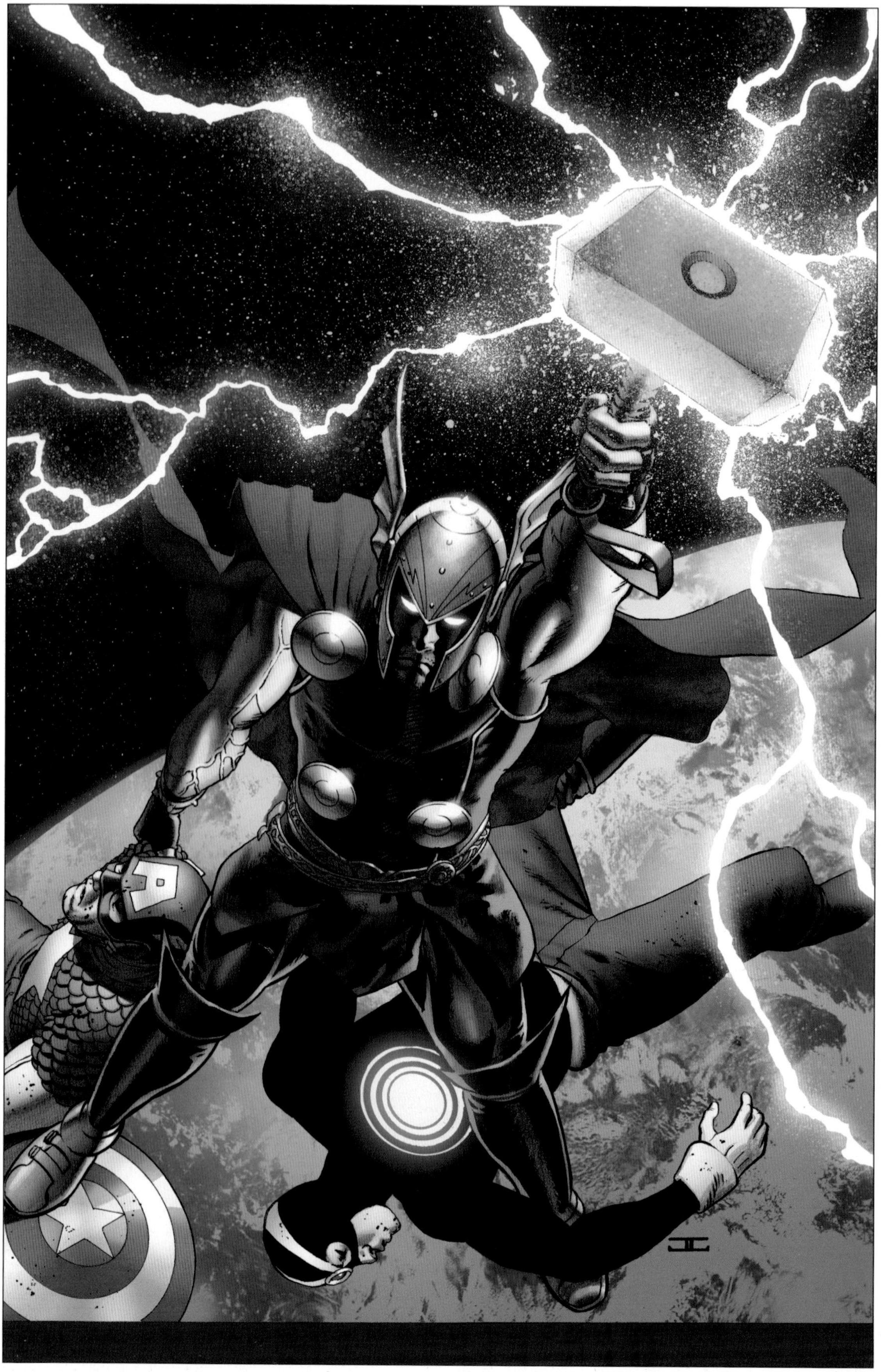

MINUTES AGO, THE SUMMERS FAMILY WAS RETURNING HOME FROM A VACATION IN ANCHORAGE, ALASKA.

NOW CHRISTOPHER SUMMERS FIGHTS BACK TEARS AS HE STRAPS HIS ELDEST SON SCOTT INTO THE ONLY INTACT PARACHUTE.

IT DOESN'T GO UNNOTICED BY YOUNGER BROTHER ALEX.

YOU HOLD ON TO ALEX AS TIGHT AS YOU CAN, SCOTT, *YOU HEAR ME?*

O-OKAY, DAD...I WILL.

BE *BOLD* AND *FEARLESS.* LOOK TO YOUR HEARTS FOR STRENGTH TO FACE THE FUTURE.

WHEN YOU CAN'T FIND IT THERE, LOOK TO *EACH OTHER.*

PROMISE ME YOU'LL TAKE CARE OF EACH OTHER. *PROMISE.*

WE WILL, MOM. I PROMISE.

ALEX CAN MANAGE ONLY A *WHIMPER,* HIS THROAT *SWOLLEN* IN GRIEF.

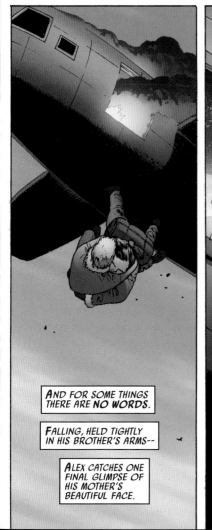

AND FOR SOME THINGS THERE ARE *NO WORDS.*

FALLING, HELD TIGHTLY IN HIS BROTHER'S ARMS--

ALEX CATCHES ONE FINAL GLIMPSE OF HIS MOTHER'S BEAUTIFUL FACE.

SLOWLY WAVING GOODBYE.

AS IF THE BOYS WERE MERELY GOING TO SCHOOL.

AS IF THEY WOULD ALL BE TOGETHER SOON.

AND THEN SHE WAS *GONE.*

IN A MOMENT THAT ALEX WILL *RELIVE* FOR THE REST OF HIS LIFE.

A LIFE SPENT *DESPERATELY* TRYING TO PROVE HIMSELF AND MAINTAIN SOME *SEMBLANCE* OF CONTROL...

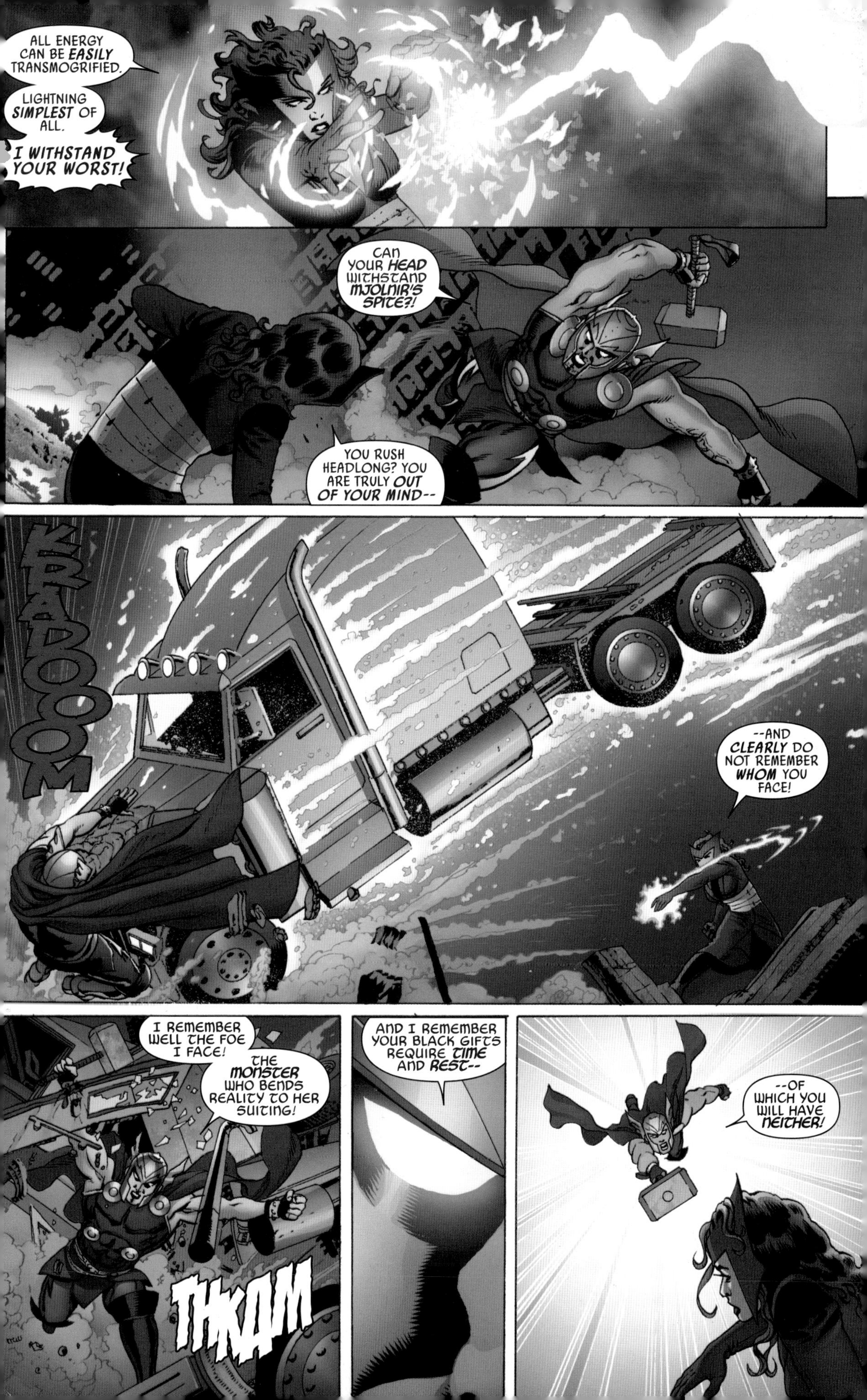
ALL ENERGY CAN BE EASILY TRANSMOGRIFIED.
LIGHTNING SIMPLEST OF ALL.
I WITHSTAND YOUR WORST!
CAN YOUR HEAD WITHSTAND MJOLNIR'S SPITE?!
YOU RUSH HEADLONG? YOU ARE TRULY OUT OF YOUR MIND--
KRADOOOM
--AND CLEARLY DO NOT REMEMBER WHOM YOU FACE!
I REMEMBER WELL THE FOE I FACE!
THE MONSTER WHO BENDS REALITY TO HER SUITING!
THKAM
AND I REMEMBER YOUR BLACK GIFTS REQUIRE TIME AND REST--
--OF WHICH YOU WILL HAVE NEITHER!

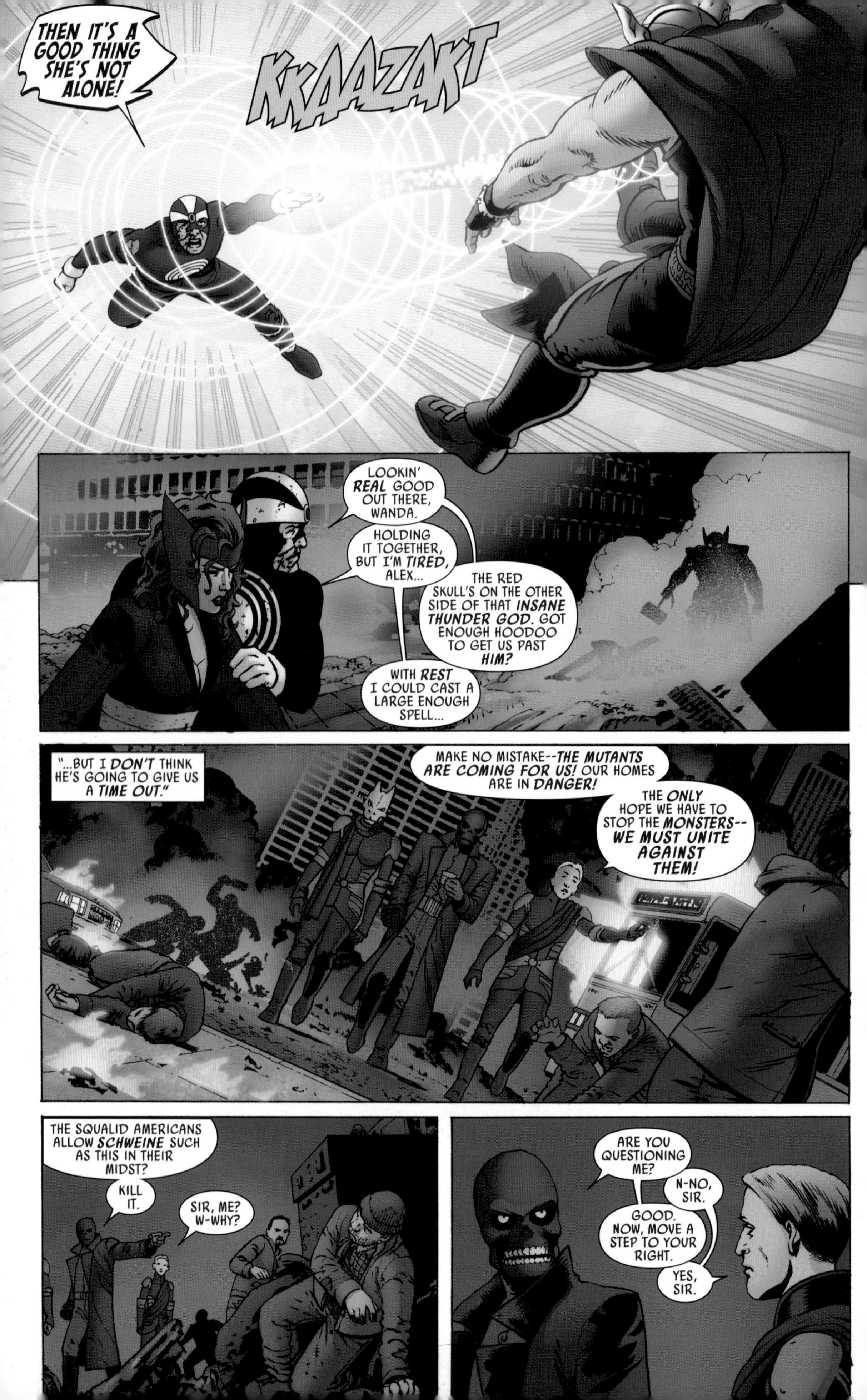
THEN IT'S A GOOD THING SHE'S NOT ALONE!
KKAAZAKT
LOOKIN' REAL GOOD OUT THERE, WANDA.
HOLDING IT TOGETHER, BUT I'M TIRED, ALEX...
THE RED SKULL'S ON THE OTHER SIDE OF THAT INSANE THUNDER GOD. GOT ENOUGH HOODOO TO GET US PAST HIM?
WITH REST I COULD CAST A LARGE ENOUGH SPELL...
"...BUT I DON'T THINK HE'S GOING TO GIVE US A TIME OUT."
MAKE NO MISTAKE--THE MUTANTS ARE COMING FOR US! OUR HOMES ARE IN DANGER!
THE ONLY HOPE WE HAVE TO STOP THE MONSTERS--WE MUST UNITE AGAINST THEM!
THE SQUALID AMERICANS ALLOW SCHWEINE SUCH AS THIS IN THEIR MIDST?
KILL IT.
SIR, ME? W-WHY?
ARE YOU QUESTIONING ME?
N-NO, SIR.
GOOD. NOW, MOVE A STEP TO YOUR RIGHT.
YES, SIR.

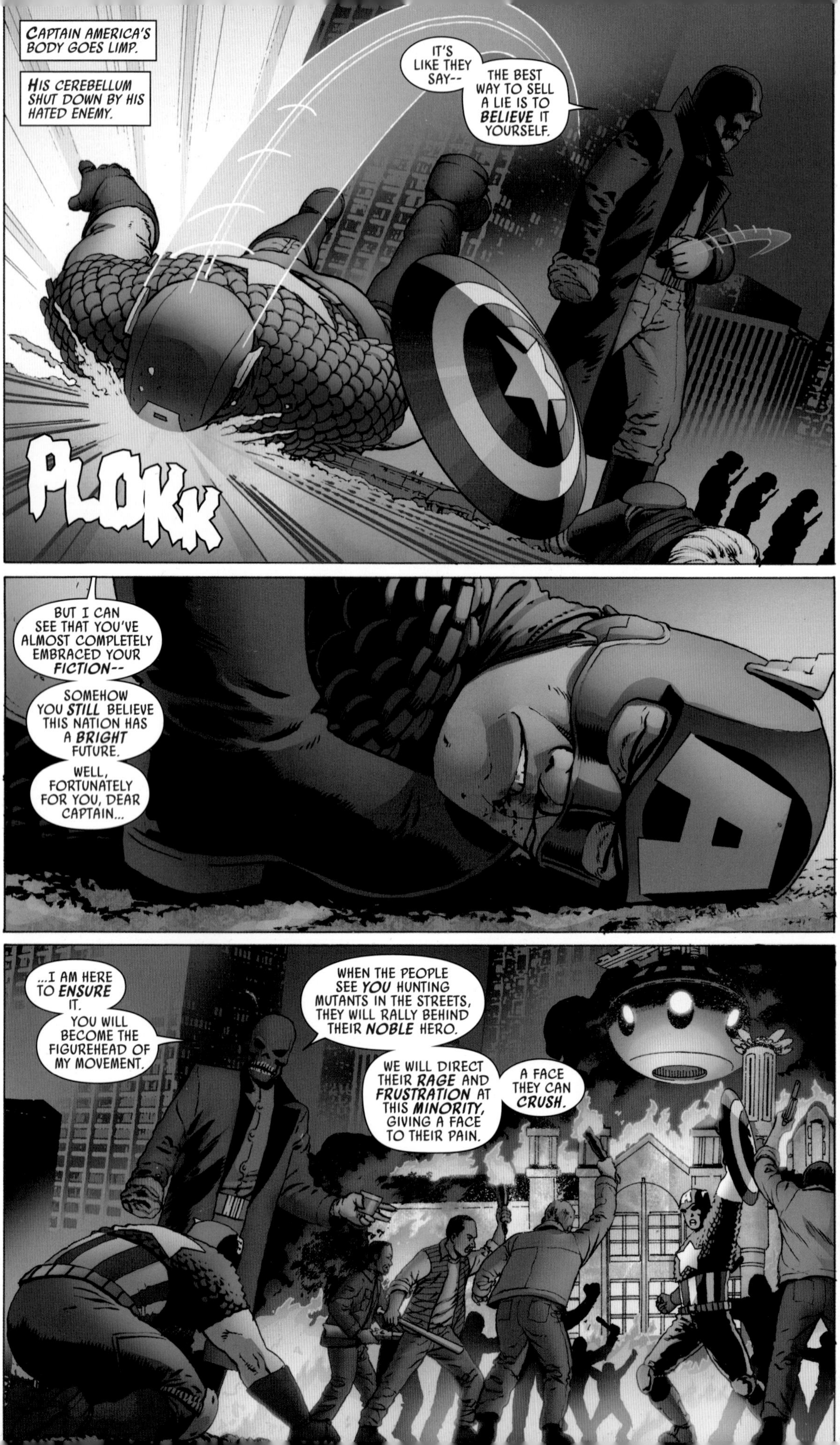
CAPTAIN AMERICA'S BODY GOES LIMP.
HIS CEREBELLUM SHUT DOWN BY HIS HATED ENEMY.
IT'S LIKE THEY SAY--
THE BEST WAY TO SELL A LIE IS TO BELIEVE IT YOURSELF.
PLOKK
BUT I CAN SEE THAT YOU'VE ALMOST COMPLETELY EMBRACED YOUR FICTION--
SOMEHOW YOU STILL BELIEVE THIS NATION HAS A BRIGHT FUTURE.
WELL, FORTUNATELY FOR YOU, DEAR CAPTAIN...
...I AM HERE TO ENSURE IT.
YOU WILL BECOME THE FIGUREHEAD OF MY MOVEMENT.
WHEN THE PEOPLE SEE YOU HUNTING MUTANTS IN THE STREETS, THEY WILL RALLY BEHIND THEIR NOBLE HERO.
WE WILL DIRECT THEIR RAGE AND FRUSTRATION AT THIS MINORITY, GIVING A FACE TO THEIR PAIN.
A FACE THEY CAN CRUSH.

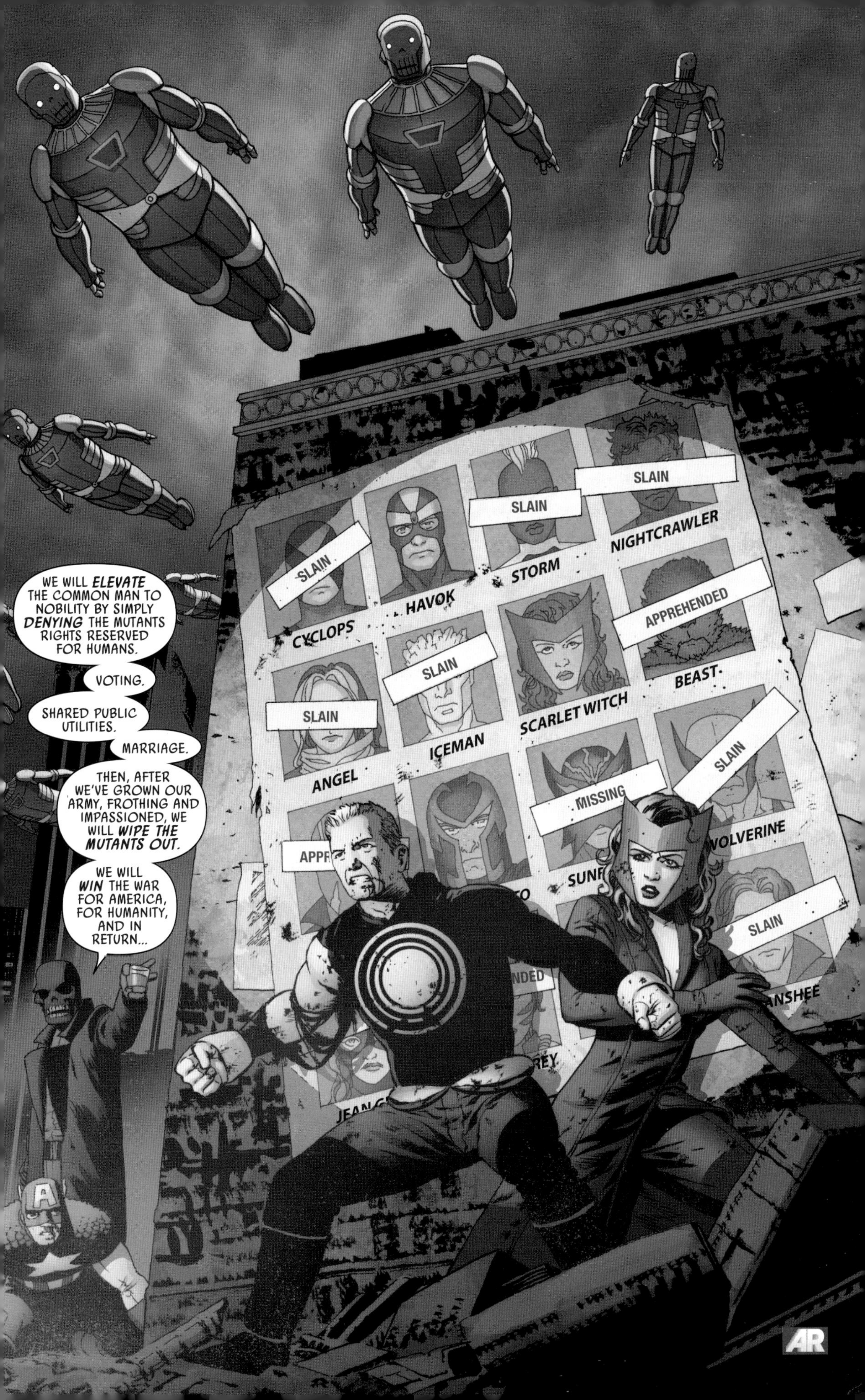
WE WILL *ELEVATE* THE COMMON MAN TO NOBILITY BY SIMPLY *DENYING* THE MUTANTS RIGHTS RESERVED FOR HUMANS.
VOTING.
SHARED PUBLIC UTILITIES.
MARRIAGE.
THEN, AFTER WE'VE GROWN OUR ARMY, FROTHING AND IMPASSIONED, WE WILL *WIPE THE MUTANTS OUT.*
WE WILL *WIN* THE WAR FOR AMERICA, FOR HUMANITY, AND IN RETURN...
SLAIN
CYCLOPS
HAVOK
SLAIN
STORM
SLAIN
NIGHTCRAWLER
SLAIN
ANGEL
SLAIN
ICEMAN
SCARLET WITCH
APPREHENDED
BEAST
SLAIN
MISSING
WOLVERINE
SLAIN

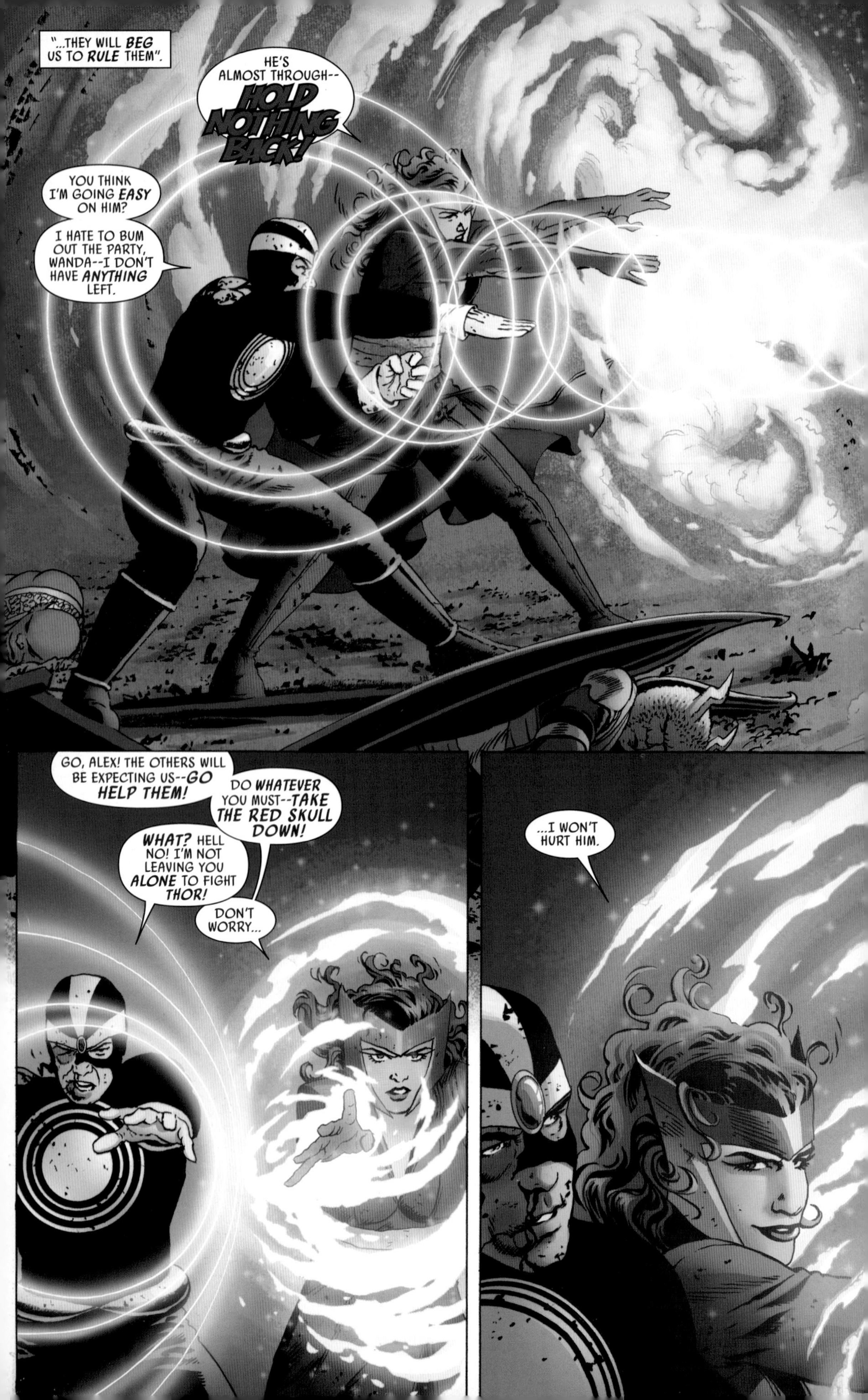
"...THEY WILL BEG US TO RULE THEM".
HE'S ALMOST THROUGH-- HOLD NOTHING BACK!
YOU THINK I'M GOING EASY ON HIM?
I HATE TO BUM OUT THE PARTY, WANDA--I DON'T HAVE ANYTHING LEFT.
GO, ALEX! THE OTHERS WILL BE EXPECTING US--GO HELP THEM!
DO WHATEVER YOU MUST--TAKE THE RED SKULL DOWN!
WHAT? HELL NO! I'M NOT LEAVING YOU ALONE TO FIGHT THOR!
DON'T WORRY...
...I WON'T HURT HIM.

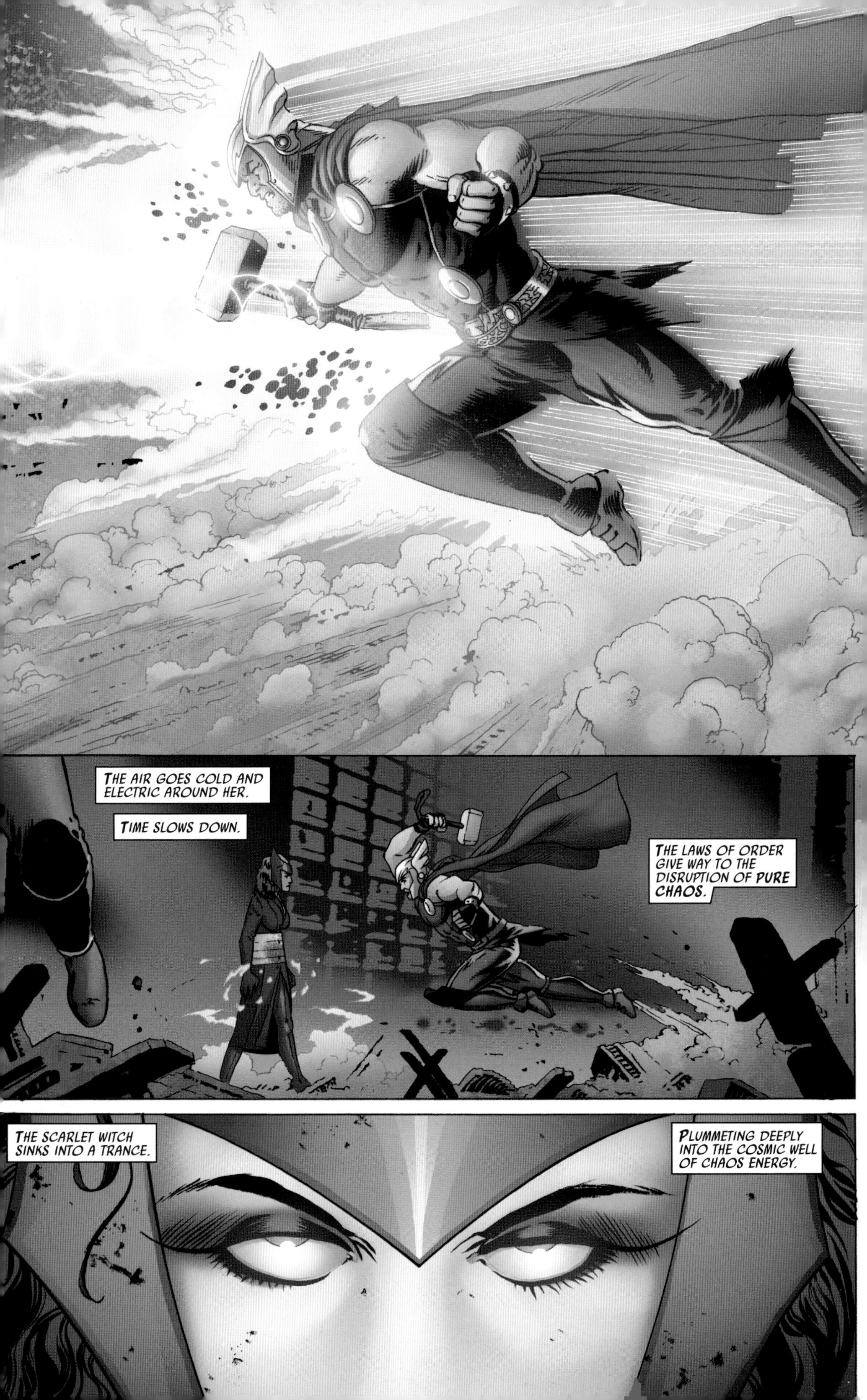
THE AIR GOES COLD AND ELECTRIC AROUND HER.
TIME SLOWS DOWN.
THE LAWS OF ORDER GIVE WAY TO THE DISRUPTION OF PURE CHAOS.
THE SCARLET WITCH SINKS INTO A TRANCE.
PLUMMETING DEEPLY INTO THE COSMIC WELL OF CHAOS ENERGY.

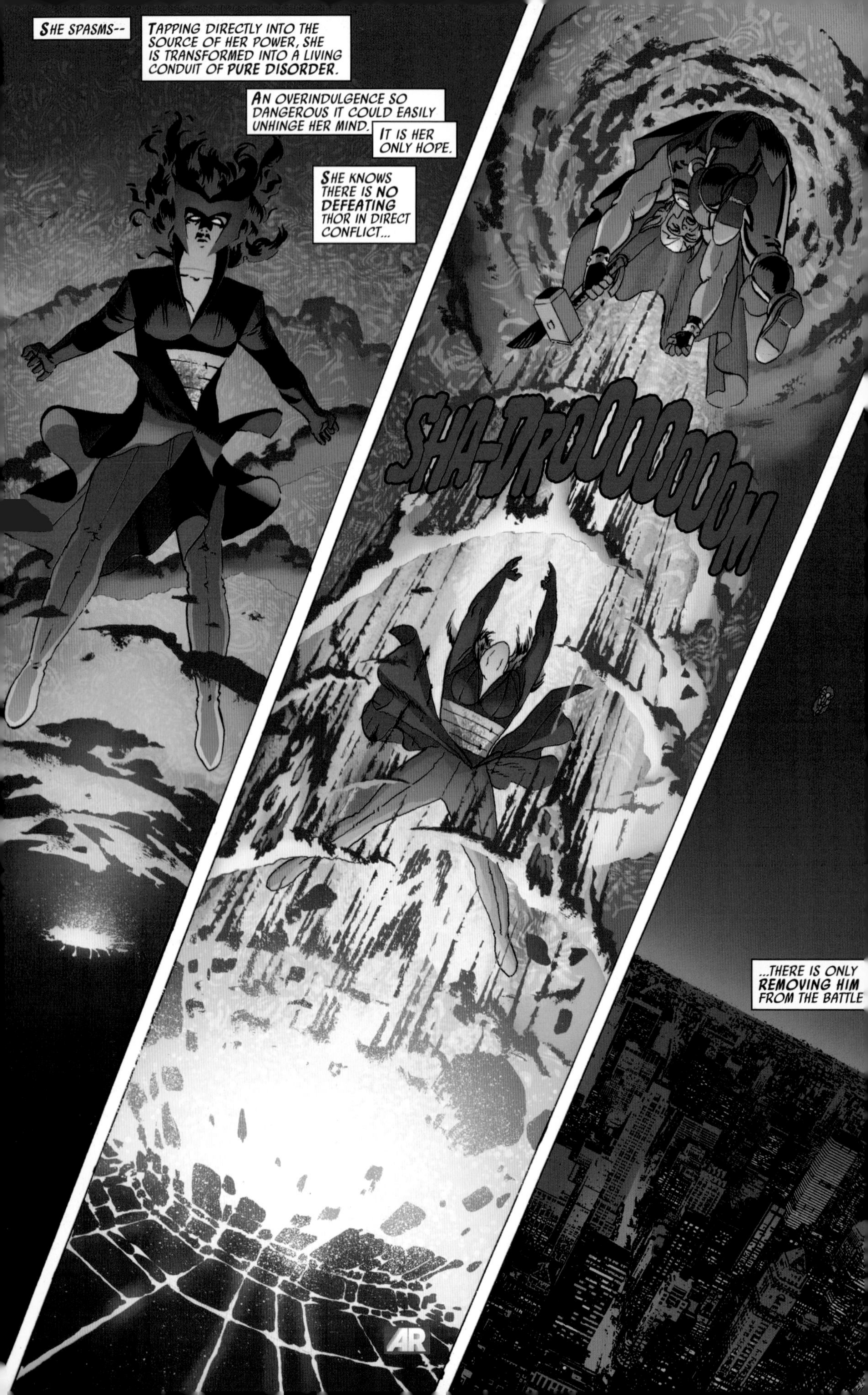
SHE SPASMS--
TAPPING DIRECTLY INTO THE SOURCE OF HER POWER, SHE IS TRANSFORMED INTO A LIVING CONDUIT OF PURE DISORDER.
AN OVERINDULGENCE SO DANGEROUS IT COULD EASILY UNHINGE HER MIND.
IT IS HER ONLY HOPE.
SHE KNOWS THERE IS NO DEFEATING THOR IN DIRECT CONFLICT...
SHA-DROOOOOOOOM
...THERE IS ONLY REMOVING HIM FROM THE BATTLE
AR

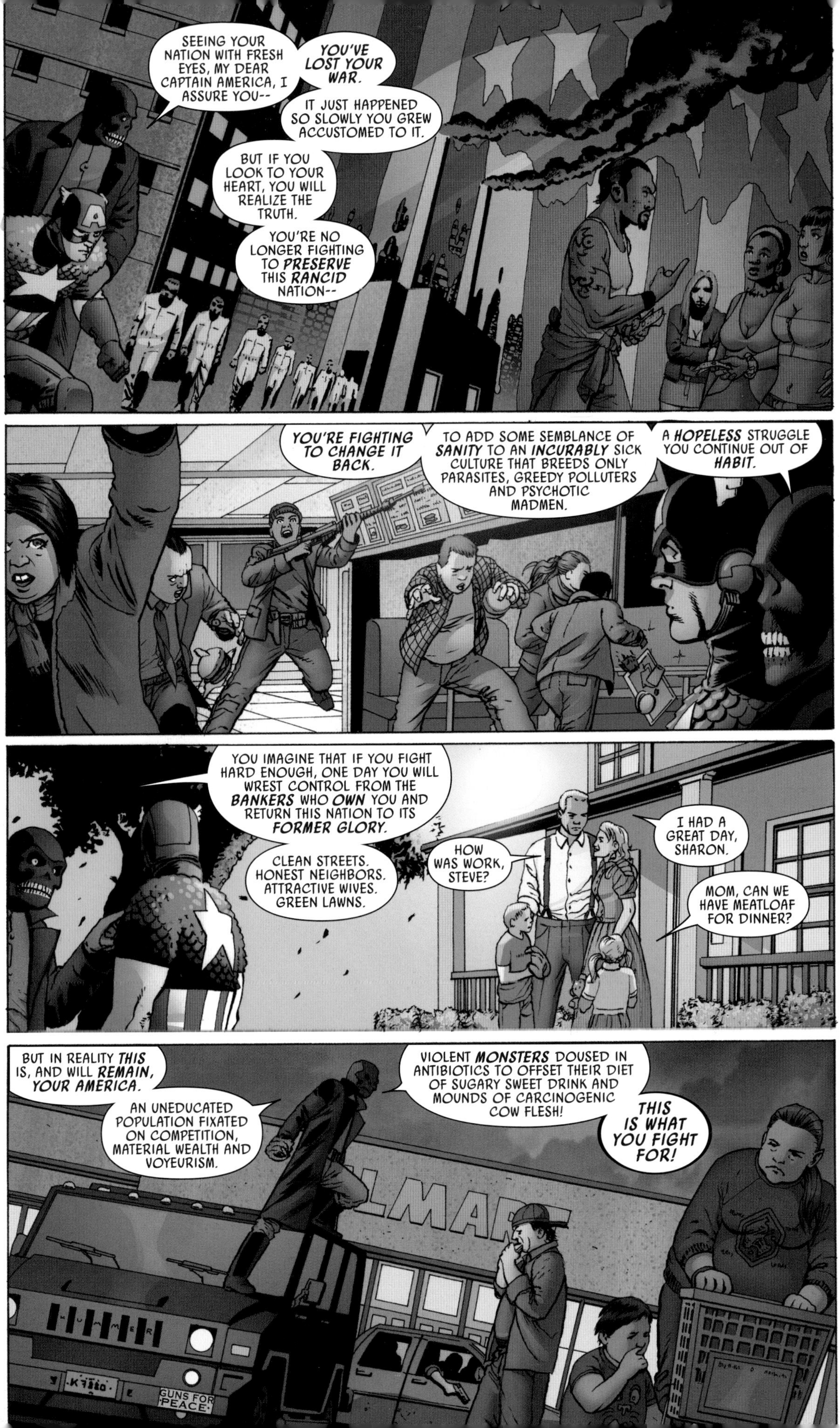
SEEING YOUR NATION WITH FRESH EYES, MY DEAR CAPTAIN AMERICA, I ASSURE YOU--
YOU'VE LOST YOUR WAR.
IT JUST HAPPENED SO SLOWLY YOU GREW ACCUSTOMED TO IT.
BUT IF YOU LOOK TO YOUR HEART, YOU WILL REALIZE THE TRUTH.
YOU'RE NO LONGER FIGHTING TO PRESERVE THIS RANCID NATION--
YOU'RE FIGHTING TO CHANGE IT BACK.
TO ADD SOME SEMBLANCE OF SANITY TO AN INCURABLY SICK CULTURE THAT BREEDS ONLY PARASITES, GREEDY POLLUTERS AND PSYCHOTIC MADMEN.
A HOPELESS STRUGGLE YOU CONTINUE OUT OF HABIT.
YOU IMAGINE THAT IF YOU FIGHT HARD ENOUGH, ONE DAY YOU WILL WREST CONTROL FROM THE BANKERS WHO OWN YOU AND RETURN THIS NATION TO ITS FORMER GLORY.
CLEAN STREETS. HONEST NEIGHBORS. ATTRACTIVE WIVES. GREEN LAWNS.
HOW WAS WORK, STEVE?
I HAD A GREAT DAY, SHARON.
MOM, CAN WE HAVE MEATLOAF FOR DINNER?
BUT IN REALITY THIS IS, AND WILL REMAIN, YOUR AMERICA.
AN UNEDUCATED POPULATION FIXATED ON COMPETITION, MATERIAL WEALTH AND VOYEURISM.
VIOLENT MONSTERS DOUSED IN ANTIBIOTICS TO OFFSET THEIR DIET OF SUGARY SWEET DRINK AND MOUNDS OF CARCINOGENIC COW FLESH!
THIS IS WHAT YOU FIGHT FOR!
GUNS FOR PEACE

TOGETHER WE WILL *CLEAN* THIS NATION.

TRANSFORM IT TO ONE MORE BEFITTING BOTH OF OUR *HIGH* IDEALS.

ARE YOU SIMPLY *TOO ARROGANT* TO SEE WHEN YOU ARE *WRONG?*

NO...I'LL NEVER...

LOOK AT YOUR FUTURE!

ARE THESE *IGNORANT REDNECKS* THE GOAL OF YOUR *AMERICAN DREAM?*

NOW, DON'T YOU GO DUMPIN' ON REDNECKS, NAZI...

...WE'RE *AWFUL* HAZARDOUS WHEN RILED.

WHAT HAVE YOU DONE--

TAKEN THIS UGLY GAL'S POWERS AN' *TURNED OFF* THE TELEPATHY YOU STOLE FROM CHARLES XAVIER--BUT THE *REAL* FUN IS STILL TO COME.

AS I CRUSH YOUR SKULL WITH MY BARE HANDS!

STUPID GIRL.

I, OF COURSE, HAVE *OTHER* WEAPONS.

COSMIC ENERGY SEARS THE RED SKULL'S FLESH--THE SHOT GOES WIDE.

BLAM!

ROGUE'S INJURY IS **NOT** FATAL...

...HAVOK'S PLANS FOR JOHANN SHMIDT **ARE.**

TWUKK

OOF--!

HIS ENERGY SPENT, HAVOK IS LEFT WITH A MORE PRIMAL METHOD OF ATTACK--

--AND THAT SUITS HIM JUST FINE.

YOU'RE LIKE THE CLOSETED JOCK WHO BEATS ON GAY KIDS! YOU DON'T **HATE** MUTANTS--

PLOKK

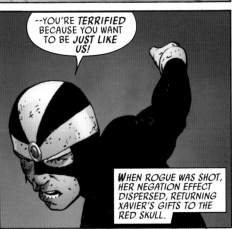

--YOU'RE **TERRIFIED** BECAUSE YOU WANT TO BE **JUST LIKE US!**

WHEN ROGUE WAS SHOT, HER NEGATION EFFECT DISPERSED, RETURNING XAVIER'S GIFTS TO THE RED SKULL.

OBLIVIOUS, HAVOK BEATS ROGUE MERCILESS, SEEING IN HER THE FACE OF HIS FOE.

KROKK

FIGHT! PUNCH! ZAP! POOR MUTANT FOOL-- YOU HAVE **NO HOPE** OF TURNING BACK THIS TIDE.

IT'S LIKE THEY SAY, THE BEST WAY TO SELL A LIE--

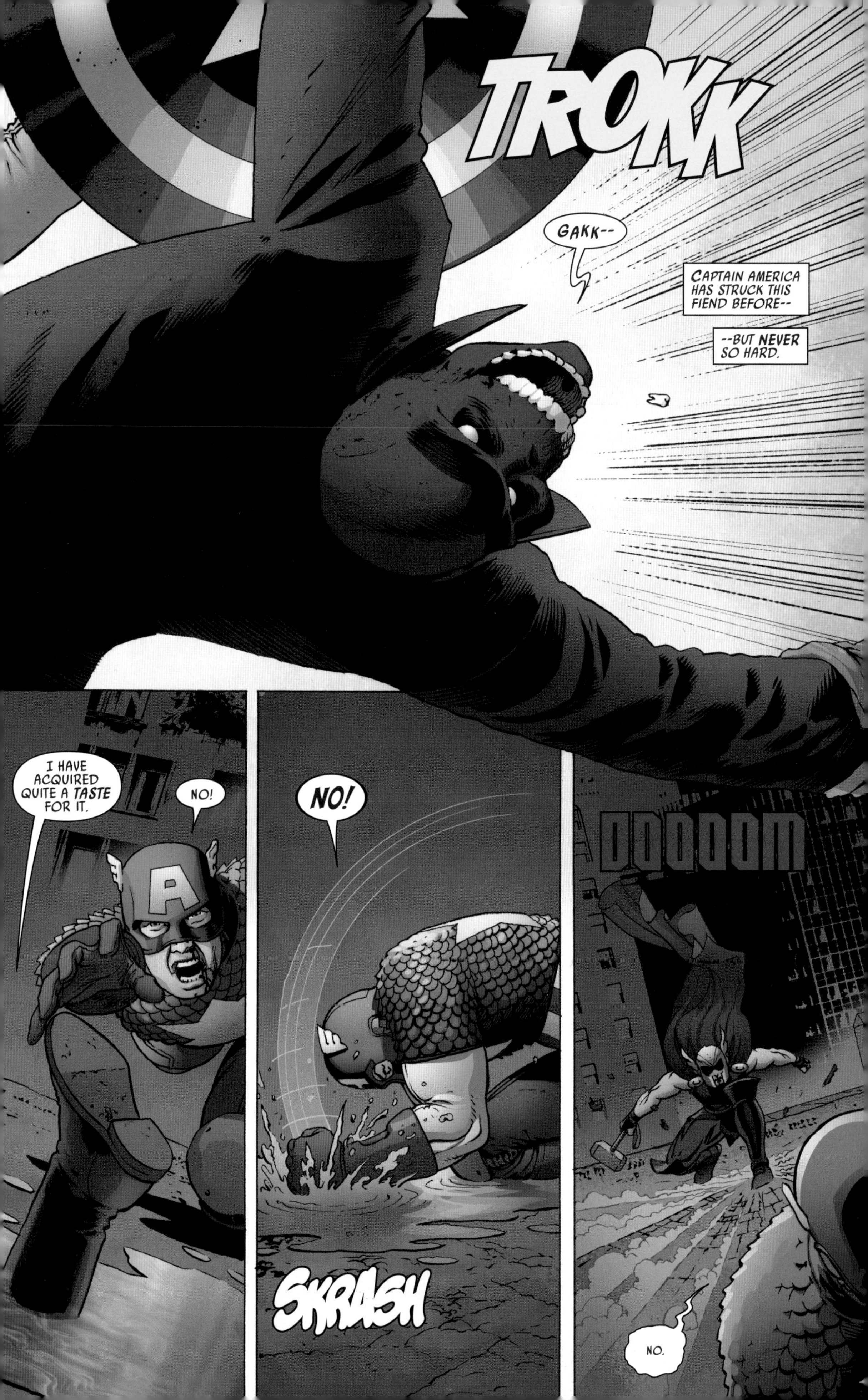
TROKK
GAKK--
CAPTAIN AMERICA HAS STRUCK THIS FIEND BEFORE--
--BUT NEVER SO HARD.
I HAVE ACQUIRED QUITE A TASTE FOR IT.
NO!
NO!
SKRASH
DOOOOM
NO.

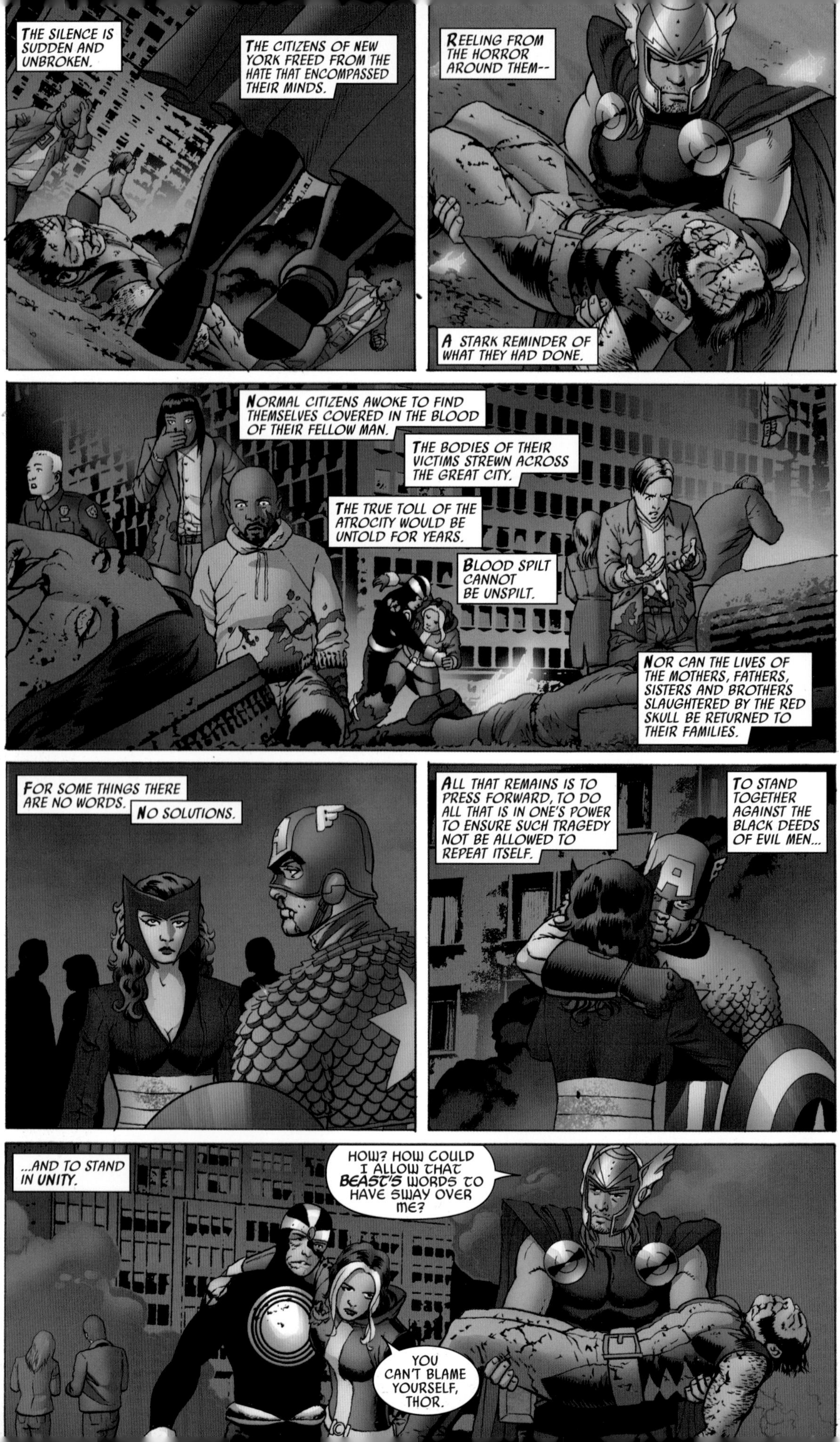
THE SILENCE IS SUDDEN AND UNBROKEN.
THE CITIZENS OF NEW YORK FREED FROM THE HATE THAT ENCOMPASSED THEIR MINDS.
REELING FROM THE HORROR AROUND THEM--
A STARK REMINDER OF WHAT THEY HAD DONE.
NORMAL CITIZENS AWOKE TO FIND THEMSELVES COVERED IN THE BLOOD OF THEIR FELLOW MAN.
THE BODIES OF THEIR VICTIMS STREWN ACROSS THE GREAT CITY.
THE TRUE TOLL OF THE ATROCITY WOULD BE UNTOLD FOR YEARS.
BLOOD SPILT CANNOT BE UNSPILT.
NOR CAN THE LIVES OF THE MOTHERS, FATHERS, SISTERS AND BROTHERS SLAUGHTERED BY THE RED SKULL BE RETURNED TO THEIR FAMILIES.
FOR SOME THINGS THERE ARE NO WORDS.
NO SOLUTIONS.
ALL THAT REMAINS IS TO PRESS FORWARD, TO DO ALL THAT IS IN ONE'S POWER TO ENSURE SUCH TRAGEDY NOT BE ALLOWED TO REPEAT ITSELF.
TO STAND TOGETHER AGAINST THE BLACK DEEDS OF EVIL MEN...
...AND TO STAND IN UNITY.
HOW? HOW COULD I ALLOW THAT BEAST'S WORDS TO HAVE SWAY OVER ME?
YOU CAN'T BLAME YOURSELF, THOR.

"...LOOK TO **EACH OTHER**."

WE SCOURED THE CITY FOR THEM...

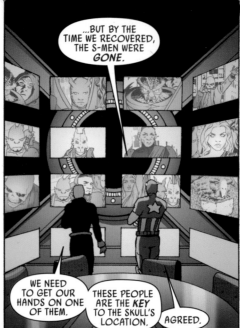

...BUT BY THE TIME WE RECOVERED, THE S-MEN WERE **GONE**.

WE NEED TO GET OUR HANDS ON ONE OF THEM.

THESE PEOPLE ARE THE **KEY** TO THE SKULL'S LOCATION.

AGREED.

GRADE-A **BAD TIMES**, STEVE.

YOU KNOW, GIVEN **WHO** WE'RE UP AGAINST HERE, IF YOU WANT TO TAKE THE CHAIR ON THIS, I **WOULDN'T** BE OFFENDED--

NO.

THE AVENGERS **UNITY SQUAD** IS IN EXCELLENT HANDS WITH YOU IN CHARGE, ALEX.

I'M **ALWAYS RIGHT** ABOUT ONE THING--WHEN SOMEONE HAS **WHAT IT TAKES.**

HEH--WELL, TO BE FAIR, I DON'T THINK YOU CAN SELF-APPLY **"ALWAYS RIGHT"**, CAP, BUT THANK YOU...

"...I'LL TRY NOT TO LET YOU DOWN."

ANNA MARIE. I ONLY NEED A MINUTE.

TIMER'S STARTED.

I WANTED YOU TO KNOW...I UNDERSTAND YOUR **TREPIDATION** ABOUT ME.

BUT I NEED YOU TO BELIEVE ME-- I'LL **NEVER AGAIN** BE WIELDED AS A MADMAN'S WEAPON.

EVEN WITH THE POWER OF CHARLES XAVIER, THE RED SKULL COULDN'T MAKE ME CAST THAT SPELL.

IF YOU DECIDE TO STAY ON, I'D LIKE TO START OVER.

I'D LIKE US TO BE **FRIENDS.**

I'M SORRY, WANDA.

I DON'T CARE **WHAT** YOU SAY--I THINK YOU'RE A **DANGEROUS MESS.**

I'M STICKING AROUND FOR TWO REASONS: BECAUSE IT'S WHAT **CHARLES** WOULD **WANT...**

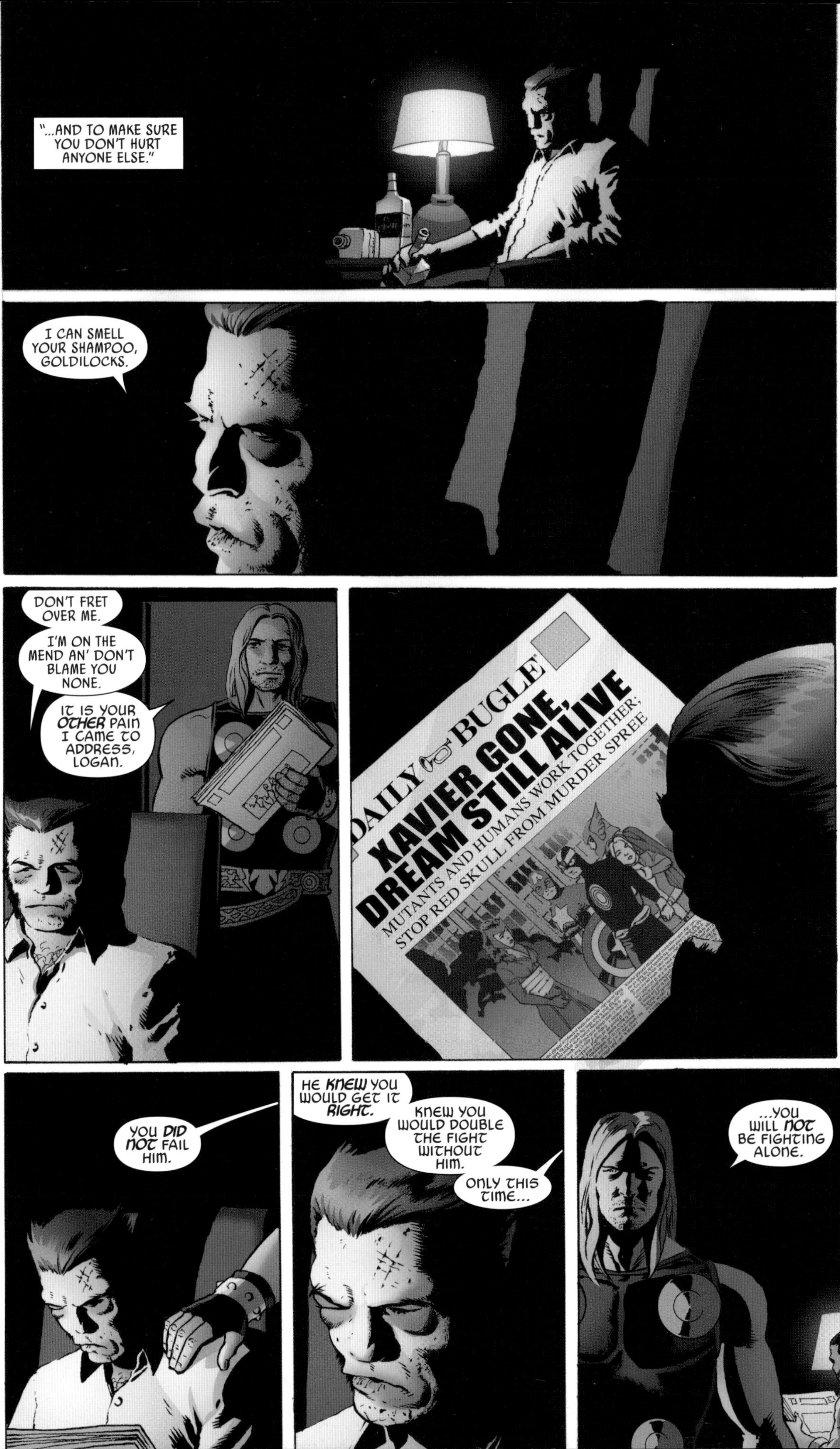
"...AND TO MAKE SURE YOU DON'T HURT ANYONE ELSE."
I CAN SMELL YOUR SHAMPOO, GOLDILOCKS.
DON'T FRET OVER ME.
I'M ON THE MEND AN' DON'T BLAME YOU NONE.
IT IS YOUR *OTHER* PAIN I CAME TO ADDRESS, LOGAN.
DAILY BUGLE
XAVIER GONE, DREAM STILL ALIVE
MUTANTS AND HUMANS WORK TOGETHER; STOP RED SKULL FROM MURDER SPREE
YOU *DID NOT* FAIL HIM.
HE *KNEW* YOU WOULD GET IT *RIGHT*.
KNEW YOU WOULD DOUBLE THE FIGHT WITHOUT HIM.
ONLY THIS TIME...
...YOU WILL *NOT* BE FIGHTING ALONE.

THREE MONTHS FROM NOW

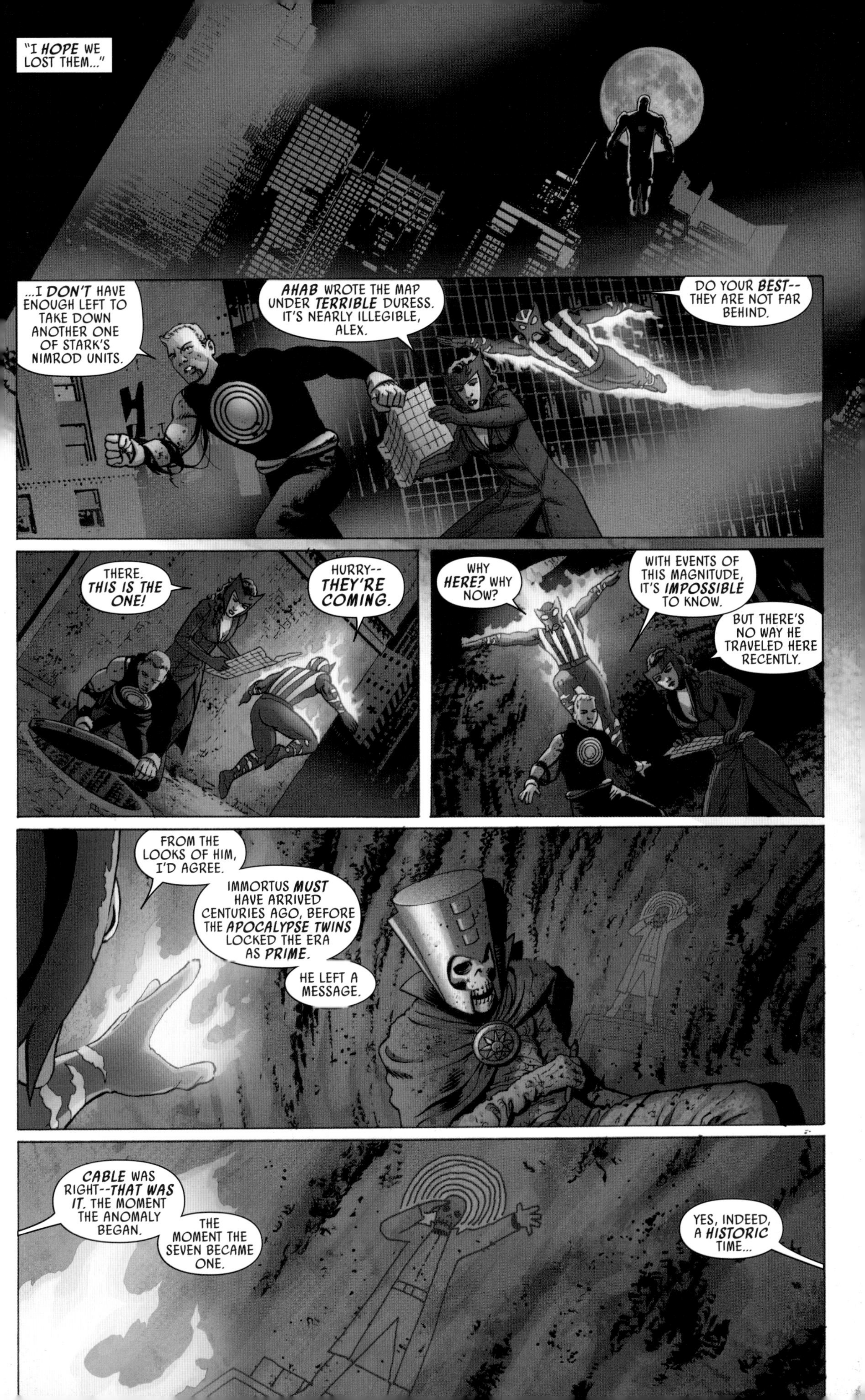
"I HOPE WE LOST THEM..."
...I DON'T HAVE ENOUGH LEFT TO TAKE DOWN ANOTHER ONE OF STARK'S NIMROD UNITS.
AHAB WROTE THE MAP UNDER TERRIBLE DURESS. IT'S NEARLY ILLEGIBLE, ALEX.
DO YOUR BEST-- THEY ARE NOT FAR BEHIND.
THERE. THIS IS THE ONE!
HURRY-- THEY'RE COMING.
WHY HERE? WHY NOW?
WITH EVENTS OF THIS MAGNITUDE, IT'S IMPOSSIBLE TO KNOW.
BUT THERE'S NO WAY HE TRAVELED HERE RECENTLY.
FROM THE LOOKS OF HIM, I'D AGREE.
IMMORTUS MUST HAVE ARRIVED CENTURIES AGO, BEFORE THE APOCALYPSE TWINS LOCKED THE ERA AS PRIME.
HE LEFT A MESSAGE.
CABLE WAS RIGHT--THAT WAS IT. THE MOMENT THE ANOMALY BEGAN.
THE MOMENT THE SEVEN BECAME ONE.
YES, INDEED, A HISTORIC TIME...

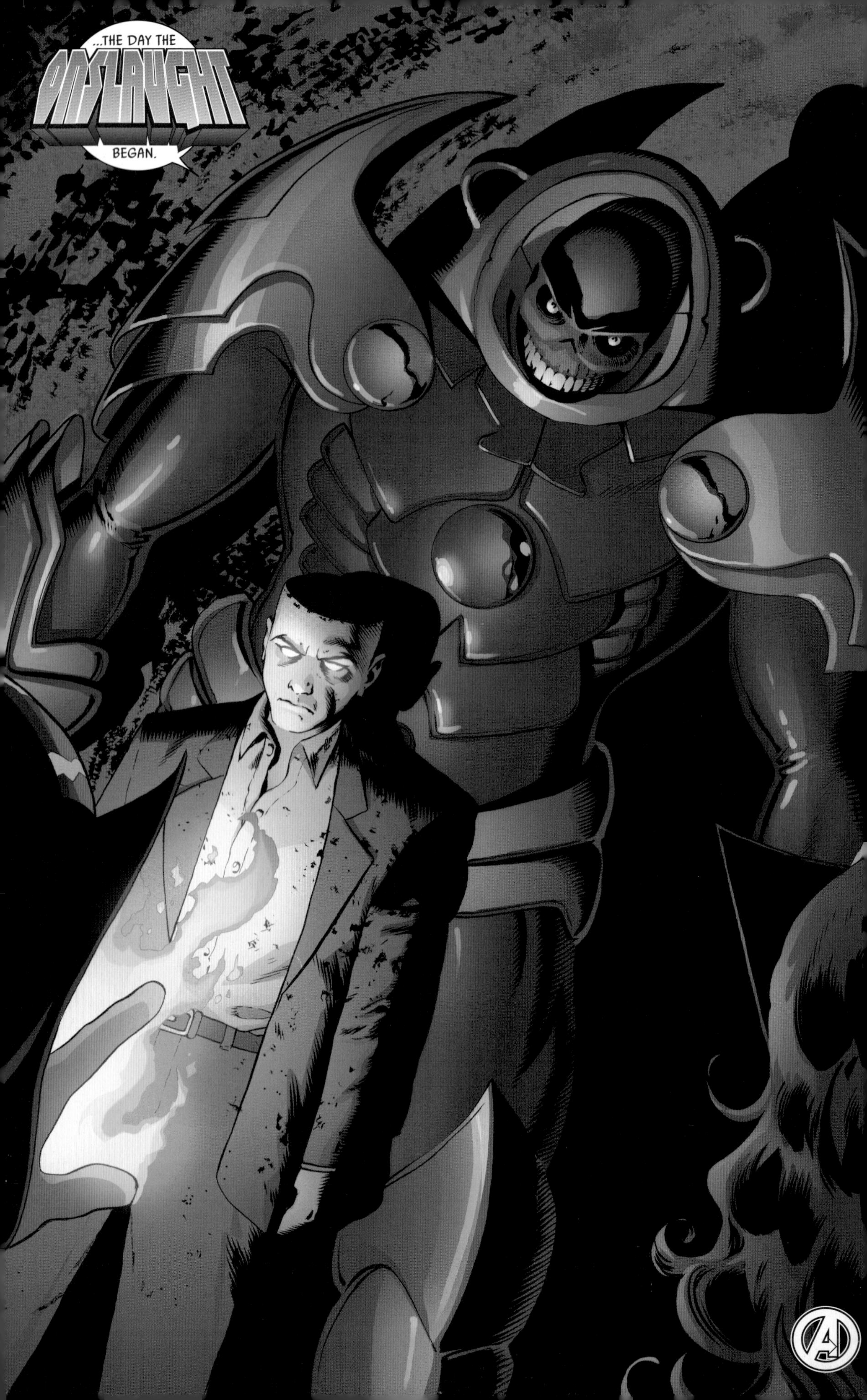
...THE DAY THE
ONSLAUGHT
BEGAN.

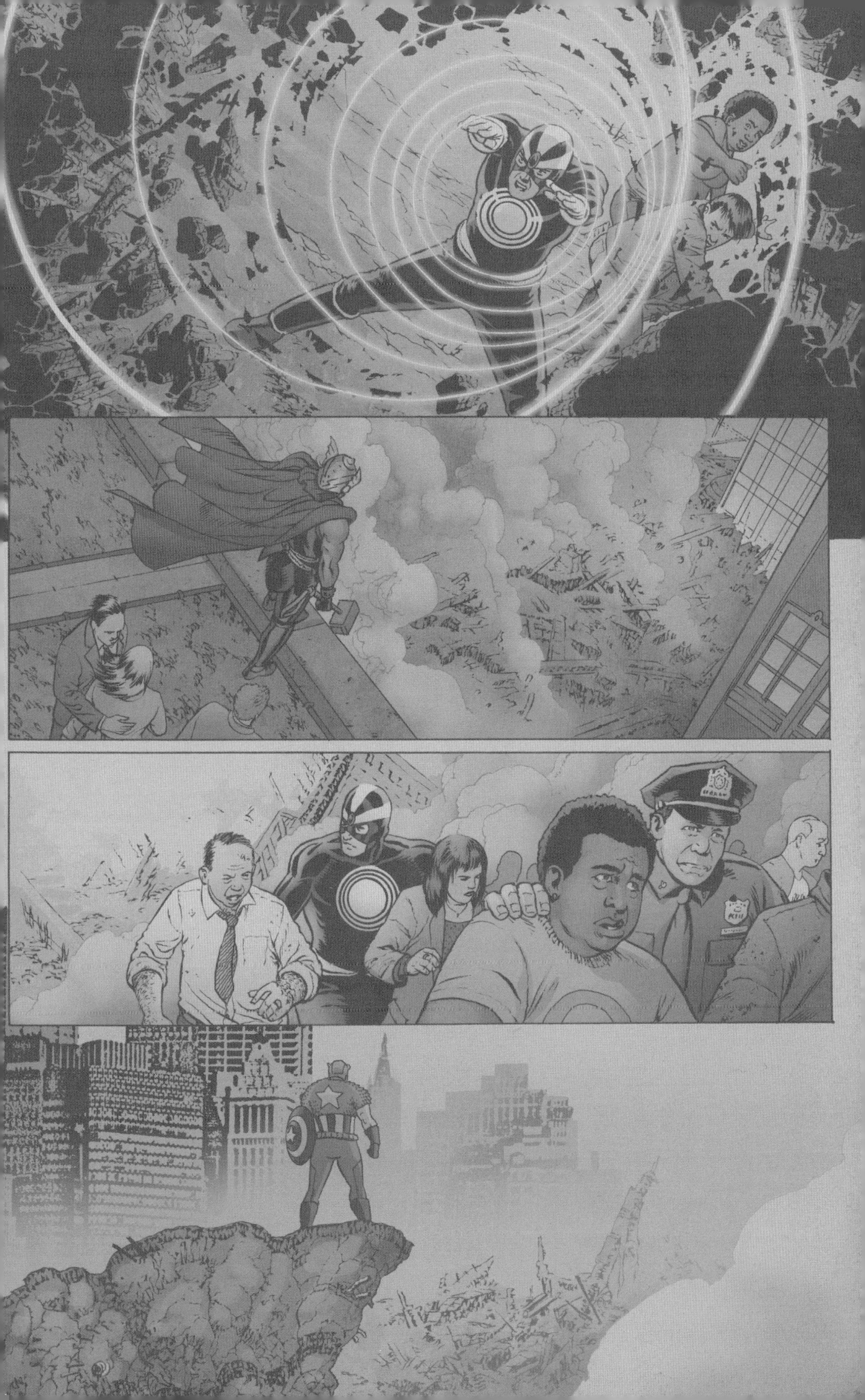

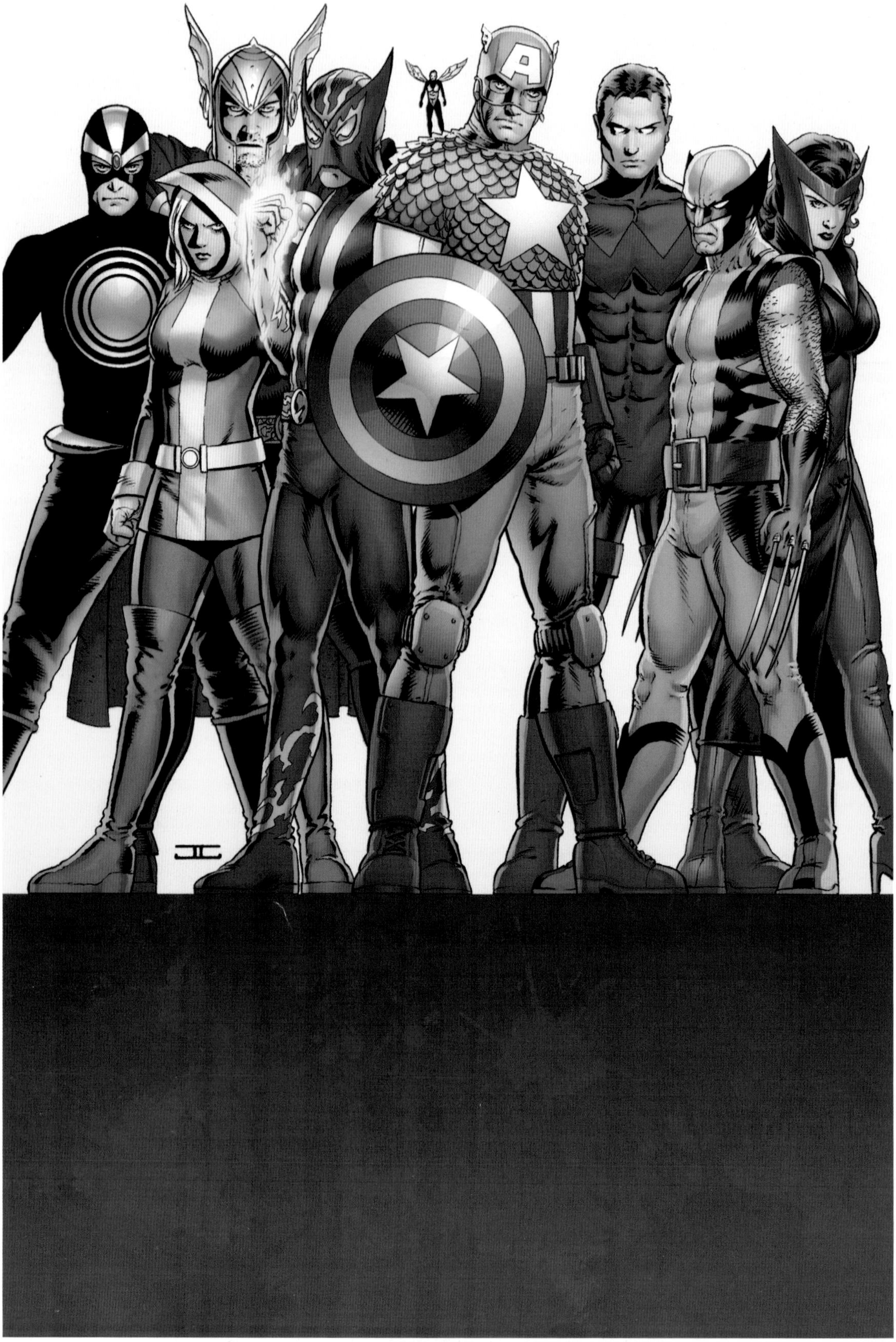

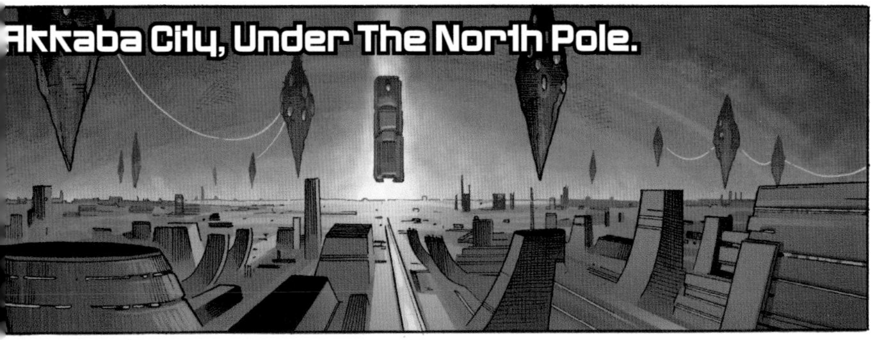
Akkaba City, Under The North Pole.

I HAVE STRUGGLED SINCE THE DAYS OF THE PHARAOHS TO STOP THIS CELESTIAL ***MANIPULATION.***

HAVING EXPLOITED ***ALL*** THE MYRIAD POWERS AT MY DISPOSAL AND GREAT SWATHS OF TIME TO THE ENDEAVOR.

BUT IT HAPPENS ***REGARDLESS--***

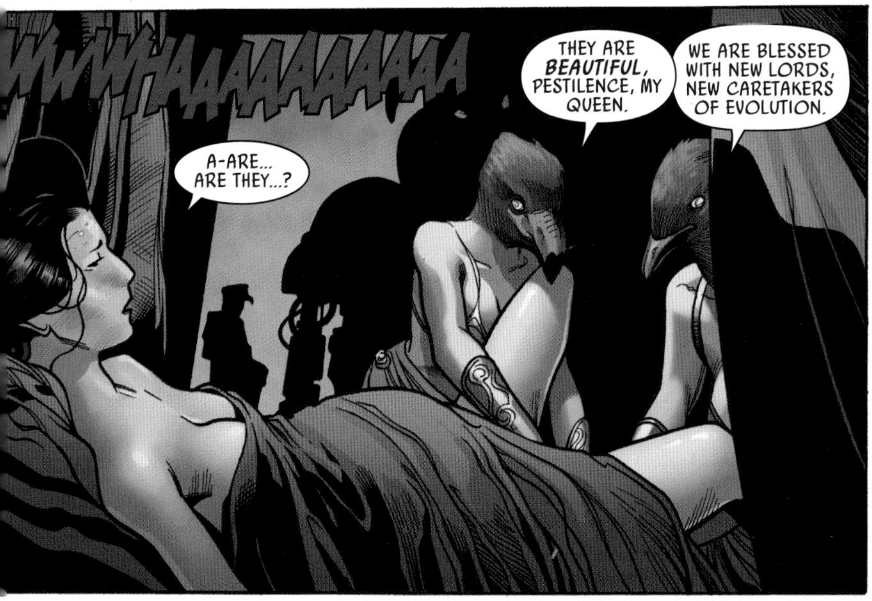
WWWHAAAAAAAAAAA
A-ARE... ARE THEY...?
THEY ARE ***BEAUTIFUL,*** PESTILENCE, MY QUEEN.
WE ARE BLESSED WITH NEW LORDS, NEW CARETAKERS OF EVOLUTION.

THE APOCALYPSE TWINS, RAVAGERS OF MANKIND, ARRIVE WITH LITTLE FANFARE.

YET THEIR INFLUENCE INFECTS ***ALL*** FUTURES.

AND THERE IS ***NO*** SIMPLE WAY OF UNDOING IT.

THEIR INCEPTION AND TIME IN UTERO--ALL OF IT ***SAFEGUARDED.***

THIS ENTIRE ERA NOW ENCLOSED IN A CHRONOS DAM OF ADAPTABLE TACHYONS.

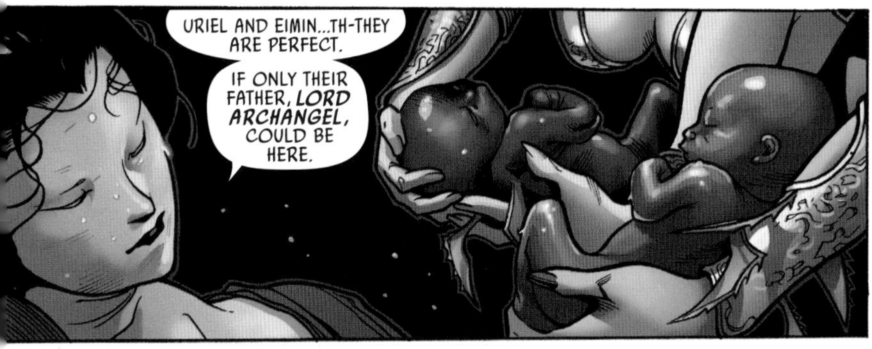
URIEL AND EIMIN...TH-THEY ARE PERFECT.
IF ONLY THEIR FATHER, ***LORD ARCHANGEL,*** COULD BE HERE.

SOME UNSEEN HAND IS ***GUARDING*** THE BIRTH OF THESE TWINS.

NARROWING THE SPECTRUM OF POSSIBLE OUTCOMES.

FEW OF THEM TO ***MY*** SUITING.

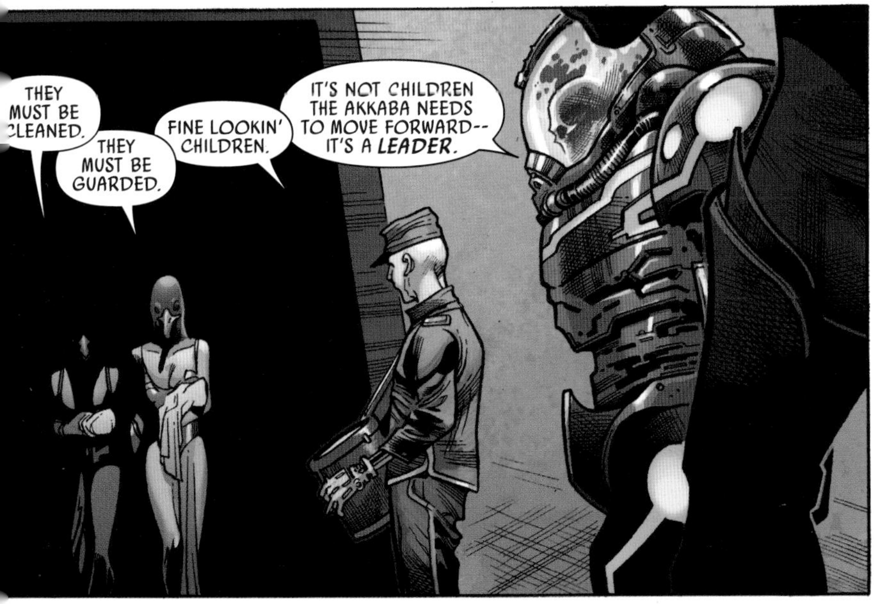
THEY MUST BE CLEANED.
THEY MUST BE GUARDED.
FINE LOOKIN' CHILDREN.
IT'S NOT CHILDREN THE AKKABA NEEDS TO MOVE FORWARD-- IT'S A ***LEADER.***

TO STOP THESE VERMIN, ALTERATIONS TO HISTORY MUST BE MORE ***SEVERE.***

REARRANGING EVENTS IN A MANNER THAT SUITS ***MY*** PURPOSE, SECURING ***MY*** FUTURE.

I HAVE REORGANIZED THE BOARD IN INCALCULABLE PERMUTATIONS.

IF TIME COULD BE MEASURED WHILE OUTSIDE THE STREAM, I WOULD HAVE AGED ***HUNDREDS*** OF YEARS.

NO MATTER MY EFFORTS TO THE CONTRARY, I LEARNED TO ACCEPT THAT PREVENTING URIEL'S RULE IS *FUTILE*.

OTHERS *QUICKLY* STOOD TO FILL HIS PLACE.

THE CLONED BOY.

THE TRUE SON.

THE SISTER.

THIS WORLD WILL NEVER BE FREE OF THESE EVOLUTIONARY CARETAKERS, THESE CELESTIAL PAWNS.

AN UNSTOPPABLE TSUNAMI INSTIGATED BY A COSMIC WILL FAR TOO GREAT TO TRULY COMPREHEND, A WILL DEMANDING FORWARD MOTION OF GENETIC PROGRESS.

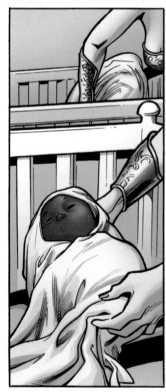

BUT I WILL NOT BE CORRALLED.

MY FATE IS MY OWN.

I WILL STAND AGAINST THIS EVOLUTIONARY WILL...

...I HAVE DISCOVERED HOW TO DERAIL THESE TWINS AND THE *APOCALYPSE* THEY WILL BRING TO MANKIND.

AFTER THOUSANDS OF PERMEATIONS, THOUSANDS OF JUMPS BACKWARDS AND FORWARDS--

I HAVE *FINALLY* SOLVED THIS CONUNDRUM.

BE STILL, LITTLE ONES.

THIS TIME--THIS *PRECISE* ARRANGEMENT OF THE PIECES WILL LEAD TO A RESOLUTION MUCH MORE TO *MY* LIKING.

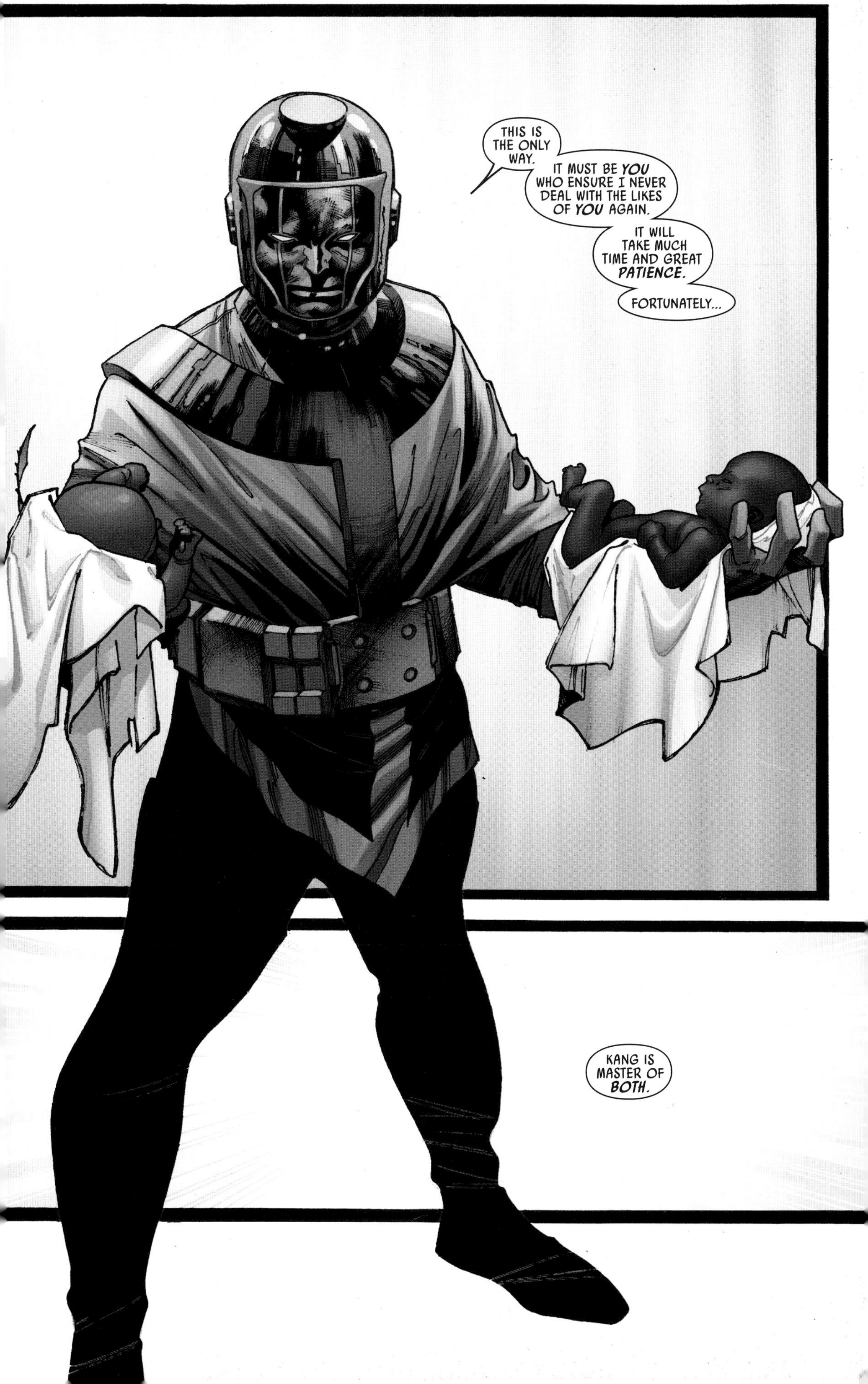
THIS IS THE ONLY WAY.
IT MUST BE YOU WHO ENSURE I NEVER DEAL WITH THE LIKES OF YOU AGAIN.
IT WILL TAKE MUCH TIME AND GREAT PATIENCE.
FORTUNATELY...
KANG IS MASTER OF BOTH.

"...AND CHAOS IS THE *LAST THING* I NEED MORE OF IN MY LIFE."

SO IT'S TRUE. YOU FOOL. SHE HAS DRAWN YOU BACK TO HER.

WASP AND WONDER MAN-- DNA CONFIRMED.

WELCOME HOME, AVENGERS.

NOT EXACTLY JARVIS, IS IT?

NOTHING IS QUITE LIKE THE OLD DAYS, SIMON.

IT'S AVENGERS MANSION, THOUGH. EVEN WITHOUT JARVIS, IT FEELS A LOT LIKE *HOME* TO ME.

LISTEN, I KNOW IT WAS HARD FOR WANDA TO COME TO YOU, BUT SHE *NEEDS* YOU HERE.

SHE'S DEALING WITH A LOT OF MISTRUST FROM THE MUTANTS...

...AND, FRANKLY, EVEN MOST OF THE AVENGERS.

MY FRIENDSHIP ISN'T LIKELY TO EARN WANDA POINTS WITH THE OTHER AVENGERS.

I'M *FAIRLY* UNPOPULAR AMONG THE OLD CREW.

YEAH, GETTING STEVE TO SIGN OFF ON YOU WAS NO EASY FEAT.

BUT HE UNDERSTANDS JUST *HOW MUCH* WANDA NEEDS YOU HERE.

SHE'LL NEED OLD FRIENDS TO SUPPORT HER. AND, TO BE HONEST--

SO DO I.

WE'RE THROUGH THE LOOKING GLASS HERE.

NOTHING QUITE LIKE THIS HAS EVER BEEN ATTEMPTED BEFORE.

NO IDEA EXACTLY *WHAT* TO ANTICIPATE, BUT FROM WHAT I KNOW ABOUT THE X-MEN...

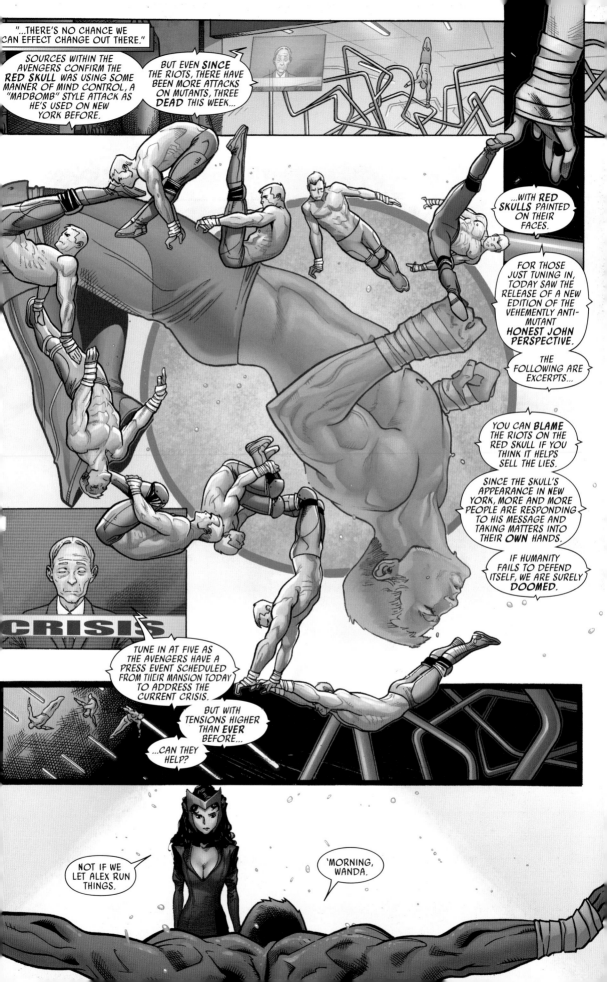

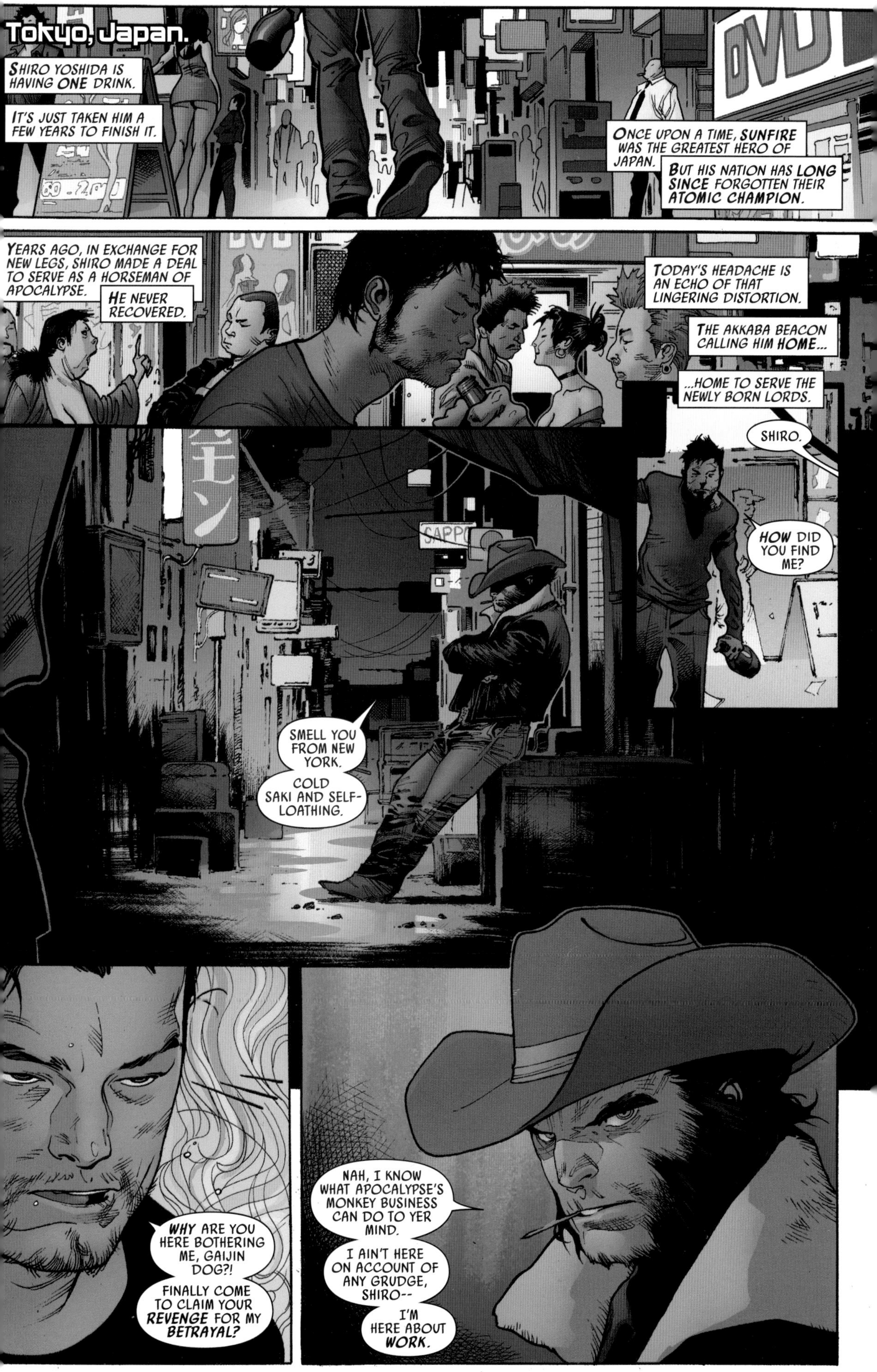

Tokyo, Japan.
SHIRO YOSHIDA IS HAVING ONE DRINK.
IT'S JUST TAKEN HIM A FEW YEARS TO FINISH IT.
ONCE UPON A TIME, SUNFIRE WAS THE GREATEST HERO OF JAPAN.
BUT HIS NATION HAS LONG SINCE FORGOTTEN THEIR ATOMIC CHAMPION.
DVD
YEARS AGO, IN EXCHANGE FOR NEW LEGS, SHIRO MADE A DEAL TO SERVE AS A HORSEMAN OF APOCALYPSE.
HE NEVER RECOVERED.
TODAY'S HEADACHE IS AN ECHO OF THAT LINGERING DISTORTION.
THE AKKABA BEACON CALLING HIM HOME...
...HOME TO SERVE THE NEWLY BORN LORDS.
SHIRO.
HOW DID YOU FIND ME?
SMELL YOU FROM NEW YORK.
COLD SAKI AND SELF-LOATHING.
WHY ARE YOU HERE BOTHERING ME, GAIJIN DOG?!
FINALLY COME TO CLAIM YOUR REVENGE FOR MY BETRAYAL?
NAH, I KNOW WHAT APOCALYPSE'S MONKEY BUSINESS CAN DO TO YER MIND.
I AIN'T HERE ON ACCOUNT OF ANY GRUDGE, SHIRO--
I'M HERE ABOUT WORK.

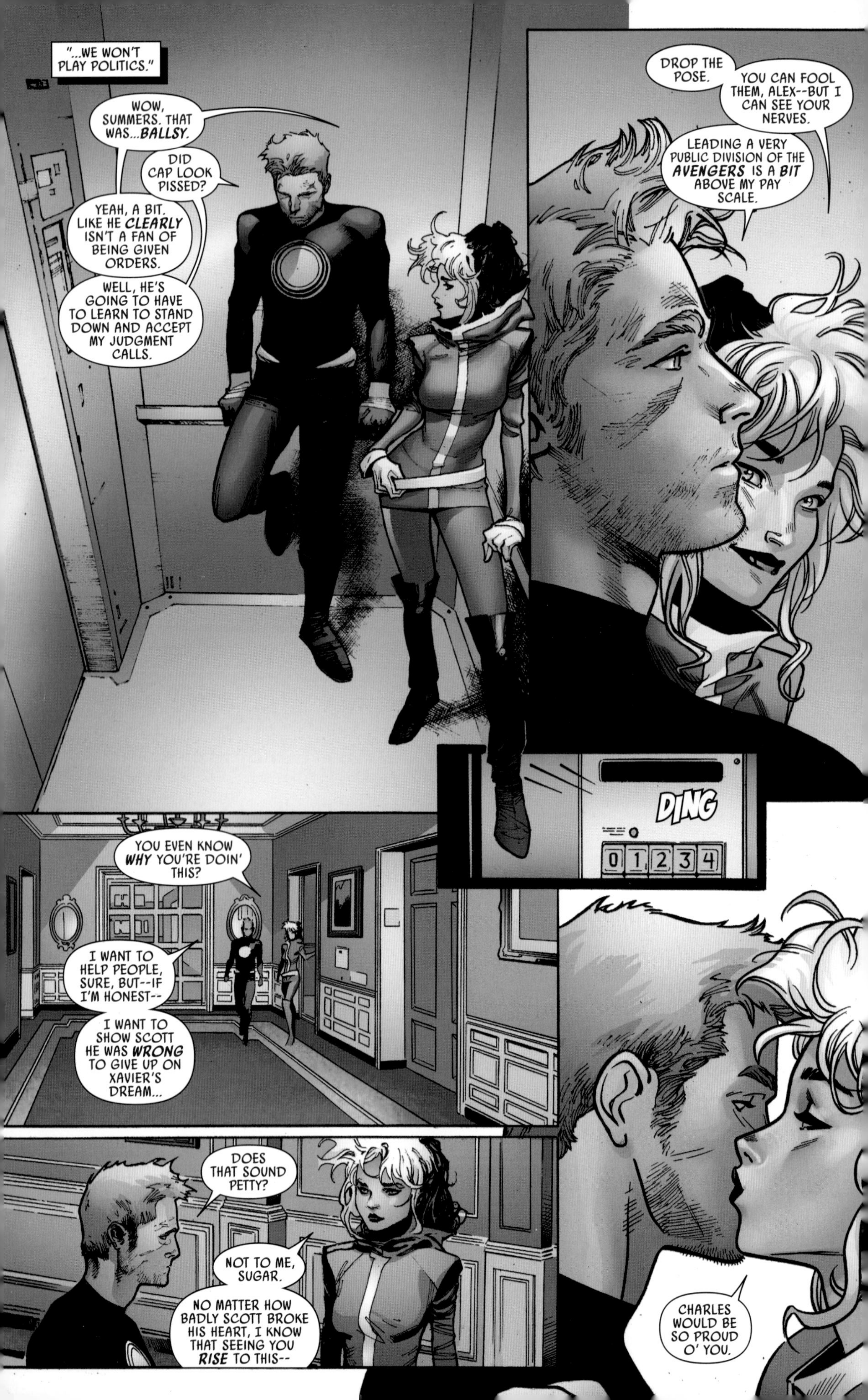
"...WE WON'T PLAY POLITICS."
WOW, SUMMERS. THAT WAS...BALLSY.
DID CAP LOOK PISSED?
YEAH, A BIT. LIKE HE CLEARLY ISN'T A FAN OF BEING GIVEN ORDERS.
WELL, HE'S GOING TO HAVE TO LEARN TO STAND DOWN AND ACCEPT MY JUDGMENT CALLS.
DROP THE POSE.
YOU CAN FOOL THEM, ALEX--BUT I CAN SEE YOUR NERVES.
LEADING A VERY PUBLIC DIVISION OF THE AVENGERS IS A BIT ABOVE MY PAY SCALE.
DING
01234
YOU EVEN KNOW WHY YOU'RE DOIN' THIS?
I WANT TO HELP PEOPLE, SURE, BUT--IF I'M HONEST--
I WANT TO SHOW SCOTT HE WAS WRONG TO GIVE UP ON XAVIER'S DREAM...
DOES THAT SOUND PETTY?
NOT TO ME, SUGAR.
NO MATTER HOW BADLY SCOTT BROKE HIS HEART, I KNOW THAT SEEING YOU RISE TO THIS--
CHARLES WOULD BE SO PROUD O' YOU.

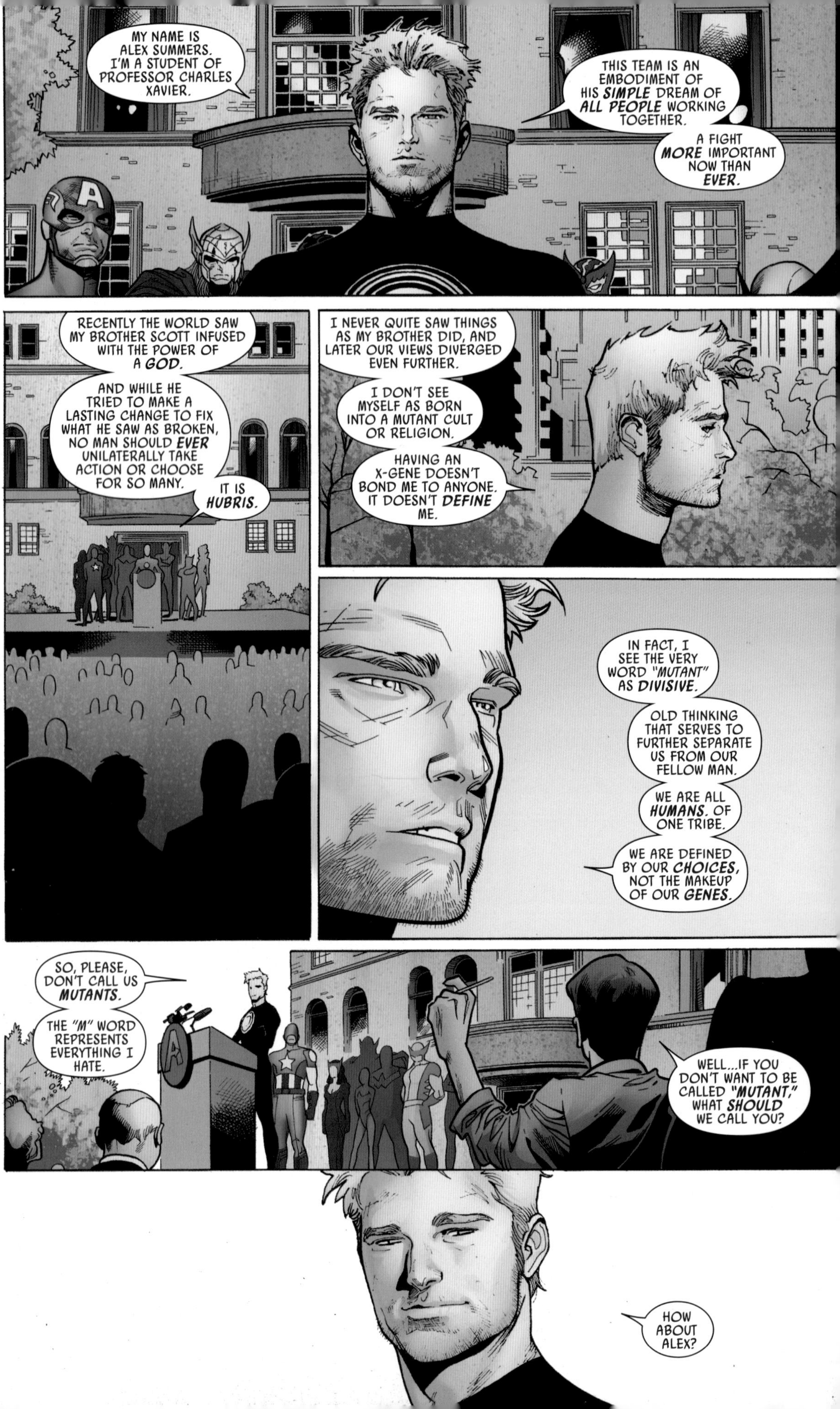
MY NAME IS ALEX SUMMERS. I'M A STUDENT OF PROFESSOR CHARLES XAVIER.
THIS TEAM IS AN EMBODIMENT OF HIS SIMPLE DREAM OF ALL PEOPLE WORKING TOGETHER.
A FIGHT MORE IMPORTANT NOW THAN EVER.
RECENTLY THE WORLD SAW MY BROTHER SCOTT INFUSED WITH THE POWER OF A GOD.
AND WHILE HE TRIED TO MAKE A LASTING CHANGE TO FIX WHAT HE SAW AS BROKEN, NO MAN SHOULD EVER UNILATERALLY TAKE ACTION OR CHOOSE FOR SO MANY.
IT IS HUBRIS.
I NEVER QUITE SAW THINGS AS MY BROTHER DID, AND LATER OUR VIEWS DIVERGED EVEN FURTHER.
I DON'T SEE MYSELF AS BORN INTO A MUTANT CULT OR RELIGION.
HAVING AN X-GENE DOESN'T BOND ME TO ANYONE. IT DOESN'T DEFINE ME.
IN FACT, I SEE THE VERY WORD "MUTANT" AS DIVISIVE.
OLD THINKING THAT SERVES TO FURTHER SEPARATE US FROM OUR FELLOW MAN.
WE ARE ALL HUMANS. OF ONE TRIBE.
WE ARE DEFINED BY OUR CHOICES, NOT THE MAKEUP OF OUR GENES.
SO, PLEASE, DON'T CALL US MUTANTS.
THE "M" WORD REPRESENTS EVERYTHING I HATE.
WELL...IF YOU DON'T WANT TO BE CALLED "MUTANT," WHAT SHOULD WE CALL YOU?
HOW ABOUT ALEX?

Let The Good Times Roll

UNCANNY AVENGERS

Variant Cover Gallery

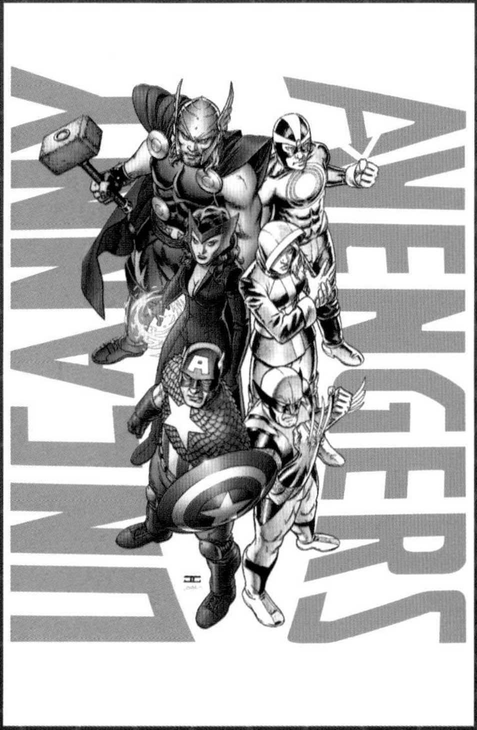
UNCANNY
AVENGERS

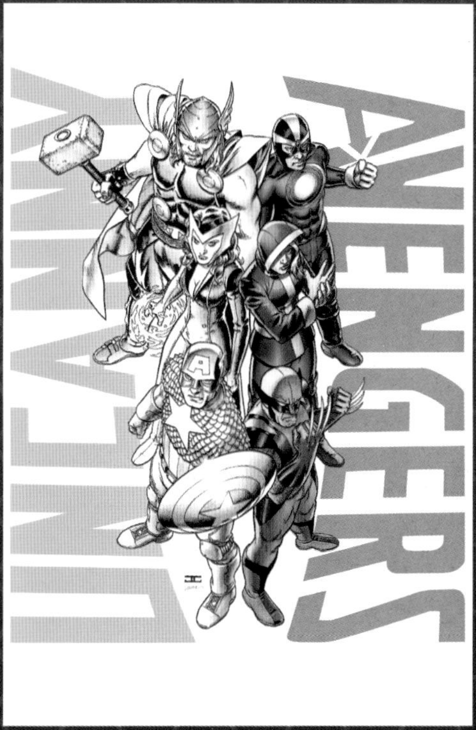
UNCANNY
AVENGERS

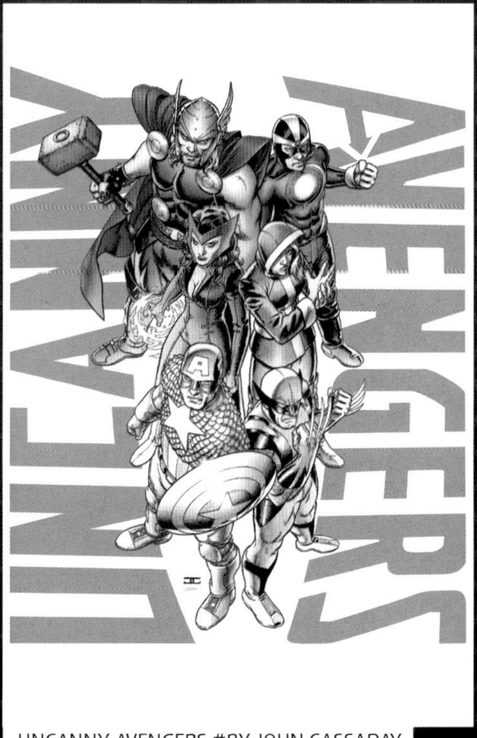
UNCANNY
AVENGERS

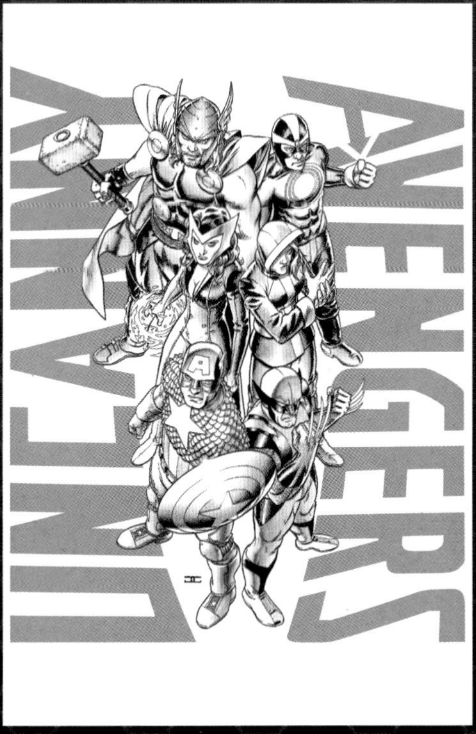
UNCANNY
AVENGERS

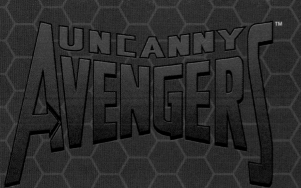

UNCANNY AVENGERS #BY JOHN CASSADAY

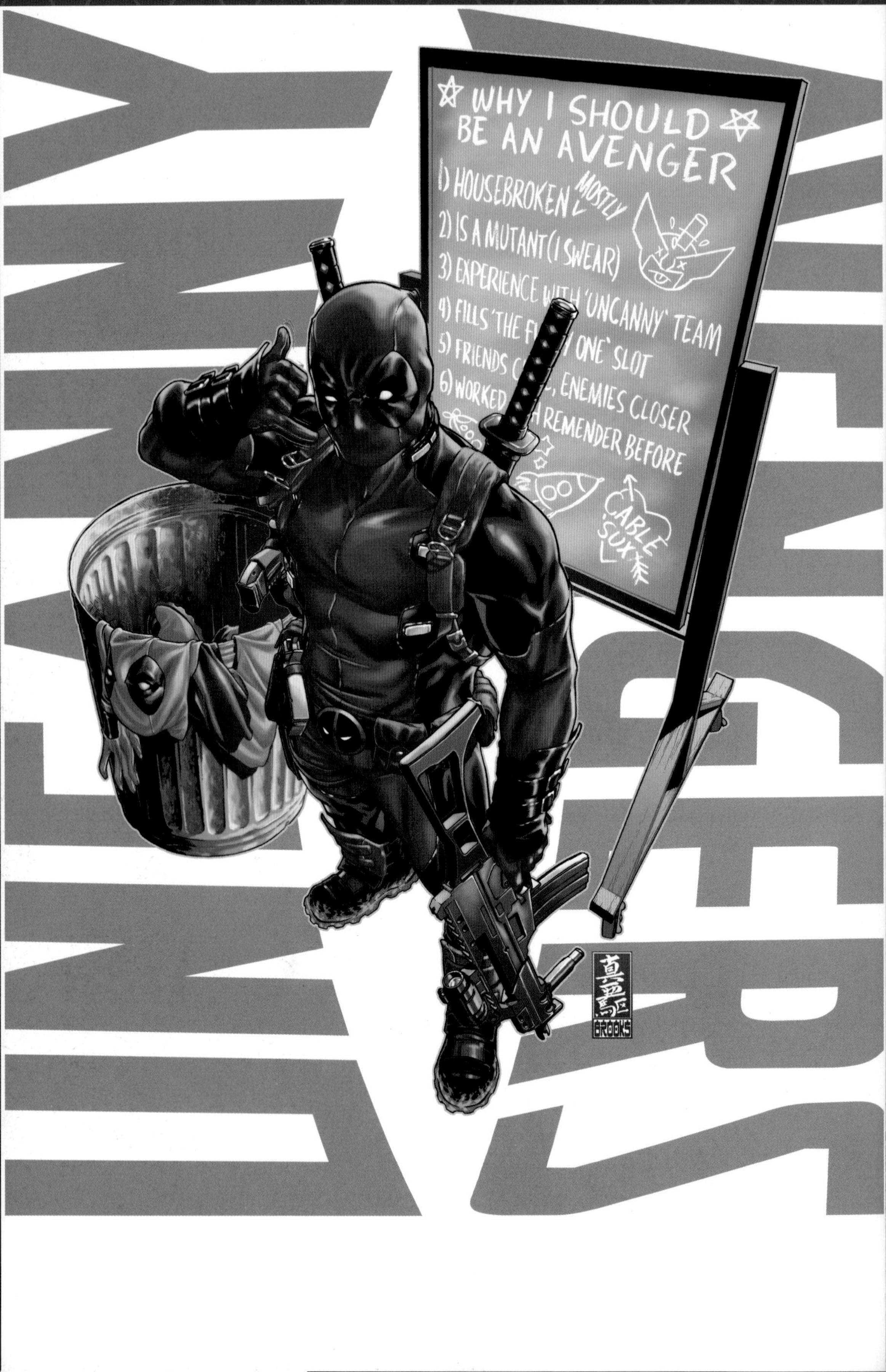
WHY I SHOULD BE AN AVENGER
1) HOUSEBROKEN
MOSTLY
2) IS A MUTANT (I SWEAR)
3) EXPERIENCE WITH 'UNCANNY' TEAM
4) FILLS 'THE FU
ONE' SLOT
5) FRIENDS C
, ENEMIES CLOSER
6) WORKED
H REMENDER BEFORE
CABLE SUX
BROOKS

UNCANNY AVENGERS #1 BY MARK BROOKS

UNCANNY AVENGERS #1 BY MARK BROOKS

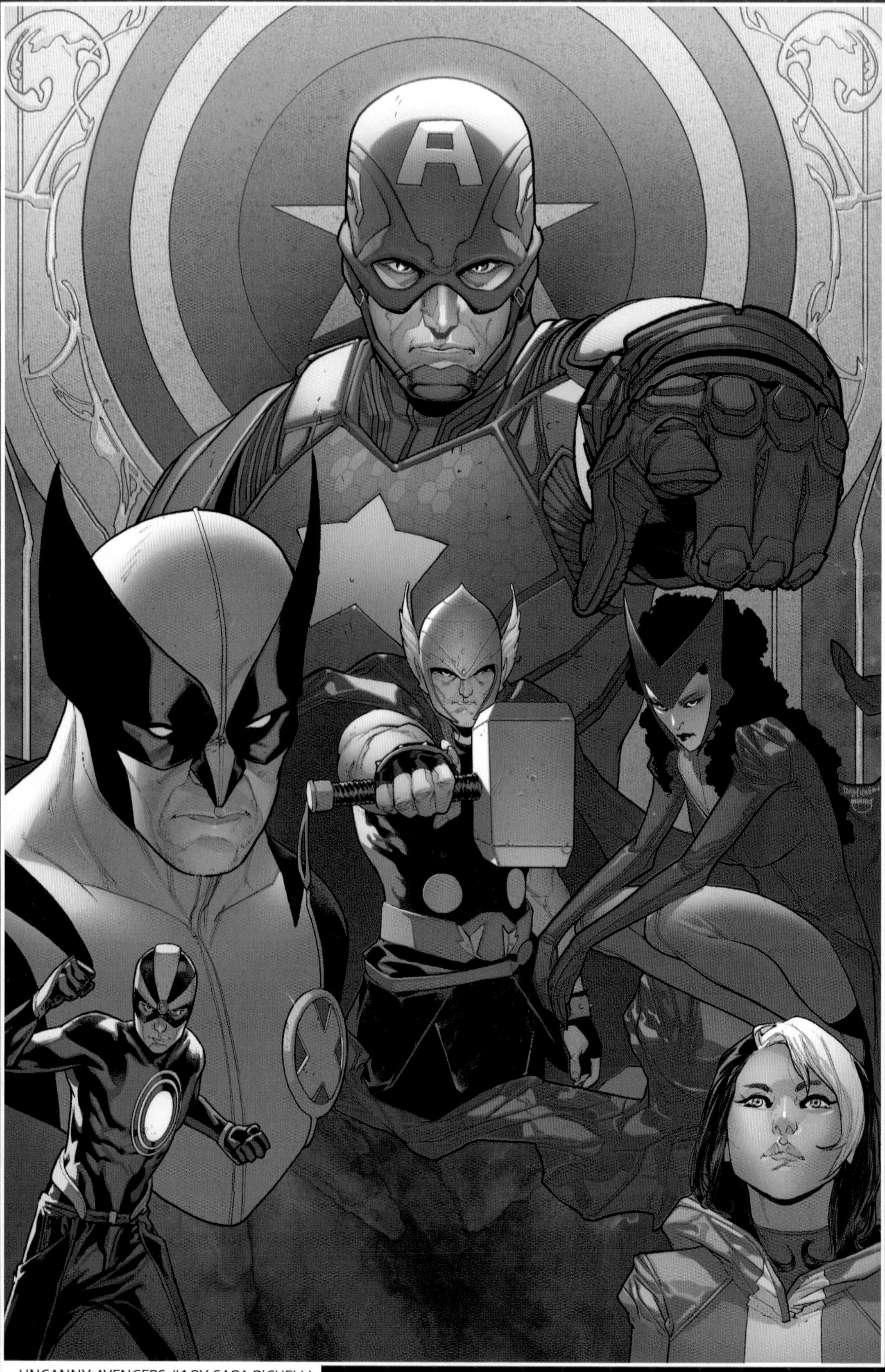

UNCANNY AVENGERS #1 BY SARA PICHELLI

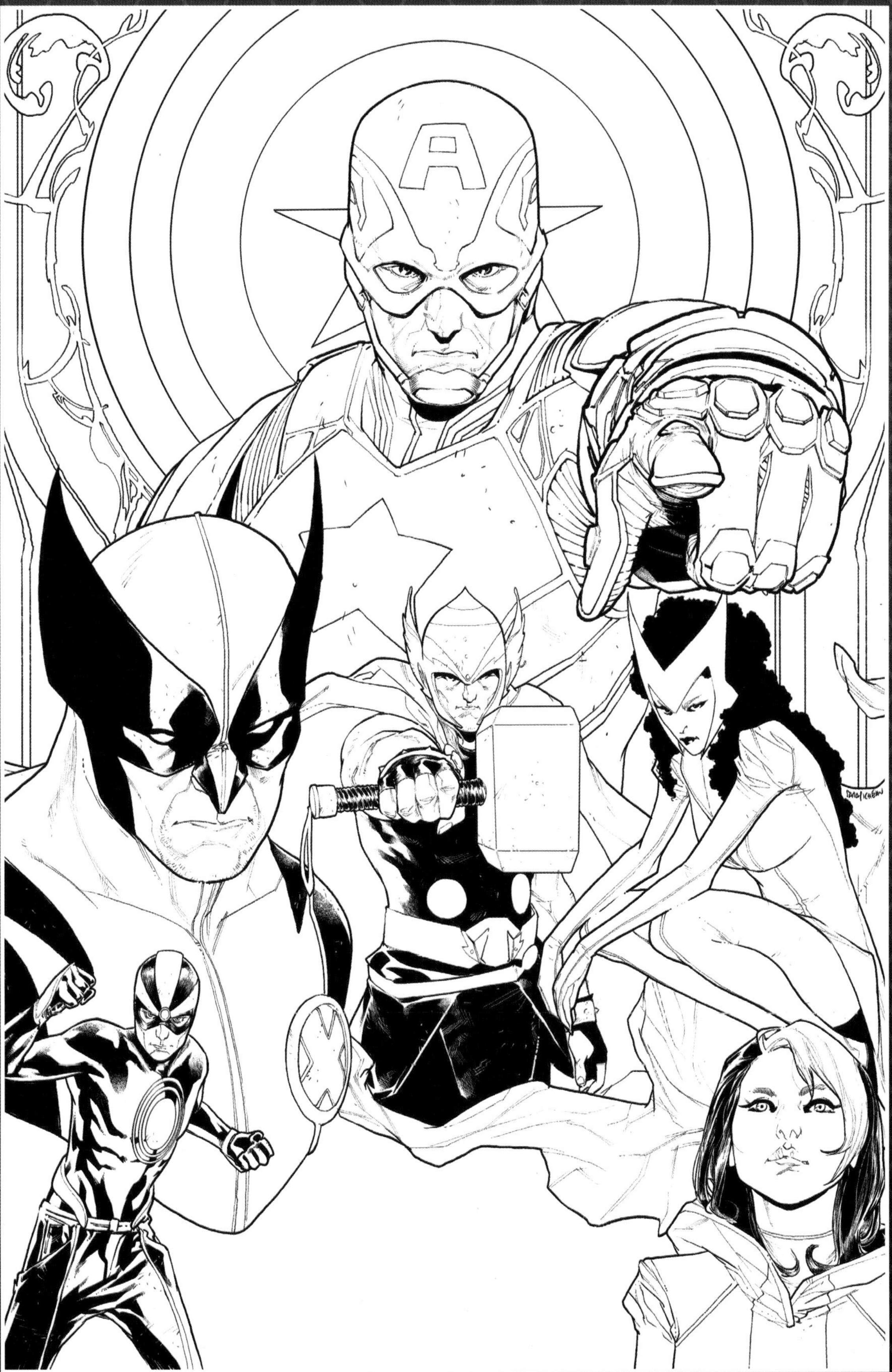

UNCANNY AVENGERS #1 BY SARA PICHELLI

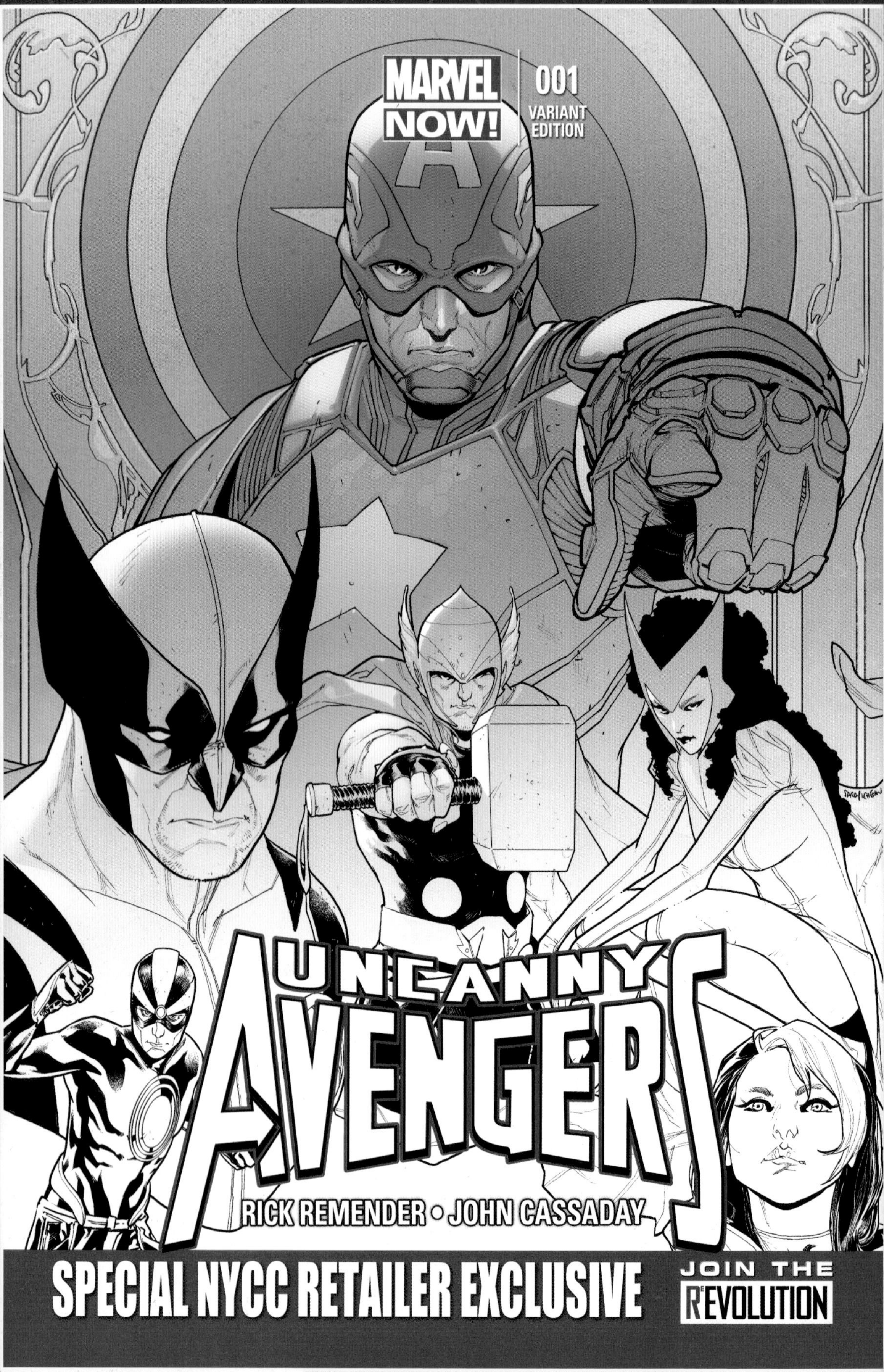
MARVEL NOW!
001
VARIANT EDITION
UNCANNY AVENGERS
RICK REMENDER • JOHN CASSADAY
SPECIAL NYCC RETAILER EXCLUSIVE
JOIN THE REVOLUTION

UNCANNY AVENGERS #1 BY SARA PICHELLI

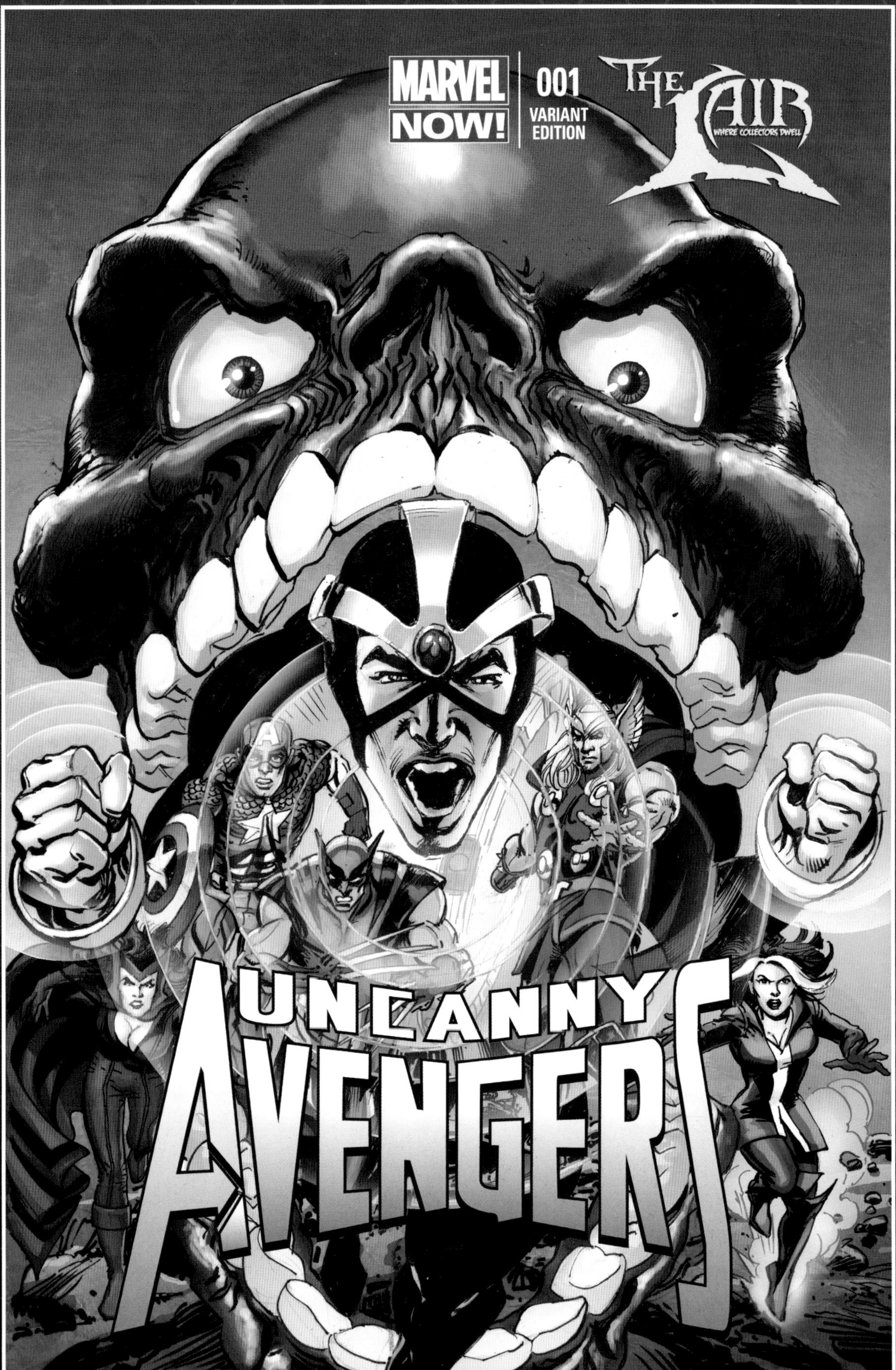
MARVEL
NOW!
001
VARIANT
EDITION
THE LAIR
WHERE COLLECTORS DWELL
UNCANNY
AVENGERS

UNCANNY AVENGERS #1 BY ART ADAMS

UNCANNY AVENGERS #1 BY ART ADAMS

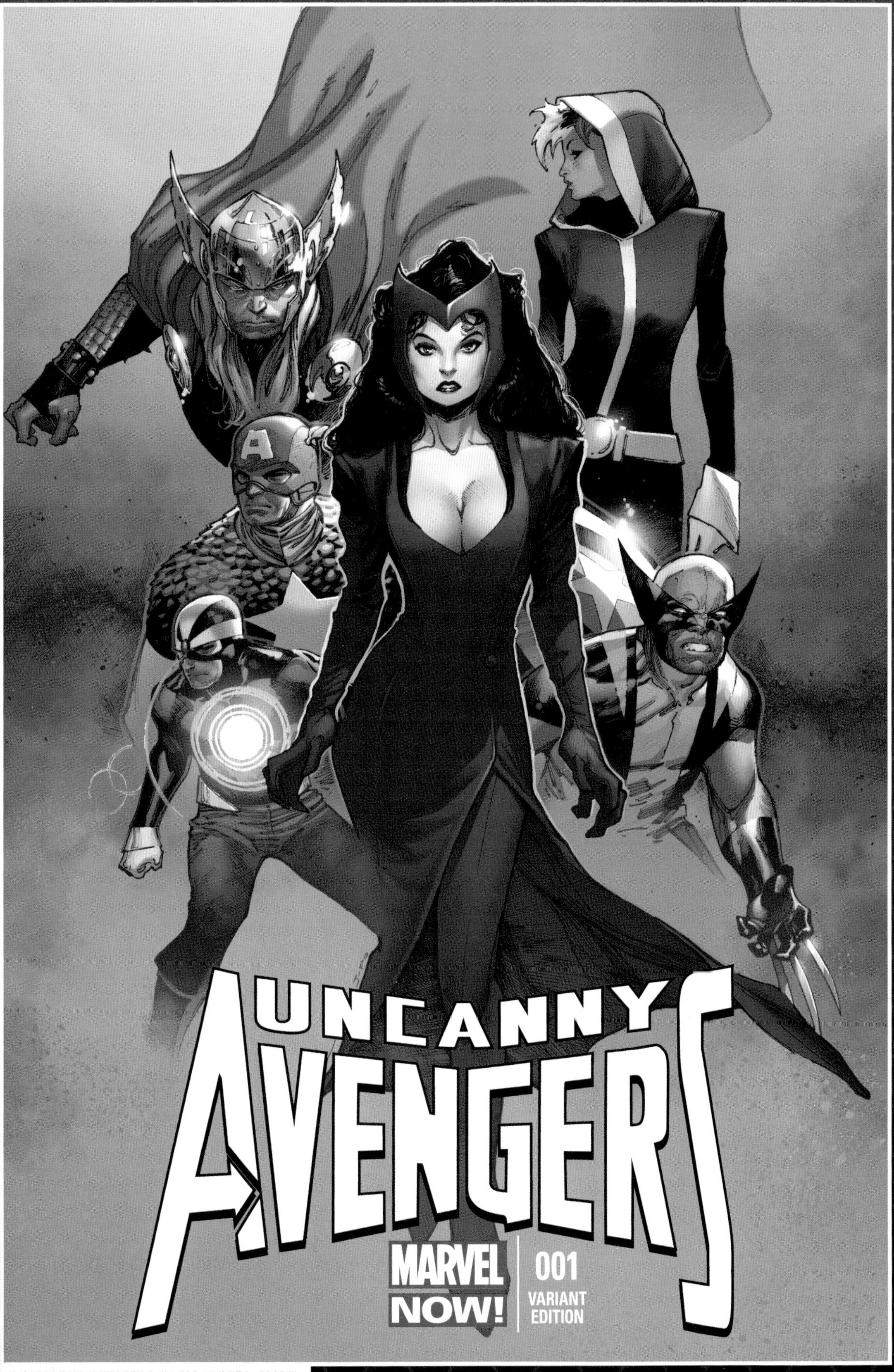
UNCANNY
AVENGERS
MARVEL
NOW!
001
VARIANT
EDITION

UNCANNY AVENGERS #1 BY OLIVIER COIPEL

UNCANNY AVENGERS #1 BY OLIVIER COIPEL

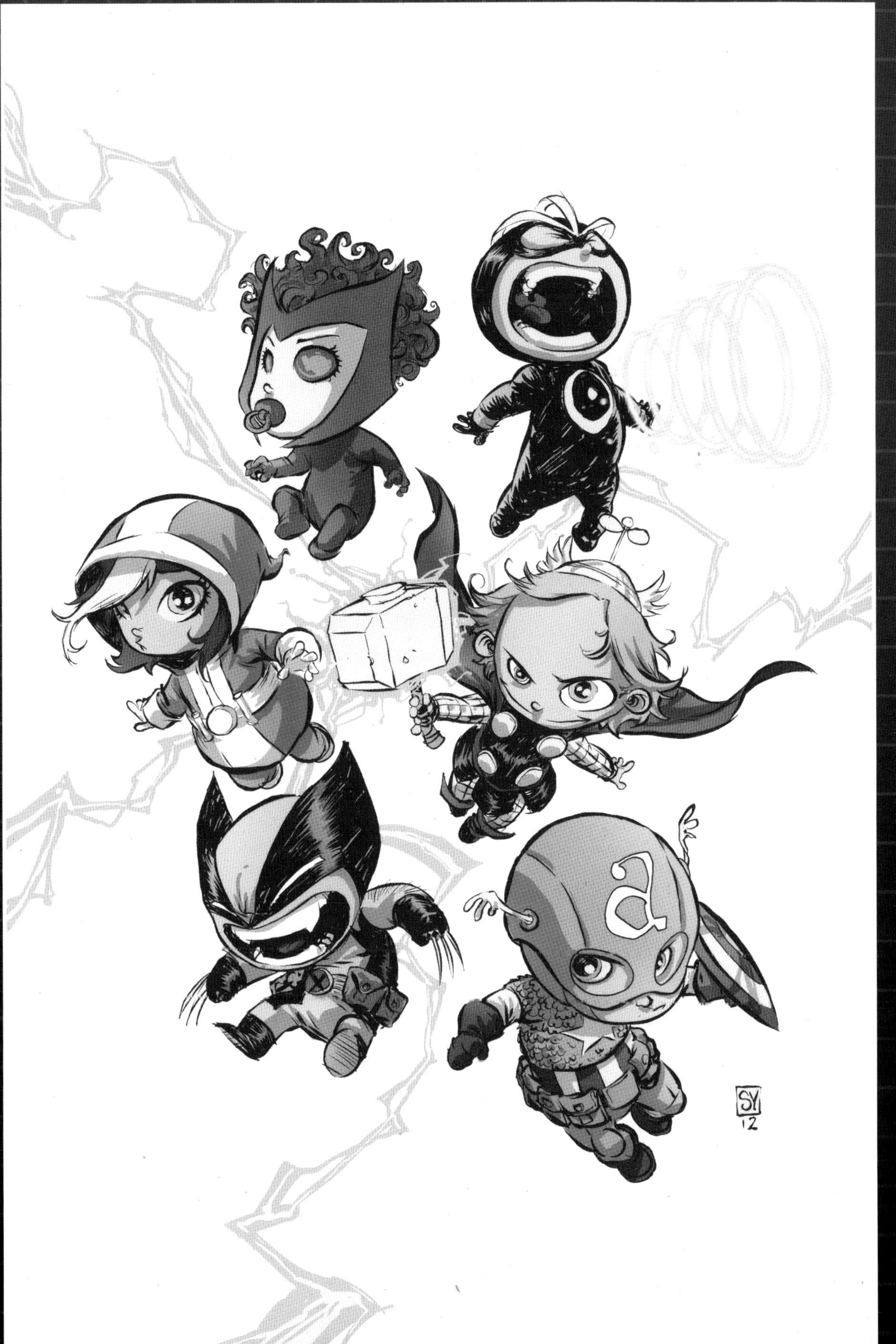
SY
'12

UNCANNY AVENGERS #1 BY SKOTTI YOUNG

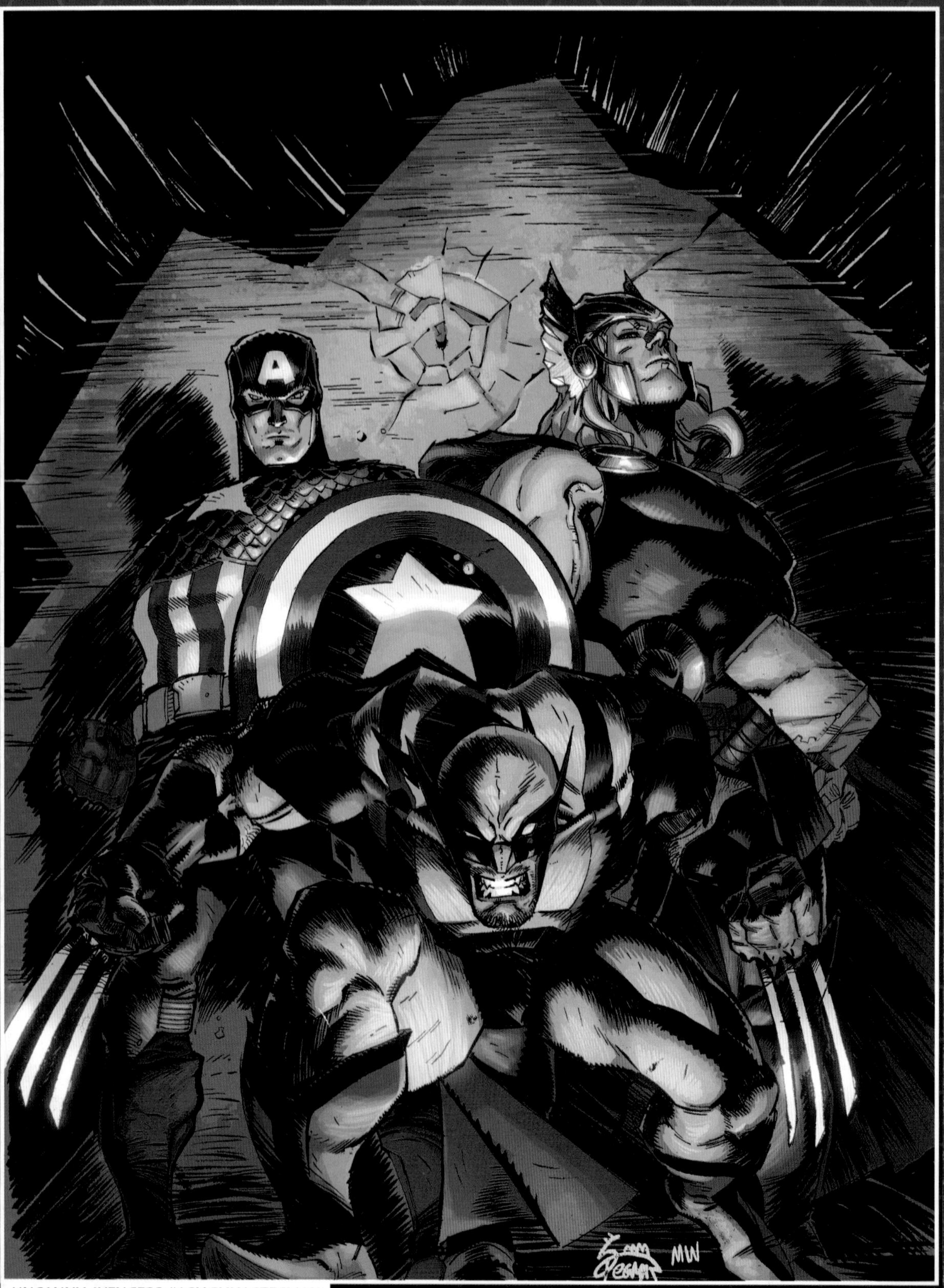

UNCANNY AVENGERS #1 BY RYAN STEGMAN

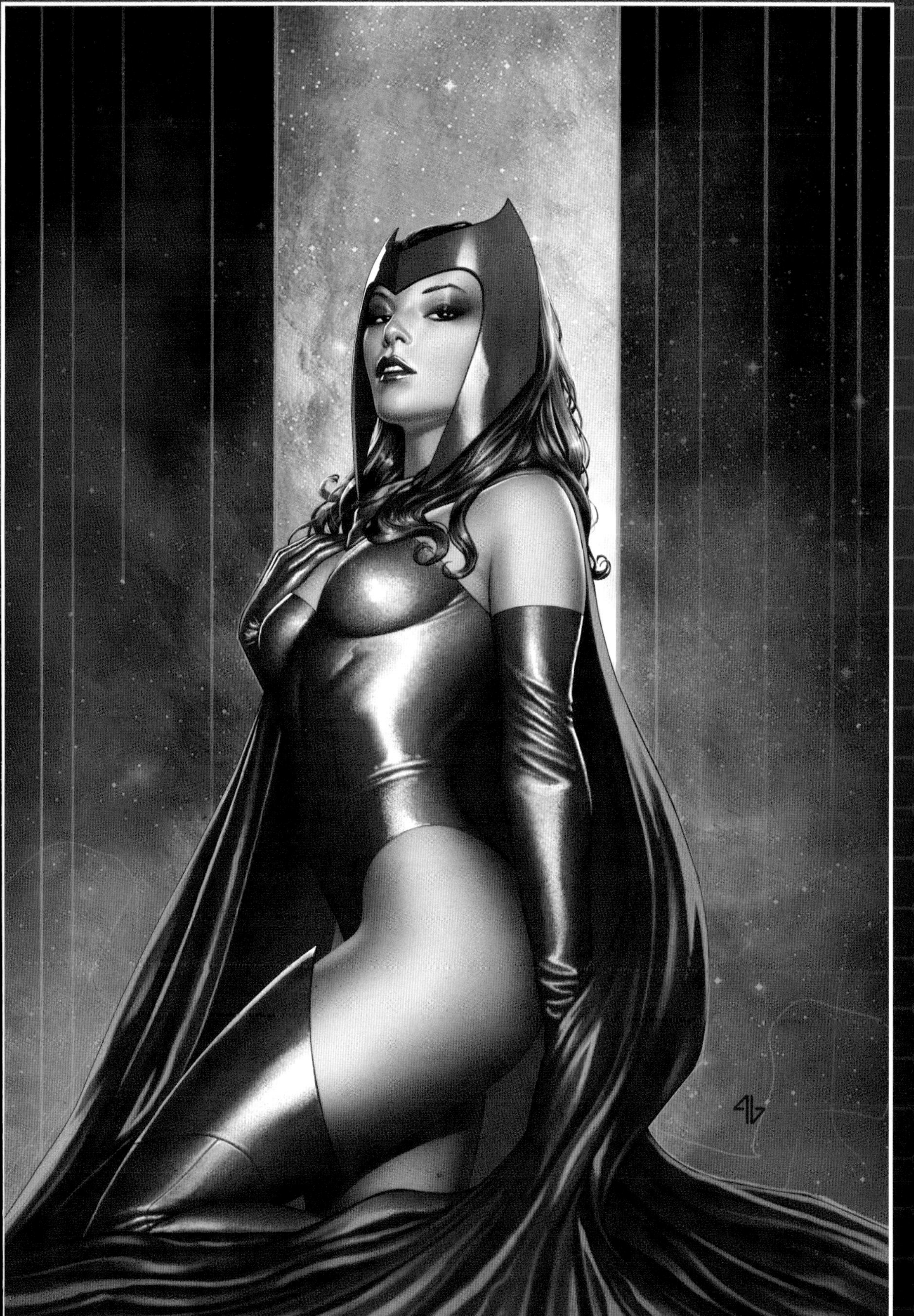

UNCANNY AVENGERS #1 BY ADI GRANOV

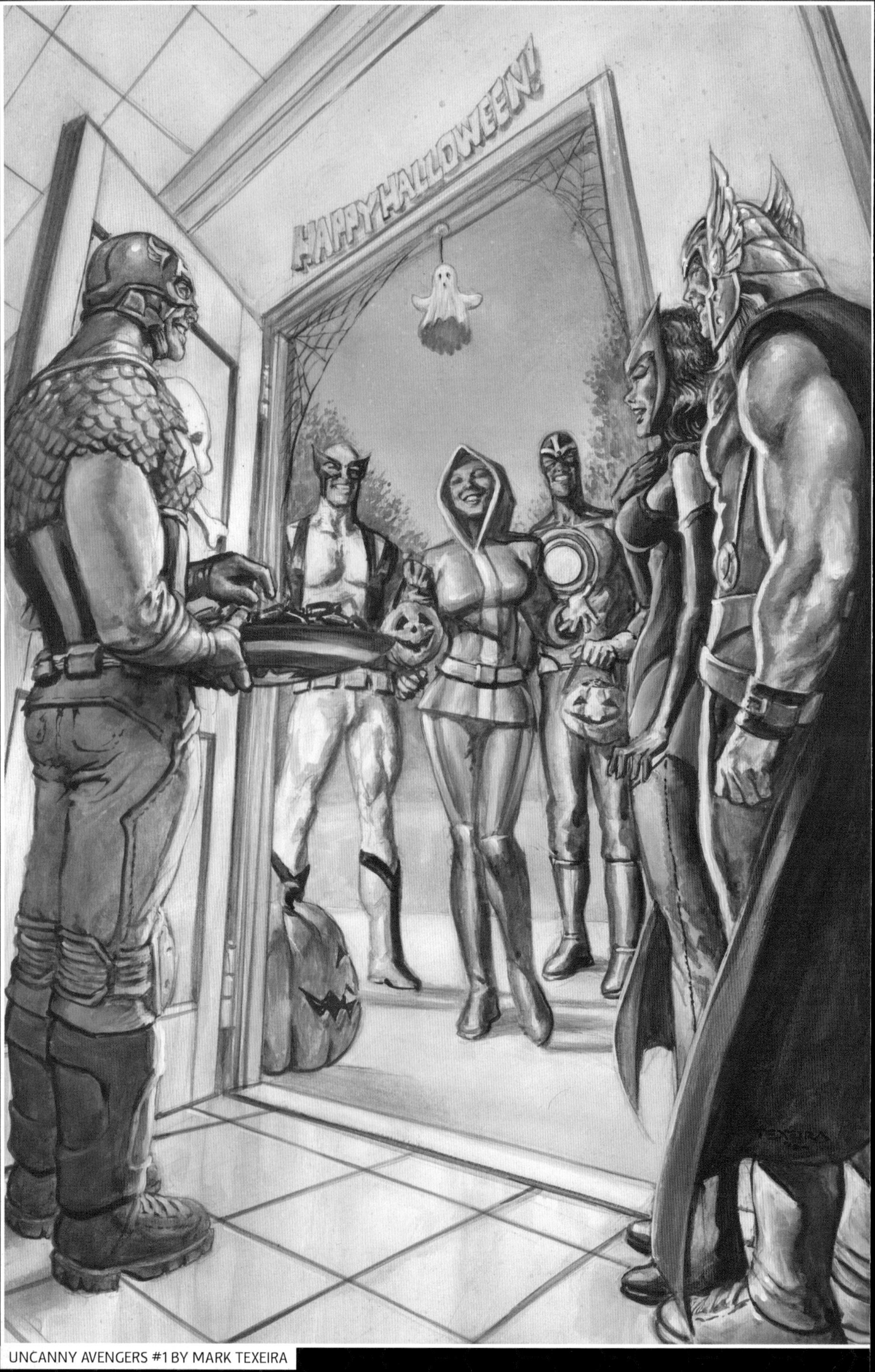
HAPPY HALLOWEEN!
TEXEIRA
UNCANNY AVENGERS #1 BY MARK TEXEIRA

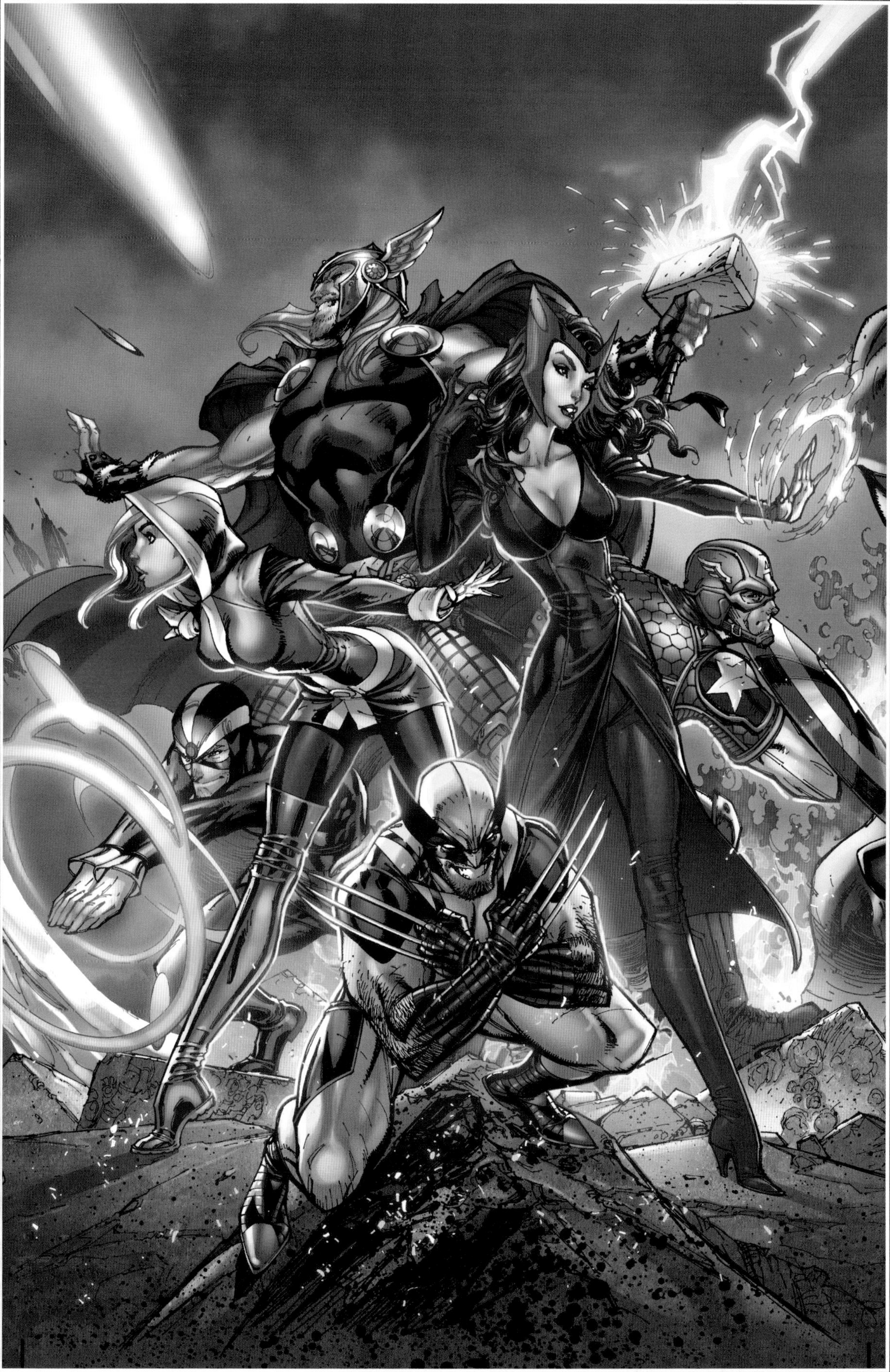

UNCANNY AVENGERS #1 BY J SCOTT CAMPBELL

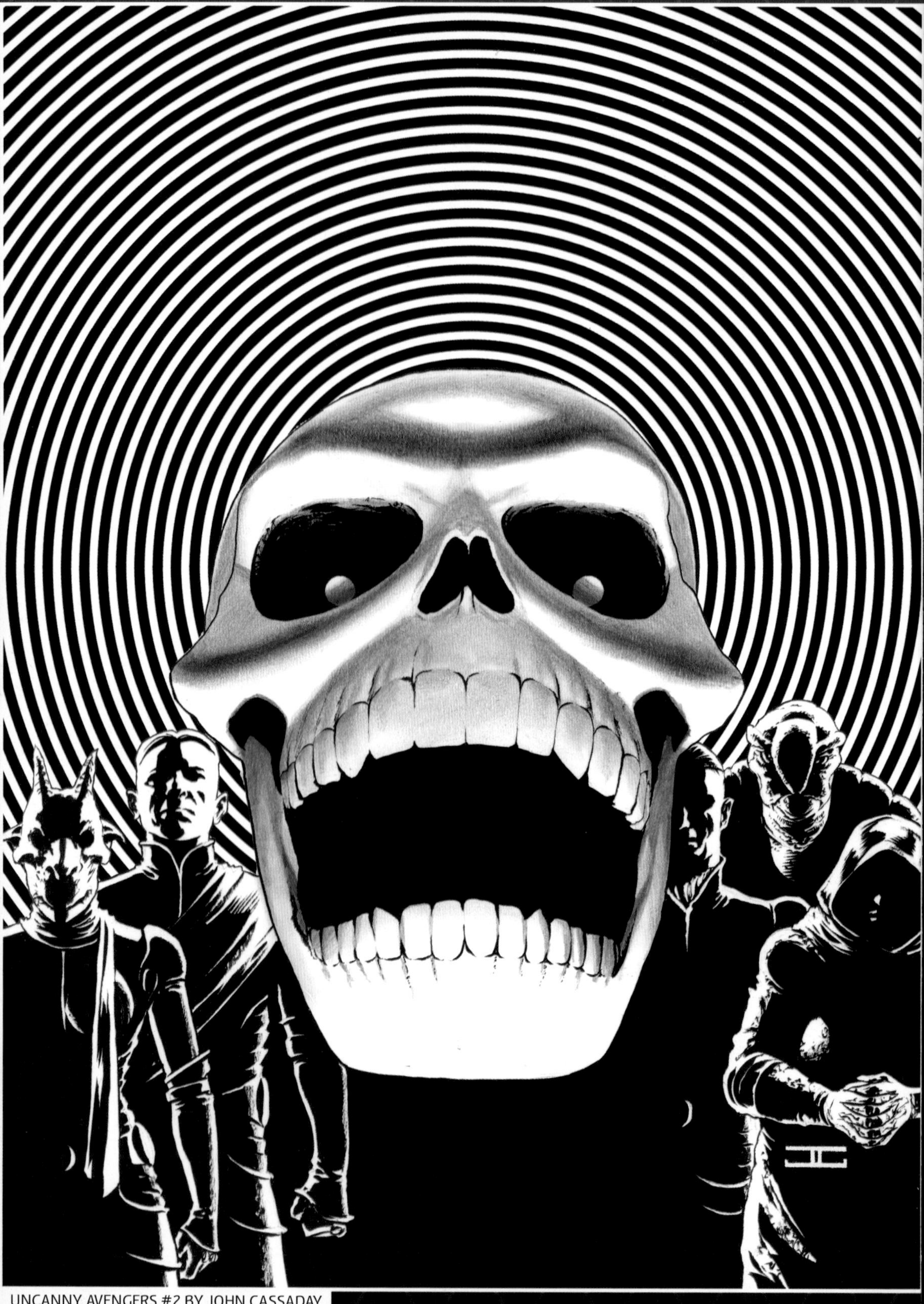

UNCANNY AVENGERS #2 BY JOHN CASSADAY

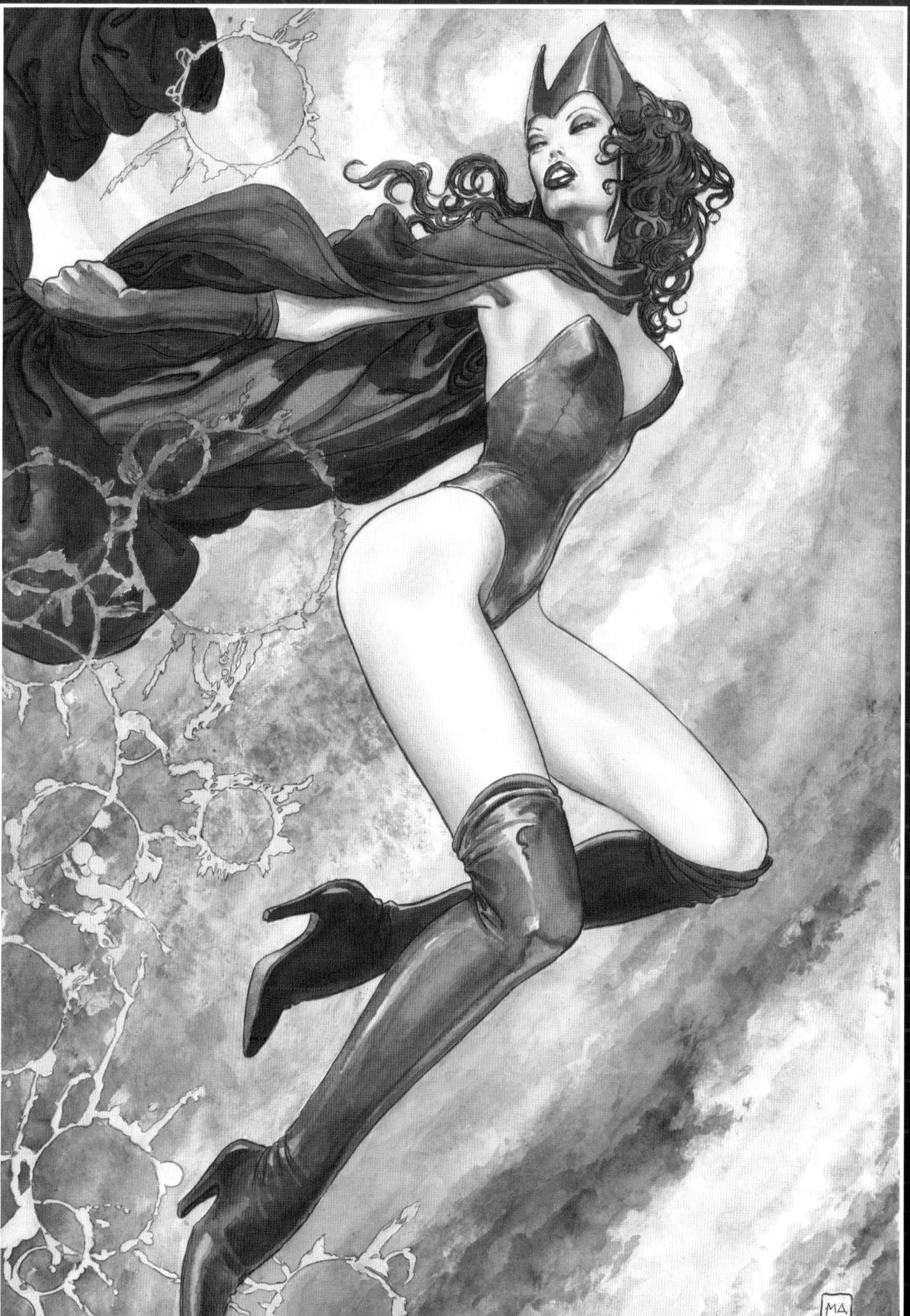
MANARA

UNCANNY AVENGERS #2 BY MILO MANARA

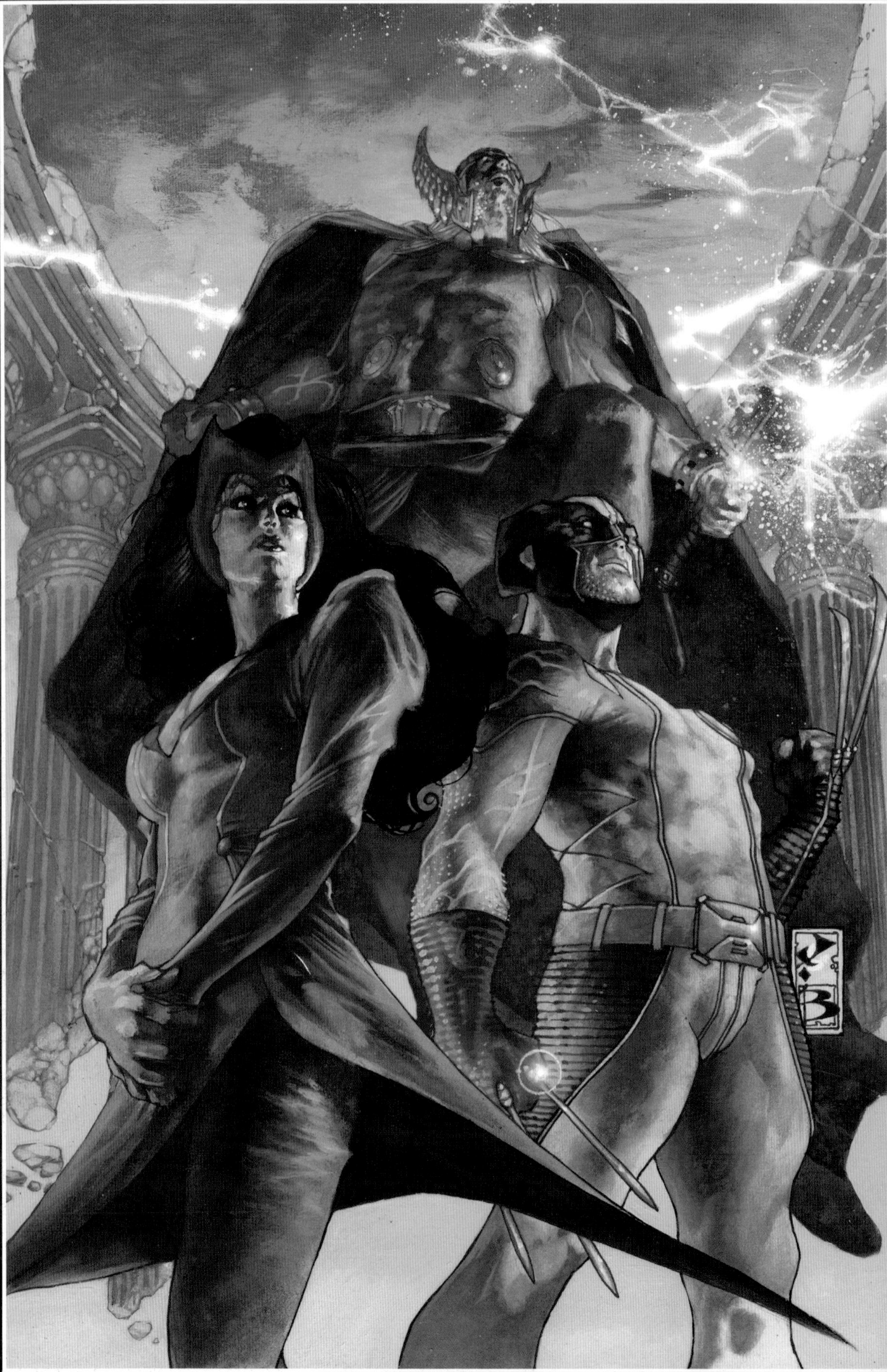

UNCANNY AVENGERS #3 BY SIMONE BIANCHI

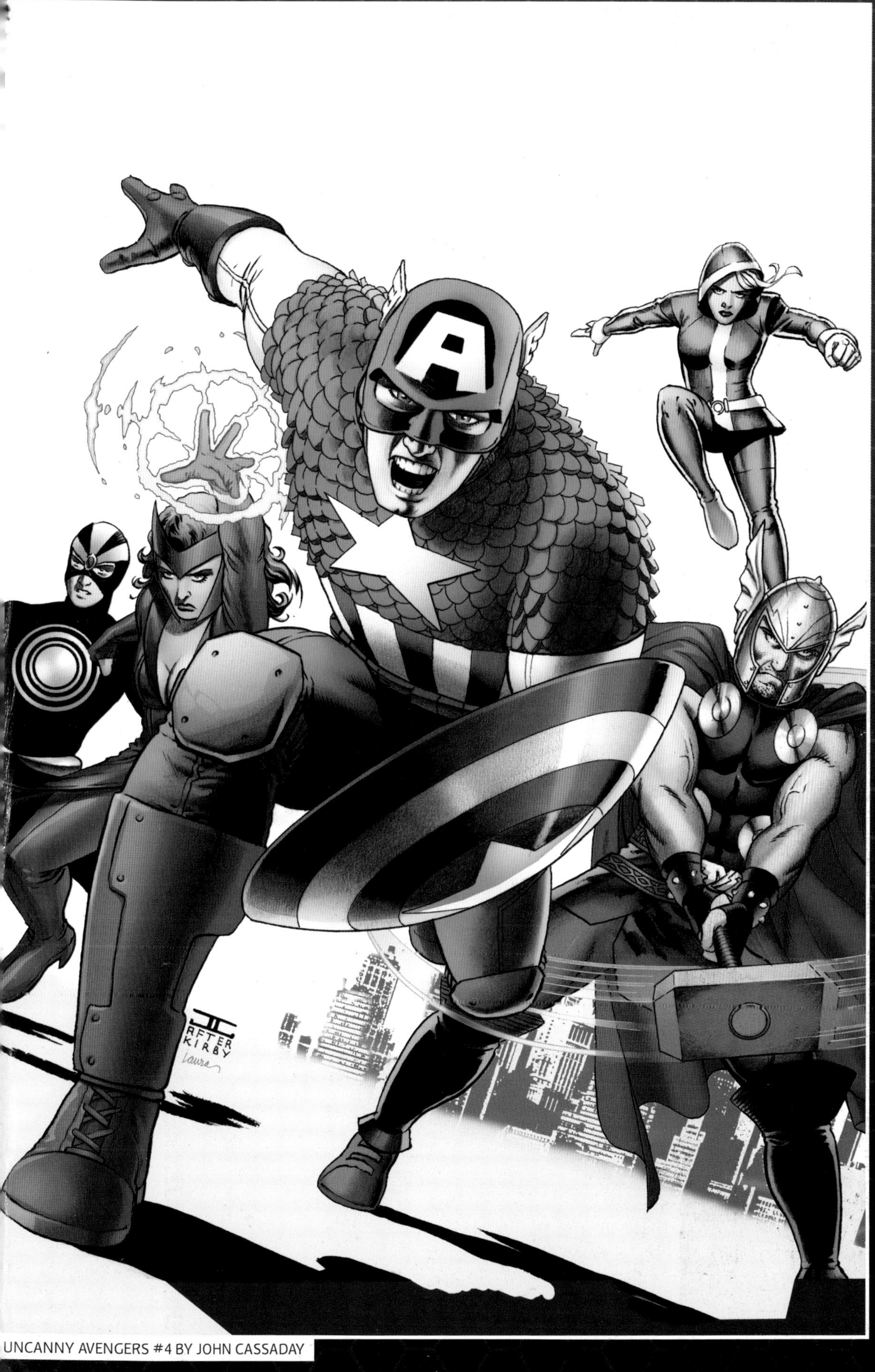
AFTER KIRBY

UNCANNY AVENGERS #4 BY JOHN CASSADAY

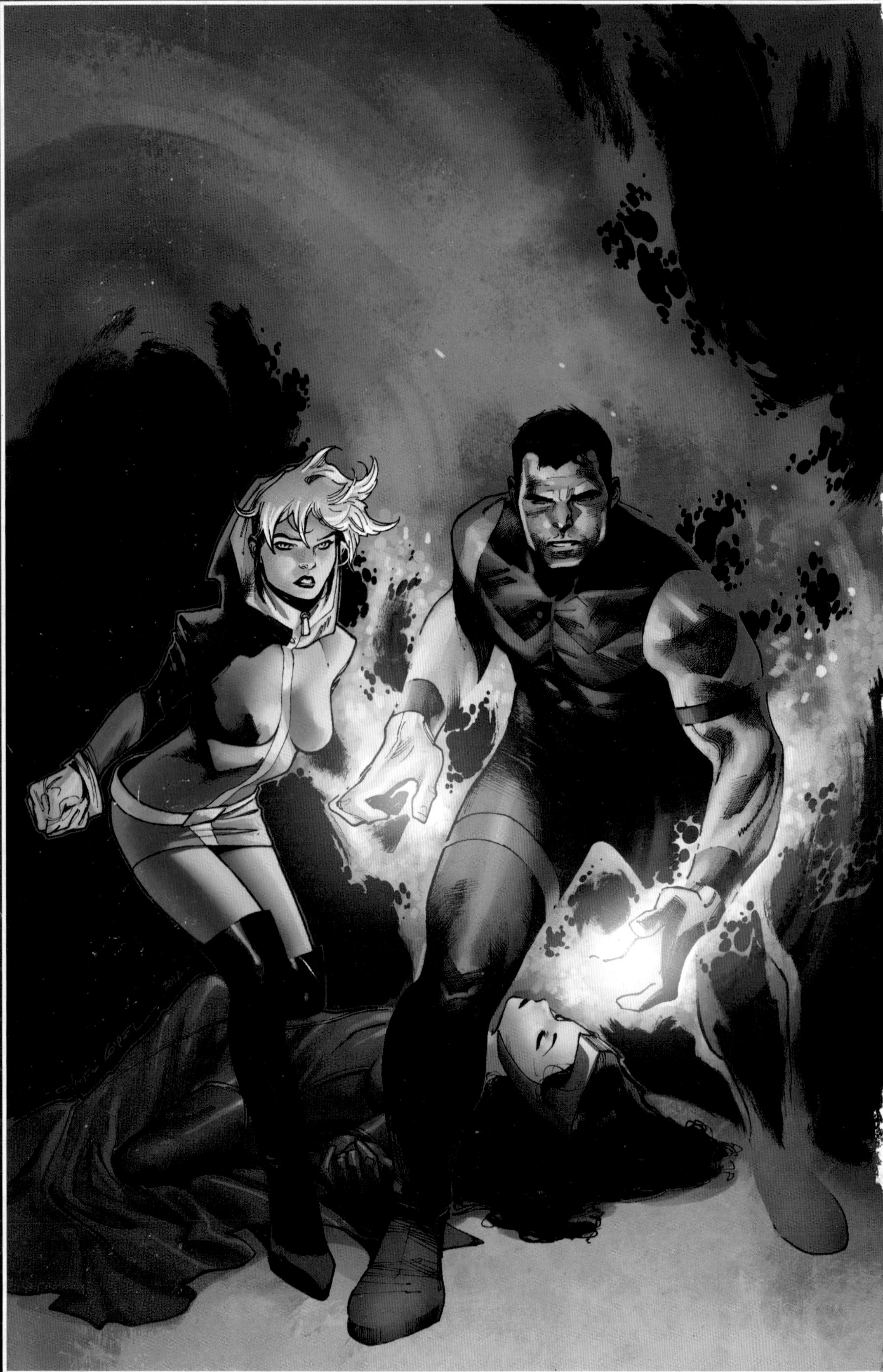

UNCANNY AVENGERS #5 BY OLIVIER COIPEL